My Alien Self

My Journey Back To Me

(Memoirs of Amanda Green)

By Amanda Green

This book contains some offensive language and sexual scenes

This book copyright ©Amanda Green

ISBN-13: 978-1493784868

First edition written and published 2012 by Amanda Green as kindle and published 2013 by Amanda Green as paperback

Copyright of the text produced herein remains the property of the writer and permission to publish is gratefully acknowledged by the author

All rights reserved

Edited by Debz Hobbs-Wyatt

No parts of this publication may be reproduced, stored in a retrieval system, in transmitted in any form, by any means, electronic, mechanical, photocopying, recording or otherwise without prior permission of the copyright owner.

For

Elizabeth (Ciss)

Never forgotten; you have a special place in my heart X

&

my mum

I love you X

Acknowledgements

To dear Debz Hobbs-Wyatt without whom I feel sure I would not have this book. When I was close to finishing myself therapy life story, I had in excess of 400,000 words but no story flow (to put that into perspective, it is around the average word count of four novels). Debz, knowing how much work there was to be done, still chose to work with me and I feel very fortunate to have worked with a great editor who has aided me, tirelessly, to mould my story into what you read here, whilst using my own words, preserving my *voice* and encouraging me to write continuously to find the appropriate writing to link my life, thoughts, people and events together, so that I essentially wrote the book with her assistance and a few sentences here and there. I am very grateful for this, as I did not want a ghost writer or to have someone else writing huge sections for me. As the amount of words grew, Debz continued to trim them down; something (being OCD) I found very hard to do myself, since I tend to just write and write the same way I talk and talk. Her dedication to my project was admirable, particularly as I have an obsessive personality, but luckily we are both perfectionists! I now not only have this special book, my life story, but I am also a far better writer, learning many new techniques from Debz along the way. Having utilised other editors in the past, who critiqued well, but wanted me to re-style everything I wrote, I am extremely grateful to Debz for this story which is my story, in my words - something I feel is important for such a personal and at times, delicate journey to write. (www.debzhobbs-wyatt.co.uk)

I also thank my local college for the short, but educational, writing courses they offered. Plus the writing retreats I went on. Both places gave me a chance to read some of my work out loud for the first time to strangers, and it was nerve wracking, but liberating and useful to do so, as it increased my confidence to write. I also thank Pearl, who showed me how to write standalone scenes from my memory, bringing out my creativity to write with more detail and description.

I am also grateful to my website developer (you know who you are) who I worked with to initially set up and create the design of all my blogs/websites during the last five years. I gave him my detailed requirements and he produced exactly what I asked for, very efficiently, whilst going far beyond his call of duty. In difficult times for me, when I was quite ill and struggling with virtually all relationships, I was hard to work with at times, but he stuck by me, forgave me and we moved on. I thank him for his support, and his understanding – a great example of someone without mental illness stigma.

To my family – without whom, of course, I would have a different story to tell. X

To Chris – Without whom I would not have had the time to write throughout my self therapy journey, this story of my life, including our tumultuous, yet affectionate, tender and passionate love story. Love and fondness forever in my heart to my best friend I've ever hung out with. I will always cherish the good times we've had! xxxxxxx

Cover 'Designed by Stuart Bache' (www.stuartbache.co.uk) – thanks for creating the perfect cover from my specification – I love it! ☺

Although writing my book has been damaging and I would not recommend it without the right support, strangely, in uncovering the past, this book might just have saved my life.

I have changed the names and the places to protect my family. But everything else you read here is how I see it or how I remember it and all the events, diary excerpts, text messages, letters and emails are real. This is me, warts n all.

Note from the author

I self published this book and am very proud of that fact, because I was able to write it exactly as I wanted it to be written, with the help from my fabulous editor, Debz Hobbs-Wyatt. Whilst a publisher and agent offer a huge amount of help, they do narrow down what is published, so I took on the journey to publish and market it myself – my story, written just how *I* wanted it to be written.

There's a sequel out too, called '39'. It's quite different, but it leads on from this one :-)

Just a few reviews from my wonderful readers!

"I found it compulsive, disturbing and ultimately inspiring. These issues are unique to the individual, but there are many more out there with similar problems, who don't have the eloquence, courage or motivation to write such a thought-provoking, honest, heart breaking inspiring book, chronicling all the pain and emotion that mental illness can load onto a person, a family... this should be read by everyone out there who has any compassion for their fellow man... it will open a whole range of new experience and knowledge, which is the first major step in removing the stigma that damns us all."

"A gripping memoir – Well written and brutally honest ... It's a moving, inspiring and exciting read from cover to cover"

"I felt so many of my own excruciating experiences shared with her, as I read it got very synchronous at times... The levels of understanding, sympathy & empathy did not stop rising until at a peak near the end. A lady who has worked hard to push through many boundaries, not just to get this book written but also to change herself, as much as one is able."

"I love the journal entries and the visceral approach to the truth as you approach healing and discovery"

"You are inspiring to have suffered so much and found the courage to write your story, which will undoubtedly help others."

"She wrote an inspiring memoir that is a must read. Plus she is an amazing advocate on mental illness"

"I think you show great insight into the world of BPD without blaming and playing the victim"

"I think you certainly have shown how it feels to live with this condition, the sense of chaos but also the ability to look so well and function so highly in front of others. Most of the time I wasn't aware I was putting on a front, I just didn't know how else to be.... You've done a great job though and on a personal level there is so much that I can relate to, especially the constant upping sticks and starting again either with location, jobs, friends or all of the above ..."

The editor (Debz Hobbs-Wyatt) adds...

This is the journey of a normal working class girl, trapped in a roller coaster world of disorder and excitement, love and joy, depression and anger – and her fight against stigma While My Alien Self would be inspiring for any sufferer, their families or medical teams in its honest insights into living with a mental illness, it also has universal appeal. For who, at times, has not felt their life spin into chaos and wondered what is normal? This story effectively and openly highlights just how fine the line is between what is normal, and what is 'mental illness' And everyone who reads it will be able to relate to it.

'**Emergence**' (supporting those affected by personality disorders) had this to say 'We very much enjoyed reading this honest and powerful account of Amanda's journey from diagnosis to recovery. We applaud such authentic and candid accounts of the devastation that can be experienced by those living with personality disorder and of the message of hope and recovery that the book conveys.'

Bon Dobbs (Anything To Stop The Pain and Author of 'When hope is not enough') said 'While there are many borderline personality disorder memoirs out now (including *The Buddha and the Borderline, Loud House of Myself, Get Me Out of Here, Girl in Need of a Tourniquet* and *Poisoned Love*), My Alien Self goes a long way to providing hope to the sufferers of BPD. By publishing the steps taken to reframe certain ways thinking, through CBT worksheets and other exercises, the author has revealed that recovery from BPD is possible.'

My Alien Self

Foreword

I have kept every little memento of my life: diaries, airline tickets, photos, letters, emails, text messages, cinema tickets and notes from people – everything and anything. I always had an inkling from a young age that my life was different, and that I might one day write my story. This was later compounded by the thought I might not have children, so who would remember me? I decided I wanted to leave my legacy in words: *my* words, *my* story, *my* perspective.

And here it is.

I've always thought how sad it is, that when people die they take their memories with them. Things they have experienced that no-one else knows are gone forever. Their house, their life's worth of objects can be sold or put in a loft and forgotten– everything that was precious suddenly seems worthless. But if they wrote it down they could at least leave their story behind. Family and friends could read it, it could be passed down to other family members, and their life would still have meaning – their words would still go on.

What could be more precious?

I want to take you into my world of *normal*. I want to take you into a world where feeling sorry for myself was not an option. I want to share with you my story; a story of highs and lows, of pain and joy.

I always wanted to write my story, but it didn't seem to have much purpose other than being a log of my life. Then, years later, I realised what was different about me – that thing I could never put my finger on – I suffered from a mental illness and dissociated from distressing events in my life. I had been having various therapies over the years, since I was in my twenties, and had been offered counselling for depression when I was fifteen. Every therapist I saw delved deeper into my past, trying to uncover the underlying reasons. When my problems and moods started to get out of control, in my thirties, I became so distressed and confused I decided to start looking into my past again – by myself. If I had had the money to have a professional therapist help me, I would have, but I didn't.

I read some childhood diaries first, and came across an eight-page typed document, describing in detail the day I was raped. I had written the story the day after the event occurred, when I was fifteen, and had obviously dissociated completely from it. You can only imagine the shock I felt when I discovered it, tucked into one of my old diaries. As I read, it was as if that person wasn't me: I guess that was my first encounter with my alien self. I stopped writing my life after that, it scared me, and then in 2008 I finally saw a psychiatrist who gave me a correct diagnosis, a name for the condition that could account for all those years of depression, chronic mood changes and dissociation. But even then I was still in denial.

I always thought of myself as a happy-go-lucky girl, as did everyone else, but I also knew the stigma of mental illness because I'd grown up with a mother with schizophrenia. Eventually I knew I had to open the *Pandora's Box* of my life memories – it would be the only way to get everything out in the open, to understand how I turned into that alien me and then maybe I could find myself again and close the box forever. All I wanted was to move on and concentrate on being happy in my future.

So I wrote my story as a type of self-therapy, but it took every bit of strength to do it, and it caused my issues to escalate, as the dark events of the past came back, one by one. At this time I also read memoirs by other sufferers, which helped me to understand myself a little more, and also made me feel less alone with my problems. Not that I wanted anyone else to be going through the same traumas, just to know there were others suffering as I was, at times, became a great comfort. So with that in mind, I decided to turn my story into a book that might help others too, so that something good could come out of the pain. But it's not all sad; like all journeys the story of me and my alien self is one of growing up, teenage rebellion, the need to escape. It's about family, about love ... and I'd like to think it's a story about hope.

So come with me. But prepare for a bumpy ride.

And, finally, my most important message to you about reading my book ...

"To read the beginning is nothing until you've come to the end."

Prologue

My life is a landscape; a lot of mountains, one after the other, and occasionally a deep, dark cave that I cannot see until I trip up and find myself falling to the bottom in the pitch black.

I must first get out of the cave, then continue trudging up the mountain. It's a long way up, equally long down, and there are hardly any plateaus on this landscape. Either up or down I go, plodding through this never-ending scene.

The sun doesn't shine much, the clouds get thicker, the rain harder, and the winds howl in my ears. I cannot escape. The caves along the way give a little respite, but they are dark, damp and dingy and full of noises and things moving. I cannot sleep, so I have to keep moving. I must find the rainbow at the end of this path.

When I come to a cave with sunlight beaming through, Chris waits for me there. It's the cave of fun. We bury ourselves under the covers of his massive bed and hide together. We say it's like being back in the womb, innocent and unaware and we hold each other and just for a few moments, we hide from the world. Then we cannot breathe, and we have to come up for air, and the outside world gets back into us once again.

Part 1

Outward Journey

Every journey begins with a single step

Chapter 1

What's wrong with me?

August 2008, Age 34

We're almost late for the first appointment with Dr Jones.

I take a quick deep breath before getting out of the car and rushing up the road to his office.

"I'm a bit nervous seeing a psychiatrist," I say, glancing at Chris. "I wonder what he's going to say about me?"

"Don't worry, I'll be there and that's what we're here for, remember? To find out what's wrong." Chris is so calm, like he always is, as we hurry up the street. I feel safe with him. I'm glad he's here. He really dislikes walking fast but today he doesn't complain.

A staircase leads us up to the reception. A little out of breath by now, I berate myself for my lateness. I am always late, no matter what the occasion. Introductions out of the way, we head into Dr Jones's office. It's an incredibly small, plain room and if it wasn't for the window I know I'd feel claustrophobic. As I study Dr Jones, I feel at ease. He's old enough to have experience, speaks in a quiet yet assertive manner, and his greying beard makes him look all the more 'professional' yet friendly – like a professor crossed with Santa Claus.

"So, why are you here – what's wrong?" He starts his conversation very seriously and remains the same throughout, even if we're laughing.

"I'm depressed and angry a lot and have terrible mood swings, happy, sad and excitable and although I have had various therapies over the years, I don't seem to be getting any better."

I feel stupid at the beginning of our chat. Do I really need help or am I wasting his time or looking for attention? I shuffle my bum in the seat.

"Do you have anyone with any mental disorders in your family?"

Oh yes, I certainly have.

Now he leans towards me – waiting for me to say something.

"Yes," I say.

Again there he is watching me; waiting.

"My mum."

And there it is.

I talk; I tell him about her, about my mum and he listens and then he says it. He says: "Do you hear voices, Amanda?"

Are you like her? That's what he means. Am I? But I don't hear voices. I'm not like her. I'm not.

He's looking at me, waiting for me to say something. It's my biggest fear, being like her.

"No," I say. "No, I don't hear voices."

"OK, in chronological order, I want you to tell me about your life – the main events."

Oh shit, here we go again – this must be the thirtieth time I will have given out the facts of my life. I don't express these thoughts to him, of course.

But honestly – where do I start? How do I start?

I have been through my life so many times with various therapists, I feel a little sick that I must go through it all again, but I'm afraid that Dr Jones doesn't know any of it yet, so here we go. I wish I could just transfer the notes from one therapist to another and then I wouldn't have to say much.

Before I start I fumble through my bag for my little note book that Mum bought me from the zoo – it has a picture on the front of the adorable resident Orangutan there, since she and most people know that they are my favourite creatures. Being a bit of an expert (so I like to think) at this therapy game, I had taken a pro-active approach to this appointment and had written down lots of words and notes as to how I was feeling and why my life was so unbearable. I live my life through lists – obsessed with them, in fact.

But he doesn't want lists; he wants my story – all of it. He wants me to let him know, tell him everything... so that's what I do – in short.

This is my life...

Chapter 2

My normal self

1973

I was born ten days early. It's probably the first and last time I have been early for anything.

I had black hair, big sideboards and was, apparently, beautiful but don't the nurses always say that? Aren't they supposed to say that?

My baby photos show such an innocent child, with big blue eyes set in my soft, round face. It's hard to see that this tiny child would end up promiscuous, attention seeking and out of control.

I guess life moulds us all.

I remember the family home, growing up. We moved there when I was one, from a two-bed bungalow. We needed the space. You always needed space when there were six of you. Of course then I was just a bundle – what space did I need? So there were six of us: Mum, Dad and three brothers, Ian, David and Peter ... seven, ten and twelve years older than me. I might have been one of six, but being the only girl, and so much younger, meant I often felt like an only child. What we all had in common was living in the shadow of mental illness. Not that I knew it then.

Many doctors have asked me about my childhood and my earliest memories. And I always told them the same thing: one of my earliest memories was the feeling of being lost.

Even with such a large family it's possible to feel that way. In fact I often wonder if I've always been lost; in one way or another. Perhaps those early memories are a metaphor for my life.

I was in a department store that first time I felt truly lost. Mum and Dad hadn't noticed me wandering off. Next thing, I remember standing there on my own. I was thinking maybe they'd forgotten me. *Where were they? Maybe I did something wrong? But what did I do?* Finally I was approached by a stranger. She used the tannoy; *there is a lost child in the toy department.* Did she mean me? Was I lost?

Then we waited.

And waited.

And waited.

It must've only been a couple of minutes but it seemed like hours before they came to get me. My dad looked flustered, asking me why I'd just wandered off; *Oh Amanda, never do that again.* But seeing him there all I felt was joy, overwhelming joy that I wasn't lost anymore. I was found. I was safe. For now.

The next time I remember feeling lost was my introductory appointment at my first school, a few weeks before I started. Of course now it's a haze in my memory. So long ago. But I still remember the feeling of being lost.

We remember only fragments of childhood

I was standing in the classroom, a room full of children, strangers. They were all looking at me. I was *a lost child* again. *What was happening? What had I done?* That's when I saw them – brightly patterned pots in the middle of each table and me in that moment thinking the only thing that mattered was what was inside them. I could hear the teacher talking to Mum but in that moment the nerves dissolved to nothing. I had set my mind to those pots with their colours. I guess I stopped being lost, lost instead in the colour – the possibility of what I was to become.

When I think about it now I see how, like so many moments in life, the ability to climb inside a moment, to be absorbed by something so completely was a way of not thinking; of not seeing. You see, while I was just being a normal little girl, there was always that shadow over our family. Maybe that was what made us different, not that I would have understood it. I just always knew my mum was sick. In fact my mum had catatonic schizophrenia.

But all I knew was she wasn't the same as other mums. And that meant I wasn't the same as the other children.

Did the teachers know?

Did they know that big fancy word for what was wrong with Mum? Could they see it?

What about me?

But I wasn't like her. I could climb inside the colour and lose myself. Some kinds of lost were OK.

I recall birthdays growing up too, so many birthdays it seems when you look back, so much longer than a year in between then, as if time had a different speed. And there I was, turning six. I see it now. We played *Tom and Jerry* and *Roadrunner* on my much loved projector. It was a silent film which we projected onto the lounge door. I caught sight of Mum stood there in her in her size 18 black t-shirt, grey A-line skirt, black tights and slippers. Her hair dyed dark brown, frizzy from perming, her eyes slightly staring. So there we were, all so normal.

The six-year old me was standing there with my fingers crossed hoping Mum would act like the other mums did. *Please let this be fun.* But I needn't have worried; my little friend Harry was there too, my good friend and Mum behaved. My friends behaved. It was all fine. In fact it was a great party – one I will never forget. Mum made me feel very special that day. I was very proud of her and very happy to share my day with my friends and no hitches. Dad tells me he was there too, and remembers it well. I don't remember that, but maybe that's why it was a good day.

It was the first and last birthday party I ever had – a happy, normal birthday party just like any regular child, remembered as any normal happy child remembers fragments of childhood.

As I think of these times now, I think how sometimes you can go back to a place - see it how it was, not how it is. I can see that house now, me there, as a child. I can close my eyes and enter through the front door, into a small hall, from which one door led to a rectangle lounge/dining room where we all crammed ourselves into on the odd occasion we were all together – usually only for a Sunday roast. It has patterned wallpaper and mismatched furniture – some dark wood, some pine wood – and looks cluttered with ornaments and tacky holiday souvenirs.

I wonder when I first realised that the paintwork was supposed to be white, not nicotine yellow, or that other peoples' houses didn't have the constant aroma of cigarettes. When my family were smoking I could see the haze in the air, like we were always scarfed in a mist, like some of those early memories are now. We had a tall standalone ashtray that they could put by their side so they didn't have to get up. It was white and silver, and often full to its brim with fag butts. You put the cigarette in, pressed the middle and it span so the cigarette would disappear into the receptacle below and the lack of air in there would put the cigarette out. Mum would have washing hanging up on the curtain rail at the far end. It's funny the things you remember.

Ian is playing *Friggin' in the Riggin* by the Sex Pistols. He does that when Dad's not around. Or Human League. You know he taught me the words to all the songs, from the record inserts, by the time I was about eight or nine. I have always listened to the words of songs and learnt them, line by line, ever since.

And there's David – a fan of U2 singing *Gloria* in 1981 and *Sunday bloody Sunday* in 1983.

Of course, I had no idea what the true meaning of those songs were at the time.

Mustn't forget Peter – there he is listening to Blondie.

Sunday Girl became one of my favourites.

Music triggers memories

Finally, I see my bedroom with its bright pink curtains, wallpaper covered in a cute girl pattern, pink blankets and white sheets and a white MFI wardrobe, all crammed into the tiny box room. And that room is the same room I slept in as an adult, on and off for over thirty-five years.

There's a saying about that; we all come back to where we started – some more than others it seems.

Lastly as I take my little tour I see our black and white cat Suds, basking in the sun. An outside cat; day and night, summer or winter. Dad didn't like her in the house. I would make her cardboard box houses when the weather turned cold, which my family found funny. I often think of her now.

I've always felt a deep connection to animals.

So there I was growing up in normal suburbia. I was normal. Everything was normal.

But somehow I always knew it wasn't.

Chapter 3

Not the same

1980

My first school report:

'Amanda is a sensible girl capable of very good work. Progressing very satisfactorily. A willing, well behaved girl'.

I wasn't like Mum. Satisfactory. Willing. I got my attention by being good. Not like her, or so I was beginning to realise.

There's a school photo of that time – me smiling, with my basin haircut, I look so happy. I suppose I was.

A few weeks later Mum had one of her 'turns.' I don't suppose I really understood it then; that she was hearing voices, that she was catatonic. I might not have known the word but I see her there – motionless and emotionless, as if everything about her was blank. Like she lost all her colours. Maybe she needed one of those pots to crawl into. Or maybe her kind of lost meant she was unreachable.

In the end she was sectioned and taken into hospital again. I remember the visits but I only remember one journey – the journey home with Dad. Age six there I was huddled in the front seat of Dad's car. I stared out the side window into the darkness, so that my face was out of view as I forced back tears. I wanted to break down, to bawl, to ask questions, but I couldn't.

When would I see Mummy again? Why did she have to stay in that horrible grey hospital? Why couldn't she come home with us?

Sometimes Mum was horrible (screaming, swearing, slamming doors) and sometimes loving and soft at home, but I didn't want to leave her behind, and I sensed that she hated that place with all the old people sitting around on worn, dull settees, in a big, plain room, nothing cosy about it, more like a waiting area, with all the people waiting for visitors like me and Dad to come and cheer them up. There must have been about fifteen or so settees, scattered about and I sat on one of them with Mum and Dad and we talked, interrupted by people yelling or waving their arms around. I didn't want to look.

Most people in that place looked old – and some looked dazed and lifeless. It didn't scare me, I had Dad with me, and he would protect me. They weren't trying to harm me, but Mum said a woman in a wheelchair wanted to hurt her. She said the woman chased her up the corridor, wheeling fast, in a kind of fury. She wanted to bash her against the wall. Mum wanted to come home with us but she wasn't allowed. She didn't want electroconvulsive treatments (ECT) and medications. That's what she said.

I didn't understand.

I guess that place is what fuelled my lifelong fear of hospitals and doctors and just about any situation where I might be trapped and controlled by others. It also taught me to hide my emotions and deal with them in my own way or ignore them. The stigma surrounding my mother and her illness, and hospitalisations in a well known mental asylum, as they called them then, is what set off my urge to beat the stigma surrounding mental health much later on. I never knew then that it would be me sitting at a psychiatrist's office, a victim of the very same stigma.

The difference was, I wasn't like her: I was free.

But growing up wasn't all bad, it wasn't all about Mum and her issues.

There was always Auntie Agnes.

I recall the time I got the croup. It took me out of school for six weeks while Mum was still in hospital and I was sent to Great Aunt Agnes's. She was actually my dad's aunt and she showed me a different side to life.

I loved it at Agnes's house – it was peaceful. Auntie Agnes and Uncle Albert looked after me at their bungalow – six blissful weeks in a happy home, with no arguments, depression or moods. Auntie Agnes was seventy-nine years old at that time and was used to looking after us, particularly my brothers; she'd had Peter for the first two years of his life.

I enjoyed it. Not because I had to have time off school, and not because I was so ill with the croup that I had to be looked after, but because it was Auntie Agnes looking after me. I liked that house and Agnes's positive attitude. She understood me. Maybe she gave me what my own mum couldn't at the time – normality.

I see her now: Auntie Agnes. She wears a pinafore apron.

That's how I remember her – all those hours in the kitchen, preparing food, cooking, cleaning and washing in her twin tub. But she'd wear overalls for digging and tending to the vegetables and fruit in her garden. And when she went out she made a very good effort to look smart; always with a little face powder, blusher, lipstick and perfume, while wearing two piece outfits with brooches or colourful flowery dresses and a smart jacket, topped off with clip-on earrings, tights, scarf and low heeled sensible shoes. I still have some of her jewellery and face powder pack and they still smell like Agnes.

The hallway was always cold. There was a coat and umbrella rack and the larder at the end stacked with tins of sardines and spaghetti, homemade jams. Homely. Really homely.

The main meal of the day was lunch, and this could be anything from pork or lamb chops, to rib of beef or meat pie. She grew all her own vegetables, bought her meat from the local butcher, and made everything – pies, suet puddings, cakes and crumbles.

The dining room was the main room – a very sociable place, for eating, talking, visitors, and listening to *The Archers* on the radio, which sat in one corner of the room on a high shelf – one that I could not reach as a child. It was nice to listen to *The Archers*, as it was a story and you didn't have to look at any pictures or concentrate fully. Auntie Agnes would listen intently and she followed the whole story for years and years. Whenever I hear of something major happening in *The Archers* now I always think of Agnes and how since she passed away will never know about it.

Everything is an unfinished story.

The doorframe in that room was painted white but it had dents to show us all growing up. I had my height etched into their frame in increments.

There were also two upright armchairs in that room – old-fashioned and dark brown, with dark wood arms and frame, finished off with white and beige embroidered cushions. I would sit in the right hand chair which was always the 'Agnes chair' while Agnes was cluttering and washing up in the kitchen and I would often fall asleep. The other chair was Uncle Albert's but after he died a few years later, it wasn't used. Uncle Albert would tell me jokes: "There was an Englishman, Irishman and Scotsman…" I never totally clicked with Uncle Albert but Agnes loved him, and that's what mattered.

They'd both take me up to the Salvation Army on Wednesdays and I loved the attention I got. I think it was this exposure to the over 60s that helped me develop a real respect for my elders, as I loved being in their company, full of wisdom and memories of 'the old days.'

Agnes always had a yellow rubber duck and some bath bubbles to keep things child like for bath-time. She would laugh when I got going with the bubble bath. I would prop my legs up, and whisk my hands under my knees in a kind of paddle steamer way to get the bubbles up as high as the baths edges, giggling all the time.

Eventually, after a few weeks of incarceration, Mum came home from the hospital and I went home. Again it seemed that her illness was ours, and in my head I wanted to see her at the birthday party smiling sweetly and throwing her head back as she laughed – being normal. Or I wanted to be standing with Aunt Agnes with her homemade jams and planning what to eat around the dining room table.

Although Mum had out-patient psychiatrist appointments, not one person – carer, social worker, doctor, came to see if we were OK; if we could cope – *ever*.

I would often think about that time with Aunt Agnes.

There's a song called *Favourite Things*. I'd listen to it on the record player when Mum and I had a music session at home. I think about that song now and remember the lists I would make in my head when I needed to feel the way I did at Aunt Agnes's house or happy at home. And how, even now, they can take me back to the safe warm feeling or maybe not such a warm feeling. At least I feel something.

Smells: Roast dinner: mouth watering- too long to cook! Cut grass: Nanna's house. Smoke in the lounge – yeuk! Mint potatoes: yum. Coffee roasting. Agnes's face powder. Mum's spit and pink lipstick smells on a hankie when cleaning round my mouth.

Sounds: Mum shouting. Mum moaning. Brothers bickering. Agnes cooking and cluttering in the kitchen. Blondie, Sex Pistols and The Human League. The 'Frog Song' (the first record I ever bought).Michael Jackson's 1983 album 'Thriller'.

Sights: Mum's face – nasty. Our cat's face – cuddly. Bright green kitchen cupboards – full. Pink bedroom -- home and mine. Mum and Dad smiling down at me in the lounge as they gave me a teddy bear bigger than me for my birthday.

Tastes: Agnes's lamb chops, gravy, suet pudding and golden syrup pudding. Roast dinners. Marmite sandwiches. Jacket spuds. Vesta meals. Cherry drop sweets I would get only at the local hospital whilst waiting with my mum for her appointment.

Touch: Teddy bear's soft fur. My cat's fur. My hamster's fur. Nanna's soft face.

TV programmes: Dynasty. Dallas. Hi-de-Hi. Hart to Hart. Saturday Superstore. Grange Hill and Educated Marmalade.

Somehow, I suppose we all found our way of coping. We had to. Of course I couldn't have known then how hard that must've been for Dad.

We used to holiday in Hemsby each year, staying in a chalet, making sandcastles and digging big holes on the golden sanded beach. Eating burgers, roast turkey, hiring a quadricycle to zoom around Hemsby in and going to see the banger and stock car racing in Great Yarmouth or riding the funfair rides of Great Yarmouth seafront. I remember Ian coming with his girlfriend when he was seventeen. I was ten and they took me out for the day to the funfair. I was so pleased that Ian still made the time for me, despite his girlfriend being there, and he seemed to be nice to me, which was special (you see he'd often bully me at home, throwing darts into my feet, hitting me and warning me not to tell anyone or I'd get it worse, or even throwing boiling water at my chest). . My favourite number became seventeen after that; it still is.

When I was older, Mum, Dad and I would holiday abroad and I remember a holiday in Spain. Mum had a screaming fit at Dad while he and I sat by the busy pool area of our hotel, surrounded by guests in sunglasses and bathing suits.

"You don't care about me!" she screamed to Dad. "You just want Amanda!"

I wanted the world to swallow me up, but as she stormed off across the white tiles and through the lobby, Dad and I looked at each other and quite unexpectedly we laughed. We laugh a lot in my family. Laughter is always a good medicine; well that's what they say. We spent the rest of that day together, Dad and I, enjoying ourselves sunbathing by the pool, eating burger and chips on our laps on our sun beds. Mum by herself; somewhere. Sad when I think about that part.

But you see there are happy memories of my dad and I: amongst the turmoil of living with a sick Mum and dysfunctional family. Although now I understand that mum she couldn't help it most of the time. And she was the one who suffered the most. I still think of those happy memories. It's just they come in fragments.

But they do come.

The Fox and the Hound was the best film for me of 1981 and probably my childhood, it was such a sweet story. The following year brought the famous film *ET* and my mum and I queued all round the block to get into the cinema – I have never seen before or since so many people desperate to see a film.

Mum would often take me to the parks for the swings and slides, the feeling of the air rushing against my skin. Mum laughing, maybe as if she too was the child. And I remember people asking if she was my grandma rather than Mum. I guess she did look older. But I didn't want people to think that of her. She was my mum. My mum, no matter what people said or thought. And she did care for me – I knew that too. She was thirty-nine years old when she brought me into the world – seven years after my youngest brother. She'd dreamt about having a girl and drove my dad nuts calling out in the middle of the night: "Babies John! Babies…" She was very maternal despite her inner demons. The doctors said it was good for her to have babies, something else for her to concentrate on. But the stress, the terrible traumas she was put through in hospital and strange private world she lived in at times didn't help her. She seemed to look older before she should. She'd been a pretty brunette in her twenties, but her forties showed a worn out soul in her face and her sometimes disturbed looking eyes. My poor mum had been through, and was most likely still going through, so much.

From play time swings and the freedom of the park to other swings; darker swings; Mum's mood swings. They read as a list of adjectives: happy, excited, depressed, loving, angry, vicious or just plain difficult. But it was like they were bigger than her, bigger than us and from one moment to the next I never knew what to expect. I remember when she was in a foul angry mood how she would go on and on at Dad – and one day I was in the kitchen and I heard her shouting and screaming. So I stood still, listening, trying to work out what was happening, then Dad started shouting back and I heard a slapping sound and it went quiet for a few seconds. Then Mum shouted again.

"You hate me, I hate you!"

I stood there crying, not knowing what to do. I was too young to really understand. I remember how I ran upstairs; slamming the door to the bedroom, wishing I could shut it all away, lose myself completely.

I was only seven.

It seemed as though Mum wanted to punish Dad and all of us, as if she detested anyone enjoying themselves. When I think about, and I mean really think about it, maybe I know why she was like this. It's not hard to imagine how her life was ruined by illness and how Dad was the one who kept sending her to hospital – no wonder she resented him. Maybe she felt that he had ruined her life by *sectioning* her so she wanted to ruin things for him in return, payback. And then there were the doctors, imagine what they put her through: forced electroconvulsive treatments without her consent, medications that made her lose herself completely and ice cold baths, all of which were facilitated there. The thing is, with schizophrenia of any kind, and other mental illnesses, the person only knows what *they* really feel, see, hear, taste or smell or think. That is their reality. And the doctors and Dad tried to change that. I cannot imagine how awful my mum's life was – years of torment both from within herself in the voices and hallucinations telling her to kill herself and then on top of that to be sent to a prison like place and be tortured by all those processes, restrained against her will, despite her best efforts to avoid them. Awful beyond imagination.

Since communicating with someone from that hospital, I now realise what went on, and I have always wanted to find out the truth. I don't blame her for trying to kill herself so many times before I was born – she'd be found on Summerville Beach wading into the sea, or sleeping on benches. Police would be involved. Although her ever-changing moods were nothingweren't anything to do with catatonia, they may have been to do with voices in her head, paranoia, who knows. I have never discussed her illness or moods with her. She's always changed the subject if I brought it up. But what I do know is that I am not surprised she was the way she was; the mood swings. Was she just supposed to come out of hospital after years, months or weeks of incarceration, and be fine and dandy about it, happy with her life? Her life was awful at times, and I don't know who to thank for her still being alive and me being able to have a relationship with her. I feel blessed by that, because in those days as a child, I could only see what was there, without understanding. It's only now I realise what a victim she was; so much more than me. And knowing how much I have wanted to die at times because I couldn't stand myself, I can only imagine how harrowing my mum's life might have been, on and off. She still causes issues, we still walk on eggshells and she is seventy-seven now, but she doesn't suffer like she did then and I can give her back some love now, that I feel she deserves.

At times she was hell bent on spoiling everything, and she was good at it too. She could create an all-enveloping darkness, like a cloud descending; anywhere or at any time she chose (although when I think of it now how much of it was really by choice?) Maybe she was jealous of how we all got on so well with Dad. Everyone had to be on someone's side, and if she thought it was anyone's side but hers, she couldn't stand it. Other times it came from stress – perhaps a family get together. Dad saying she had to 'behave.' I guess none of us really knew what she might do, and many a time she would refuse to come to family events and get away with it – my eldest brother's wedding, birthday celebrations, my dad's work dos, she just couldn't handle them.

She would pick an argument, slamming doors as she fled and Dad or someone would have to placate her and coax her out of her room. These are not symptoms of catatonia or schizophrenia, but the product of confusion and resentment; of gruelling medications and physical treatments in the psychiatric hospital. It must have been hard for him. In fact, though I was far too young to know what was happening at the time, I can only imagine just *how* hard it was for him to see her catatonic, have her brought home after suicide attempts, section her and have her sent back. Sent back to the mental hospital; sent back to the place she hated so much. One time my dad and young brothers had to barricade the door with their bodies so she couldn't go out, which she desperately wanted to do when she knew the doctors were coming for her.

Of course my brothers saw so much more of her illness than I did, they remember those times. I was born after the worst of it. The incident when I was six was her last hospitalisation, and the only one she'd had since I was born, but she'd been in and out for over twenty years before that, sometimes for many months at a time. In the early days, she didn't know my dad at all, and he would visit the hospital nearly every day and write her letters every day to try to get her to remember who he was – her husband. When she came out after the longest stay – the first one which happened two weeks after their marriage – she was just like a child again, and my dad had to teach her the smallest of things, like how to pay for something with money. Imagine that? Maybe it is why she spent years wasting money, buying things every day and hoarding them in her bedroom – as a reaction to freedom or maybe just because that was the first thing she learnt to do when she came out.

I admire his patience and commitment to his marriage, and so do many others. But my mum and dad both have their own experience of their marriage, very different ones. I blame the ECT and drugs they gave her for numbing her brain. She has always had trouble having any kind of serious conversation, and even has trouble taking in how to use a remote control past the programme selector and volume control. BUT, she wasn't simple. Just ill.

And there I was, a child growing up in all of that. I can see myself standing there looking at Dad, pleading with him: "Daddy, please get rid of Mummy. I don't like her. I want her to leave the house. I don't want her as my mummy anymore."

I've often wondered if that's how someone will feel about me.

Even though he didn't come to the school parent evenings or show a lot of interest in my school work, I always had Dad. I felt a closeness to him I didn't have with Mum, maybe borne out of respect as I came to understand that he loved her no matter what. He was going to be true to his marriage vows. Even though neither of them could ever talk about their emotions, and they still can't.

From that, a pattern emerged of loving and hating all at the same time. Like picking off the petals of a rose – *love her, love her not.* I guess that's how Dad and I coped. I guess it's how we all coped, a way of weathering the storm. And like all patterns we find in life they stay with us, leave their echoes. And I see something else too – how their arguments and their fights, mainly my Mum's part in them, somehow reflect in my behaviour as an adult. As you will see when I tell you about Chris.

My brothers shared only one similarity – getting completely drunk. I guess we all form our own patterns. My mum recently told me that sometimes when David, Peter and Ian were really drunk, her and Dad locked them out and they had to sleep in the garage. Punishment? To teach them a lesson? I knew it was what my mum wanted. I knew Dad liked to do what she wanted. That's his pattern, I guess. It's easier, he'd say. Mind you, those boys were a handful.

Peter was the quiet one. He did well at school, was very good at art, and he became a Christian later, partly due to the shared beliefs he found with his Christian wife, Mel, who he met aged twenty. All I remember about him from my childhood was that he ate *Weetabix* for breakfast, worked in town in insurance and liked drinking alcohol with his friends. He was hardly ever at home and moved out when I was about six.

David was the serious one. Always inquisitive, loved his food and was thoughtful. He made up a game to play with me. He would surprise me by coming into my bedroom, saying *"Azzamadoo, Azzamadoo!"* Sometimes I didn't like it, him invading my space like that, but mostly I did as it was a good game. He would talk and act like a wizard waving his arms and speaking slowly in a low tone. Basically, he would cast his *Azzamadoo* spell, then I would need to look under my pillow to see if *Azzamadoo* had left me any money. Sometimes he did, and sometimes he didn't. I guess it was his way of giving me pocket money.

He liked to drink pints and went to beer festivals. He met Linda when he was in his twenties, who he married fifteen years later.

Ian was the raucous one. He was funny, angry, popular and protective. He couldn't be bothered with school, and bunked off a lot, opting to work in a garage since he was fifteen. He still does that now, spraying cars. He got into lots of fights and won them, he was always weight training and Arnold Schwarzenegger was his idol. He drank a lot down the local pub where he was very well known. He crashed a lot of cars and the police knew him by name. Perhaps, like me, he went wild because of his childhood. I caught the edge of his aggression when he bullied me. He was Mum's favourite. He made an effort with her by performing and being jolly like me – or maybe I copied him. He had a few long term relationships and was not without a girlfriend for long. Handsome and funny I think many would say to sum him up, as he has always been a popular guy. Over time, he calmed down a lot, and as an adult he can be a thoughtful, caring person, albeit still childish and grumpy at times. We have our similarities. He is also brave and has taken health issues in his stride with little complaint.

Having a full rein to go out, with no particular rules at times and with Dad not always around to keep an eye on things when at work, I found ways to cope. My friends and I would go over to the woods and field wasteland, called *The Wreck*. We would make camps – proper ones with shelves and saucepans and curtains all taken from the local tip that we'd fasten into the branches of trees – and it amused us for hours. There were remnants of glue sniffing bags and pornography magazines scattered about as we walked through the trees. Thinking about it now, we knew it wasn't a good idea to go over there, so we didn't tell our parents, but the excitement would fuel my need for 'feeling something'. Maybe I didn't learn my emotions properly, but I learnt how to press the 'excite' button and release my frustrations that way.

Later I found another way to release my frustrations. I was only nine. I didn't know what it was, or there were times and places for that. But in 1983 this strange thing happened to me.

Chapter 4

But it was normal, wasn't it?

1983

"Amanda, can I have a word?" said my teacher. "It's about that thing you do in class. It's very wrong and it has to stop."

I didn't know it was called masturbation. How could I know it was called masturbation? What *was* masturbation? All I knew was that it felt good.

It was a wonderful way to relieve my stress at school. It started as a regular habit at home in bed and in private, but I soon took it into the classroom. I had worked out that if I added pressure to the bottom of my pubic bone with the fingers of both hands and moved my fingers in a circular motion as I sat on a chair, my legs would go out in front of me, and start splaying and moving out to the side and back to the middle, and it felt good. I would be fully clothed in a t-shirt and skirt, and I did my act through my clothes.

The good feeling inside of my parts would intensify as my legs moved more frantically, and my face felt blank, almost paralysed – unable to look or take in anything outside of what I was doing. I would tingle, and then a huge powerful desperation would come over me, as I knew that relief was coming. My legs shook and splayed faster and faster, and I felt the strain in my face, concentration and desperation, and then it would come – a wave of pleasure in my parts and throughout my body and I would massage my parts a little as the intensity died down. My legs would slow to a stop and I would come back to the real world of the school classroom again – friends looking strangely at me, in shock, surprise or a look that implied I was weird.

My body would relax and I would realise that I was sweating. I knew something was not quite right with these actions, but I didn't know what, other than the fact that no-one else did it. All I knew was that the comfort it gave was wonderful. I had problems in my head: confusion, loneliness and fear of being bullied at home and in school, and this helped me to deal with them and escape for a few minutes.

Our class was made up of around twenty-five children, all seated on small grey plastic chairs with a metal frame, around square tables – four to five children to a table – so when I did my 'act' it would be directly in front of others. The teacher didn't seem to notice, so it happened a few times before he asked me to stay after class for a 'chat.' He broached the subject directly, that's when he said it: "It's about that thing you do in class. It's very wrong and it has to stop."

So I did.

I wanted to erase it from my memory. Although my classmates at the time didn't know what I was doing any more than I did, the natural course of learning about sexual subjects led them to realise when we were eleven and starting secondary school. Once they found out, they made damn sure I did – *"Amanda likes masturbating, Amanda likes masturbating!"* They'd chant it as I walked to school. They would crowd around me in a group and enjoy the whole process of humiliation. Smirking, their eyes full of pleasure and faint viciousness; they'd laugh out loud, taking in their power as a group, against little old me who was wiped of pride and life in those moments. I walked on surrounded by these girls, all eyes on me. Not the attention I liked. I was a big girl now, at big school and was trying to change. As I felt the colour wash from my face, my throat tensing, I wanted a big black hole to swallow me up and spit me out somewhere else. How could girls I have known for years do this to me? Although all my real friends were quiet, I had spent a lot of time with these other girls, trying to fit in with everyone, even stealing sweets from a shop and playing knock down ginger with them to keep them on side.

But there was no getting away from it, I was different to them. Wasn't I?

A couple of years later, I had the three senior school 'hard nuts' from my year, who I didn't know, corner me on the tower block stairs one day. It was just me and them, no-one else, and they started harassing me and pushing me about. That was the moment. I would not have it. "Don't you dare fucking talk to me like that, and don't touch me, you fucking stupid little slags! How dare you try to pick on me!" I screamed, looking directly at them, mustering my meanest face. They froze. It was a picture. They were shocked by my outburst, a very big surprise coming from quiet little old me who kept herself to herself. They thought I was an easy target, but they were wrong. They were the ones who would get back all that I had suffered. They looked at each other and left.

Later that week, one of them approached me and apologised. I was never bullied at school again. I had dealt with the situation. I had been strong.

But it wasn't only the masturbation I had been teased about in Junior School. I also had a lisp and they'd make me say 'Amanda eats saucy sausage sandwiches' to make my tongue come out on the S's so they could laugh at me. And at the same time…

My mum was sick.

And this is what happens when your *friends* find our your mum's been in a mental hospital

"Your mum stays in Hinton Hall," my *so called* friends would sneer at me when I was ten.

"Why does she go to Hinton Hall?' "

"Is she really sick?"

"Are you crazy like your mum?"

I didn't know.

News travelled fast in school and soon most of the children at my Junior School and some of their mums knew of my mum's hospital stays. I wished it wasn't called an asylum. Not many of the mums talked to her if she came to the school and she would stand alone, looking at the ground. She felt they were 'cliquey' amongst themselves she told me later in life. Although there were a couple who were nice and she still talks to them. Certainly, she had many friends away from the school. I know as I had to stand there while they talked and talked in the street and softly pinched my cheeks saying how I'd grown.

At parents' meetings the teachers would tell my mum about my progress but she'd glaze over or just nod in the right places. I don't know how much she took in but at least she came and took an interest. I loved my mum when she was nice. When she was horrid, I hated her and wanted her to leave us. And I could take a certain amount of taunting from my school friends about me but not about my mum. I wanted to protect her and could not stand to hear them being nasty, or making fun of her illness and her strangeness.

And the whole time this happened I remember telling myself that I wasn't like her, whatever they said. I might have been different but I wasn't like her.

Out of pain can come creativity. People say that, don't they? And what do you know, I could write poems and stories, and draw animal pictures. One of my favourite poems I wrote was 'The cat and mouse' –

> *That poor little mouse, scuttling around*
> *In the shed, in the straw or the drawer, and on the ground*
> *Where it's secretly pursued by the black and white cat...*

Maybe that's how I felt? But was I the mouse or the cat?

So there I was, growing up and yet needing to escape; a sanctuary from everyone – my whole family – space for me... in my room. I liked being alone. It's only now, many years later, I realise Mum must have felt the same way, as if the world was too big for her too; as if it was all happening around her.

Despite the teasing, I was a fairly popular girl at school; I had a desire to be *in* with everyone and I did have a few *real* friends.

I had met Julie in Infant school – she was shy, with a stutter and we grew through those years together; her picked on for her stutter and me for my lisp. I bullied her for a while, smacking her when she didn't do as I wanted, but she told her mum, who told the school, I got told off by the headmistress, and I begged Julie's mum to let us be friends again, which she did eventually. I didn't tell Mum and Dad. Then Jane and Debbie came along in senior school. Jane became my best friend, although she did muck me about, favouring others at times, and asking me on holiday only to ask someone else instead in secret. But I stayed friends with Jane until I was thirty-one. Her mum died of cancer when she was in her twenties. Debbie moved away when we were fourteen, after our school skiing holiday together, but I still saw her when her dad would come and get me and I'd stay with them sixty miles away. I still see her now and always will, I expect. She has never seen the bad side of me.

I wonder how much Jane or my other friends saw of what I was turning into it; how much they understood the problems of living in a family like mine.

We are all alone. But in different ways.

Chapter 5

Sticks and Stones

1984

Almost every day, at ten years old, I'd have Marmite sandwiches for lunch.

Or if not Marmite, then I had potted beef spread.

While the other children had different sandwiches and vitamin drinks and crisps and sweets there I was with my Marmite or potted beef. I did manage to get Dad to get me the vitamin C orange drinks sometimes and we progressed to sandwich spread. If I had a school dinner, which was a treat, there was a good chance it would be cheese flan. I hated cheese flan. I'd be forced to eat it, even though I pleaded, sobbing, with the old dinner lady to leave it. The cheese would make me projectile vomit in the school playground every time. Other times I went home for lunch: jacket spuds and brown sauce. Somehow I liked seeing my mum during the day like that. I suppose I must've missed her. Although sometimes I didn't like her, I always felt something; and I always loved her.

It's funny how even if something is bad for you, you are still drawn to it. This was to be a recurring theme in my life.

In the evenings, I remember sitting alone eating ham, egg and chips or corned beef, mash and beans. I liked to play with my food, push it around my plate for an hour, making a mash castle, filling it with beans and corned beef; making it look pretty. I guess even then food was becoming an issue.

And alcohol.

I had the taste for alcohol at a very young age – I remember one time when Dad left his bottle of sherry on the dining table. He was sitting in the same room watching TV with my mum while I secretly knocked back swigs from the sherry bottle. Mum and Dad found out later as I couldn't even get up the stairs – I had to crawl on my hands and knees. Of course I learned it from Dad – he did get drunk at one stage, and he'd sometimes sink a bottle of sherry in one go or walk round the local pubs, coming home drunk. Drinking went the same way as the judo and the other things he used to like; any hobby that could bring him enjoyment – crushed one by one by Mum. She would go on and on at him about things so much he actually lost interest in doing them, even watching TV. For the alcohol maybe that was a good thing. But as for the hobbies, well, I guess she was his hobby. She was his life, his everything.

There's a fine line between love and hate

In junior school, I received the highest mark for the 11+ that my school had ever known. I achieved double or triple gold stars for much of my work, particularly art. I asked for extra homework every day, and the other children teased me for being a 'boffin,' but it was my mission to prove my worth, intellect and skills to the teachers, who were more interested in my abilities than anyone at home. And it kept me busy.

The worst part of being eleven and starting senior school – apart from the '*Amanda likes masturbating'* chants that I got on my way to school - was when I started sweating profusely, and had to dress accordingly. Something else I had to cope with. No matter the weather, I donned a thick black cardigan over my white school shirt, one long enough to cover my bottom. I didn't know then, or in the many years of it that followed, that it was a symptom of nervousness. I was a quiet girl. Then, anyway. And shy.

Kids asked me why I wore a sweater in the hot, summery weather. I told them I was cold or I was comfortable, and I suffered the heat in secret, sweating more and more underneath my cover.

I was constantly aware of myself and of how others perceived me. Every new shirt soon had yellow stains in the armpit area, so on the odd occasion when I was not wet, I still wouldn't take my cardigan or jumper off, as it would only reveal the evidence. I didn't wear deodorant, and I worried about getting too close to anyone in case I smelled.

I felt their eyes boring into me. I heard whispers about my odd behaviour. I felt sweat trickling down my side like a mini waterfall.

Take it off, take it off, I told myself, but that would have given them even more to talk about. *Little Miss Masturbation sweats – Erghh!* I could hear it all. No, I wouldn't take it off.

My doctor said I had Hyperhidrosis. He gave me a regular supply of Anhydrol Forte, Aluminium chloride, which blocked the sweat glands. Applied at night, the irritation, itching and soreness, caused by the strong medication kept me awake. I wanted to scratch the skin off, and my armpits looked and felt as if I had been stung by a swarm of bees.

But it worked, most of the time when I could stand to apply it as it did block the sweat glands. Thank God. I could take my cardigan off, as long as I was careful which shirt or blouse I wore underneath. But it felt good at last, on occasion to wear just a shirt – I felt free, finally, at least for a few days.

So there I was – Amanda Green, doing what all normal kids do. There were challenges along the way, but isn't that just life? And yes I was a bit of a loner sometimes, but I was never truly alone. There was always God.

Although my family were atheist, I still found it comforting to pray from a very young age. I was not influenced by others, and have no recollection of how I came to think about God and Jesus, since I had not read the bible, but all I knew was they were there listening to me, watching me and helping me when I needed it.

I'd sit on my single bed in my little pink room, and close my eyes in preparation. I'd clasp my hands together tight.

"Dear God and Jesus up above, I need your help and I hope you understand. I just want everyone to be happy and stop arguing. I want my family happy, and my friends, and everyone in the world to be happy and stop suffering. And I want to be happy. Please, please God and Jesus up above please let everyone be happy. You can do it, I know you can. Please stop everyone hurting. Most of all please make Mum well. Amen."

Chapter 6

September 2008

A name

I'm back in the office. Dr Jones studies me across the desk – it's been a week since our one hour session when I told him about me, growing up, trying to put the pieces into some order – trying to find sense in the chaos and the life that was mine, only it reads like someone else's.

That's when he says it.

That's when he tells me he has a diagnosis.

And that's when he says the words that will change my life, three little words: Borderline Personality Disorder.

Borderline Personality Disorder (BPD), he explained, is a condition of the personality which is on the borderline of psychosis and neurosis. He tells me there are nine characteristic symptoms.

(1) Regular pattern of unstable personal relationships – often due partly to black and white thinking or *splitting*, where the person feels others are very good or very bad with no in-between.

(2) Variable self image.

(3) Impulsive behaviours: sex, driving, eating, spending and substance abuse

(4) Chronic feeling of emptiness.

(5) Overwhelming fear of abandonment.

(6) On reaching high stress levels, paranoid thoughts or dissociative symptoms (running on automatic or feeling 'unreal' and removed from reality) can occur. At the very worst, the person may experience psychosis (their thoughts, feelings and experiences are not shared with others).

(7) Suicidal threats, gestures or attempts and/or self-harming.

(8) Mood swings; anxiety, anger and depression. The symptoms can be very brutal, with rapidly changing from intense anger and in extreme cases, violence, to heightened excitability or depression. The symptoms can be similar to Bipolar but, unlike Bipolar these mood swings can last only minutes, hours or at the most a couple of days usually.

(9) Anger – easily triggered.

Nine symptoms. Nine ticks. Not the five required for diagnosis; I have all nine. Nine things that I can own as mine and a name; am I supposed to be happy now? Can I take a pill and make it all go away? 2% of people apparently have it. But what's more worrying is the statistic that 10% of those with BPD commit suicide.

Although Dr Jones says I've been suffering with Borderline Personality Disorder for a long time, maybe it's been bearable, but it's not now. Now I have to do something about it. It doesn't seem to me that I'm getting much empathy, let alone sympathy, so I feel inferior and the inferiority complex feeds my anxiety and anxiety leads to confusion, frustration and then anger and disruption of relationships. And it goes round...

How did I get to this point?

How much of what I told him about me growing up and being an adult led me along this path?

What happens next?

And am I ready to face it yet?

Chapter 7

A typical teenager?

1987

When I was thirteen, I broke my mum's finger.

Everyone was out of the house, leaving just Mum and I. We'd been arguing and she was shouting at me in the lounge.

"You protect your dad 'cause he's your favourite!"

"Rubbish! That's all you care about, whose side I'm on."

"Well, it's true. Since his mother's death, it's all about him."

"Shut up!"

"You hate me!"

"I said shut up!"

"Always on his side…"

"Shut up! Shut up! Shut up!"

"You don't care about me!" Her face was snarled up and the glare from her eyes pierced mine and through to my soul to inject her hate in a way that no one else's eyes could.

"How can I care about you when you're so horrible all the time?"

We faced each other on either side of an armchair. I used the armchair as a defence, but it didn't protect me from her vile mouth and she wouldn't shut up – on and on jibing about my dad, who was so sad over the recent loss of his beloved mother. Mum never liked her.

She would not stop ranting – endlessly ranting.

I thought of the neighbours, who must have heard through the wall of our semi, and when she came at me with her evil distorted face, that was it. I launched at her and swung my right arm, hard. meeting her hand with a thump. She stopped and went quiet. Her expression changed to a grimace.

"Mum, are you OK?"

"My finger…" Her voice was shaky.

"Let's see it," I said, and she presented her left hand. The little finger was bent ninety degrees at the knuckle. I drew back momentarily. I felt sick. She said she felt sick.

"Let's go out to the kitchen," I said. I held onto her and walked with her.

As I led her into the kitchen I could see better in the bright light. She had a strained look on her face, which had paled, but she said nothing, only sobbed quietly.

I was shaking. She was shaking. I knew she needed the hospital, but I couldn't leave her finger like that, so abnormal, in case it set that way. What had I done?

I told her that I would straighten it, very fast.

She didn't agree, but she didn't disagree either. She held her shaking hand out and I took a deep breath and lined up my path of action, steadying myself by leaning into the cupboard under the sink. I squeezed my eyes shut, and then opened them and bent her finger back to straight in one quick move. She cried out. I got a sharp pain in my stomach. Then I told her not to move her finger in any way.

At the hospital, the doctor said that I was brave to force her finger back into place, that if it had set crooked, he may have had to break it again to reset it. He said he would have done the same thing. His voice was kind. But what I did, that wasn't – was it?

The funny thing is when I mentioned this to her years later she said she didn't remember it. Maybe she too dissociated from painful things. But as I checked her little finger, it was slightly bent, and I knew she had just forgotten, somehow.

When I was fourteen I wrote a letter.

It was one I'd written to my friend Julie when on the plane going to Portugal...

I've been smoking on the plane can you believe it? Two. My dad is in front of me you see, and the seats are high so he didn't know. I thought that was really funny. I've just finished dinner, it was OK I suppose. This plane's quite posh. It's got a video screen. 'Shelleys' on at the moment, Tales of the unexpected has been. You have to listen to it on these special earphones...

The words take me back

When I got to Portugal Dad let me smoke – I had to ask him for permission as I wanted one every time he had one and had to resist, so I thought it best to tell him I smoked and he was fine about it and even offered me one of his as he thought I was just asking him for one. It didn't bother my mum either. It was all good after that at the time. When the teachers complained about me smoking in uniform at school, he stuck up for me.

Stuart was a real Northern lad, with a cheeky but handsome face although he did have a gold hoop earring in his left ear.

He was in fifth year, making him fifteen. I was a year younger, and had almost white blonde curly permed hair, which I would bleach myself. Looking at the photos of Stuart that I took on my pink *Le clic* camera and reading my diaries brings it all back. All the blowjobs I would give him in the caravan in his mum and dad's front drive. Him drinking so that he could wear my arm out when I wanked him. His lovely mum and dad and sister, who I'd have dinner with. Losing my virginity to him on Thursday 24th November 1988. He wouldn't wait until my 15th birthday. The condom splitting, being worried about being pregnant. Him telling me that other girls are pretty. When he told me to go away because I had my hair tied up and it looked horrible, he said he didn't want to be seen with me! He chucked me on my paper round because he was always being horrible to me and he wanted some fun with other girls! So, we split. In the meantime, I'd started clubbing and getting drunk until I was sick. I was still mixed with my brothers' older friends and girlfriends, which I had been all my childhood, and I enjoyed it. And I was still dealing with things at home. But now I was a teenager and things were about to get complicated.

Journal: 9th December

Ian hit me round the head twice because I told him his food was shit.

When I was fifteen I looked in the mirror and saw someone else.

I was growing up. It was Dad who had to explain about periods and buy me my first sanitary towels. Imagine that?

But it wasn't just that.

In the mirror, it wasn't those changes I saw. And I didn't see my skinny frame or my strained face, just the bulge in my tummy.

I resolved I had to do something about it and made a plan that would hopefully obliterate it forever. It had to be flat, end of.

I had been working quite hard on the project over the previous few months, but had found nothing that fixed the tummy issue. I'd lay on my bed with my knees propped up in my little private pink room, surrounded by posters of the Bros boys, Nick Kamen, James Dean and fluffy kittens, avidly revising the calorie counts of every type of food or drink that I might consume at some point or another. I had my head in all kinds of diet plans and books, and wrote down in a little pocket book everything that passed my lips. I stared at the list, dissatisfied. Always one too many boiled sweets or a banana, which was a whopping ninety calories.

I weighed myself a few times a day and the decrease in pounds of my bodyweight pleased me.

I had read somewhere that laxatives were good because they pushed the food through quicker and the calories and fat were less absorbed, leading to weight loss. Great idea! Off to the chemist, I bought Ex-Lax laxatives off the counter – in the form of little chocolate pieces in a cardboard packet, got home and shoved some in my mouth. Those little miracle pieces of chocolate worked a treat when I was having my 'one day of eating'. If food entered my body, it had to exit as fast as possible, so I had an answer for everything.

Sitting on the toilet a few hours later, emptying the contents of my bowel in fast succession was such a relief – I loved diarrhoea. I'd also found *Limmits* lunch bars by then – a low calorie 'meal in a bar' - and would just eat those apart from an occasional dinner. But soon it interfered with school.

Usually I would meet my friends for lunch. We'd eat our packed lunch and either hang out in the school grounds, bantering about something, or we'd rush over the school field to the public playground, where all the boys went. They loved to excite us by spinning us round fast on the merry-go-round. We'd laugh our heads off, until we thought we'd fly off it. Boys could be bad, of course.

But, I'd go home instead as part of my new routine. Each trip was nearly a mile, so I'd walk nearly four miles a day, just going to and from school and spent more time on my own with my new diet obsession.

Before long, I found myself running most nights after school. I felt free as I ran round the back roads of my town to the fields beyond. My trainers pounding the track, I taught myself how to deal with a stitch in my side – breathe all the time methodically and slowly as I ran, in through the nose and out through my mouth, and the air didn't get caught. Every step freedom, every step my body felt better, every step I pounded out the thoughts in my head – memories, events, boys, shit! All shit! Get it out. Writing my diary every day helped to erase the day, but running really pushed it all away into the recesses of my mind.

Midway through the three-mile jog, I had half a cigarette – rationed exactly. The other half would be put back in my box for another time. I enjoyed it. Being in full control of my actions, to overcome my grumbling belly and hunger, was an achievement. After two days of eating nothing, the hunger subsided, my stomach felt empty and I was full of energy to exercise even more. What a wonderful feeling, feeling so light, and to see that flat tummy in the mirror – it was worth all the effort. It was about taking control. If I couldn't control others, I *could* control myself.

But rain stopped me jogging.

If a downpour came, typically British climate, I'd put some music on in my room and do star jumps, running on the spot or dancing, intently watching how every bit of my body moved in the mirror on my chest of drawers. I particularly liked Diana Ross' *Upside down* and I loved dancing – it made me feel free. I couldn't do much as I had around four foot by two foot floor space, but I managed a sweat and I just had to do it for longer to achieve results, then straight in the shower.

My friend at the time, a skinny, pretty girl called Marcia was thinner than me. I felt fat. When it came to boys, she got most of the attention. Eventually, I had a strict routine going, which entailed no food for three days, except for three boiled sweets.

We didn't have regular meals being cooked in my house, so I was able to keep my little diet to myself. Following the three day period of starvation, I would binge, stuffing sausage rolls, cream cakes and other naughty foods in my mouth, always waiting until the house was empty. When out shopping with Dad every Friday, I would choose all these treats myself so they would be waiting in the fridge for the right moment. Standing at the end of our narrow kitchen, by the bin, I would munch my way through packets of food ravenously. I would then do one of two things. I might chew the food, spit it out into the kitchen sink and dispose of it down the plug hole so it didn't enter my stomach. Or, if I felt like a treat, I would scoff them as fast as I could, go upstairs and stick my fingers down my throat and puke the whole lot up, repeatedly purging until there was nothing left in my gut to come up or the retching and acids caused too much pain in my stomach or throat.

Next, I would eat as normally as possible for two days, everything calorie counted and logged, using *ExLax* to push it through, then back to starving – starting the six day process all over again.

I remember continuously bashing my hip bone on everything and I loved to see the bones on my chest and ribs poking through my skin. I was never, thank God, at death's door. This six stone person was fantastic at covering her body, keeping the puking a secret, and dodging all possibilities of getting caught or stopped and it lasted for several months. Although I have to confess, I still had issues with food for years afterwards.

At school, I began taking the cross country and long distance running seriously in P.E, and in our last Sports day I came second in the 1500 metre race, coming second only to a competitor for our county – a professional. Finally, the need to succeed overcame my self consciousness.

Looking at the numerous photos of myself taken a couple of years after this period, I can see that it worked and I did have a flat tummy, but there are no photos of the time of my 'diet' – an unusual gap in my life history of photos.

Dieting for days on end, bingeing and throwing up, and exercising for hours a day, took its toll and my body started giving up and my periods stopped by the summertime. I reckoned this was great, but my friends did not. I hated periods – the pain, the blood, bad, erratic moods – everything about them. I got them pretty bad. I didn't want them anymore, so this was another achievement. I suffered lots of stomach cramps two years later, which turned into severe IBS when I tried eating properly again, for which I self prescribed hot chocolate and smoking weed. It was a three-day stay in hospital that led to my diagnosis for my chronic pain, constipation and diarrhoea – (IBS) Irritable Bowel Syndrome.

My parents knew nothing about my diet and my secret routines. By the time I was thirty-two, I had had three teeth extracted and lots of root canal treatment and I think it was connected to this early abuse of my body – acids rot teeth and upset the gut, and lack of nutrition make teeth weak .

***

Excerpts of My Diary - aged 15

Friday 24th March 1989 – *Danny White came round so I went out with him in the car with his mate Ben and Tara. Danny didn't try anything!!!*

Saturday 1st April – *Went to see Auntie Teresa* (Aunt Agnes's sister) *and later, Danny and I went to the pictures and saw 'Tequila sunrise' (shit!!!) I said I was sleeping at someone called Tara's and I slept the night with him We went down the arcades and slept together all night except I only got two hours sleep.*

Sunday 2nd April – *Dad did say be home early. I got home at nearly 5. Shit!!! They were out though. Danny went and got some Jonnies (mates). We went walking in the rain, and got* soaked. Found an empty lorry front and got in. We fucked. He came three times, but I didn't. I couldn't feel him. He said he couldn't get all of his dick in me 'coz my legs were cramped up, so we will try again tomorrow.

Wednesday 5th April – *Susan* (my friend from school) *asked me if he had fucked me, so I told her yes. She warned me about pregnancy but I told her I was not going to do it as much as her!*

Thursday 6th April - *It's Danny's birthday, he's 16.*

Friday 21st April – *Went round Damian's (*Danny's mate*) tonight with Danny. I drank lots of Vodka and got totally pissed. I don't remember half of it. I threw up for ages everywhere. Slept the night. Danny woz sober so he fucked me. We then went to sleep I think. Woke up to find Damian fingering me. I nearly threw a fit coz I thought it was Danny trying to have sex.*

Danny was using me for sex – I always knew that, but hey, I was young. It seems when I look back at these diaries how I always seemed to go for the same type. It's how I learned about sex. How I learned to gain attention by giving blowjobs and opening my legs. It's how I learned that I could be recognised for being good at something.

Thursday 4th May – *I'm sure Danny's gonna chuck me. I hope not.*

Sunday 7th May – *I think Danny's trying to get me to chuck him first as a bet*

Tuesday 9th May – *Had consultative meeting at school about my weight loss. Mrs Bates has noticed it.*

Thursday 11th May – *chucked Danny*

Sunday 30th July – *off to Torremolinos, Spain*

"We're all off to sunny Spain! Vi-va España! La la, la-la-la-la-la! España por favor!"

Mum and I were excited about going to Spain, so I got her singing and clapping the little ditty on the settee, while I danced around the rectangle, drab lounge, giggling and singing at the top of our voices. Dad put his head round the lounge door, grimacing, with his fingers in his ears and then he laughed. So, off to Spain we went, just the three of us. My three brothers never got any holidays abroad like I did, but Dad couldn't afford it when they were younger, so there was one benefit to being so much younger than my siblings.

Apart from a few unforeseen incidents, Mum enjoyed herself with us, wandering around the shops and taking day trips to Gibraltar and Spanish markets. We all adored the sun, and gradually saw our skin browning like toast. It was bliss, family time.

That was until the boys turned up.

And as you can see, I never was good at staying away from boys for too long. Danny was dumped so what did I have to lose?

I owned a pair of old denim cut off shorts, *Falmer Kitten Purrfect* fit, my Amanda G shorts and I must've worn them from the age of about fifteen until I was eighteen. I wore them with little vest tops and tiny, barely there cropped tops. I bought them as jeans, cut them down and wore them until the denim was pale and faded. They were tiny; to fit my size 0 waist and petite 5ft 3ins figure.

I wore my bleached blonde hair in a curly, permed bob, and I flaunted the entire package in those old shorts. And there I was wearing them in Torremolinos on our little family holiday... so it stands to reason the boys took notice.

They soon made their daily spot in the corner of the complex, near the pool, and I watched them from beneath my sunglasses – a strong urge to be amongst them, getting their attention. Mum was at the shops because she couldn't sit still long enough to sunbathe and Dad was chilling out beside me on a sun lounger. It was nice, having a beer and smoking cigarettes, and reading magazines in his company, but I couldn't concentrate with the lads...over there... in my face.

I made my move and slid into the hotel pool wearing my tiny black and fuchsia pink bikini. I swam in their direction, stopping in the shallows in front of them, to bask in the sun and wait, listening to their banter and laughing. The pool and sun beds around it were busy with other guests and I could feel all eyes on me, but I was only interested in the boys' attention.

It didn't take long: young men could never resist my curly permed bleached blonde bob, sun freckled button nose, blue eyes and skinny figure.

"Hiya, lovely day…" one of them started. Soon, I met all the lads, who, it transpired, were in their early twenties and lived just a few miles from me in England. They invited me out for an evening of bars and clubs; perfect. I liked hanging out with older people, perhaps because my brothers were older and I'd hung out with their friends and girlfriends when they'd babysat. I said yes straight away, but that I would have to check with my dad. Two of them volunteered to come and ask my dad's permission, and they escorted me back to my lounger, where they politely introduced themselves, pointing to the rest of their group, and telling him that they lived near us back home. Dad was pleased for me to go out and have some fun, and said that they seemed like 'nice boys' so it was a done deal. I was grinning on the inside all the rest of the afternoon.

Mum, Dad and I had dinner first at the hotel. I didn't eat much. Then I met up with the lads – all nine of them and the fun began, as we trawled from bar to bar, drinking copious amounts of beer and gin.

There I was in my element, surrounded by all these fun guys, all of whom wanted to talk to me and make me laugh. I wore my little white fitted cropped vest top, which showed my bronzed skin and blonde hair off and my little cropped denim shorts. I smiled and laughed all night, taking lots of photos on my pink *Le clic* camera, which I stashed in my purple bum bag along with my money, until I found myself in the queue for the ladies, having made a rapid departure from the lad's company. I felt my stomach turning and acid was forming in my mouth. I felt dizzy. "Excuse me, I have to get in the toilet, I'm going to be sick," I shouted. I was probably lucky I didn't get a punch in the mouth for being so loud and direct in amongst a load of drunken ladies, but I got away with a few frowns and moans. "You'll have to wait in the queue like all the rest of us," I was told firmly. "OK, well I can't …" but I never finished. A string of projectile vomit arced from my mouth and landed on the wall tiles. As I looked back I saw it clinging to one of the girl's shoes. I didn't look back again.

Apart from the projectile vomit, I spent most nights with the lads for the rest of that holiday. Until it was time to go home, back to reality. And I knew I was going to miss it. I just didn't know how much of that life style I was going to miss.

All my life I've had terrible trouble dealing with the quietness when the party's over; with rapid change.

I wrote in my diary that I phoned up the bar when I got home, where all the boys said they went. The barmaid knew them all and was surprised when I said I met them in Spain. She said she'd give Gary (the one I liked) the message to phone me Tuesday. I found out his second name, looked it up and found his phone number (just in case). When I got my photos developed I stared at them for hours.

I guess you can say I was love struck, or maybe I just needed someone to like me. It was a start of an obsession with men and a need to feel wanted. But I also wanted to have fun. And I guess I wanted to be loved.

Gary eventually called and asked me to go to the cocktail bar Friday. I said 'yes' and he told me eight o'clock at *Kentucky Fried Chicken* and not to bring anyone. The next three days were filled with excitement. I really fancied him, although, to be honest, I fancied a couple of the other guys from the group more, but he showed interest in me and we got off with each other on the holiday, so I channelled my efforts and desires into him. I just wanted to have a laugh, continue the fun from the holiday and to be his girlfriend. That was until I met him on the Friday. There he was in a t-shirt, jeans, five foot six. But all he kept doing in the cocktail bar was leaving me so he could talk to his ex-girlfriend. His friend, Steve, assured me that Gary really fancied me. On the way home in his car we were quiet.

I remember how it was both awkward and charged with anticipation. He didn't have a lot to say to me as we didn't have a lot in common. My problem all along with guys was sleeping with them too early; giving them what they wanted, and then being dumped, but it didn't happen that night. I did *get off* with him in the end which was heavenly; his soft mouth meeting mine at last, his tongue touching mine, our saliva mixing. But that was all we did.

So who was I? Who did I want to be? Amanda Green in her little cropped shorts, flirtatious, getting virtually any male attention she wanted? Or the person she always felt underneath all of that, just a shy little girl who wanted to be loved? Believe it or not I was both of those things.

But I had a lot to learn.

We all have two faces

A few days later, after finishing work at the café where I'd got myself a Saturday job, I met Gary again, but we did nothing, not even a kiss. The next day, Dad took Mum and I for a ride to the same town where Gary lived. *I had looked up his address and we even found his house. He was in, I saw his car was there, but I couldn't knock, I was afraid he'd think I was a stalker*, is what I wrote in my diary.

It's funny when you think of it years later. A teenager doing what many typical teenagers do – fancying boys and partying and leading guys on to like me... what was wrong with that? I was having fun.

But three months later I was raped.

Chapter 8

A diary excerpt I found written at age 15 years – entitled 'A very horrible and gruelling experience one Tuesday afternoon on a day off from school'

3rd October 1989

Last night, well the night before actually (I can't even think straight here) on the 2nd October, I was half asleep on my mums bed when the phone rang. My mum woke me up because she thought it was going to be for me, but I wish she hadn't. Anyway, I answered the phone and it was Susan, someone I hadn't been out with for a long time. She asked me out for that night, and although I felt awful, I also felt like going out and as it was going to be to a pub, I said "yes."

If only I had of said no and gone back to sleep.

So, at 9 o'clock, Susan appeared at the door, I said goodbye to Mum and went outside to find a Y reg escort with a guy called Dave, who I kind of knew as he used to date Susan, and this other bloke, called Vinnie. He was driving.

We went to a pub called The Lobster and I had just a couple of pineapple juices and I didn't smoke much because I wasn't well. In the car I could only see the back of Vinnie's head and he seemed quite nice, turned out he wasn't. We left just after ten because we had to get Susan home and I said I'd be in early as well. During the evening I mentioned that I was having the next day off school, but I should have kept my big mouth shut.

We took Susan home and then drove back to my place. When we got there, Vinnie asked me if I'd like to go out with him for lunch the next day, and me thinking that it was a good idea, said "yes." He said he'd be round at about 11.30. I didn't really know whether he would come or not.

But he did and he was on time.

We went straight to Woodgrove parked up, spoke just normal chit chat, then we went for lunch opposite Woodgrove Station in an Indian restaurant. I got him to order for me because I knew fuck all about Indian dishes. We had red wine, which I thought was really strong. I had a feeling I might get pissed or something. Our meals came and it was all really nice, but I was actually feeling rather tipsy by the end because he only had one glass of wine because he was driving (I wonder if that was part of the plan to get me half pissed? Mind you I had no thoughts of him doing anything to me at this time at all).

We left there and went bowling. That was alright. Then he wanted to go back to my place, as I could make him a cup of tea (my arse that's what he wanted) so I said no, we couldn't. I didn't want to go home and he said that he knew of somewhere else that we could go, but didn't say where. Anyway, after a lot of driving around, we went into a road just off Station road. A couple more roads off and he stopped. He said it was where he lived and pointed at his house. He told me to wait in the car, and he went into his house. A couple of minutes later, he was back. He said to get out, so I did and he went over to this bungalow I think it was and unlocked the door. I asked him again who's house it was (he'd said his house was down south) and he said it was his sister's. I didn't know what to think. Inside, I sat down and we chatted and smoked cigarettes and he said he had to leave to pick his nephew up. He was only about fifteen minutes and he came back without a soul. I assumed that he had taken him to his house just up the road and he didn't mention a thing, only that I hadn't made him a cup of tea, so I offered, and he said that he'd just had one. Where? I thought, but I said nothing. I had been reading a magazine of his sister's (she was apparently at work) and he took it away from me, saying that reading showed that I was nervous.

I started to wonder what was going to happen next, because he mentioned that Susan had said to him the night before not to expect anything and he said that he wasn't a kid and he knows what he is doing, he's not stupid etc. Only thing was he kept on saying it here there and everywhere, and I was beginning to feel a bit uncomfortable so I lit up a fag and started to bite my nails. He then mentioned that it was another sign of nervousness and I admit that maybe I was rather nervous. I mean he is twice my weight and size and ten years older (I couldn't go out with someone with such an age gap and I had only gone for a laugh as he seemed quite nice). He had already told me he was twenty-five the night before.

I didn't know what to do; I couldn't read my magazine (his sister's) as he had ripped the page out that I was reading, told me to put it in my pocket and threw the magazine on the floor. I didn't argue, as I was sure that he had a bad temper, from little things he did or said through the day, like when I said to him that it wasn't good enough not having a stereo in the car coz I like music. I said it jokingly and he looked really quite annoyed and said that I could get out and walk if it wasn't good enough (miles from home) so I just shut my mouth after, to keep him happy.

Anyway, he put his arm around me and started fiddling with my hair and then in the middle of my ponytail, round and round. God, I was getting really annoyed and told him to stop, as I hate people playing with my head. But he didn't, he kept on. By this time I found him really creepy and I was beginning to wonder what was coming next.

He then came over to kiss me, so I did, and it didn't seem to stop! He was on the floor with me the next minute, just kissing, and he seemed to be getting a bit carried away, touching me up. God, this is making me cringe and shivery, writing this. He was rubbing my parts through my jeans and wanted to put my hand down his trousers, I resisted and said No about ten times, but he kept putting my hand down there. I didn't want to do anything like that, or him to me but I admit that I did touch him from outside his jeans, just rubbing to keep him happy, but he said he couldn't feel it and that I owed it to him to get inside properly. I owed him fuck all and I started to shit myself. What the hell should I do?

I mean, can you believe it? He seemed to actually think that because he took me out and paid out for me that I should do sexual favours for him. My God!

Anyway, I kept pulling away and told him that I didn't want to but he persisted in putting my hand there. Now I know I am hardly Miss Innocent, but Christ I have my pride. Yes that's it. That was what he said to me. Did I have my... And I finished it by saying pride and he said that he agreed totally and understood what I meant. Yeah right. He didn't stop. In the end, he just undid his trousers, so I kept my hands away. He took my hand, though, and put it down there onto his penis so I sort of started to wank him off, but not very well. I didn't want to.

We were on the floor and he pushed my top across and caressed my breasts. I admit that he must have good experience of sex and everything seeing as he is twenty-five and it did actually feel quite nice, but I couldn't enjoy it. I didn't even want to do it. How could I stop him though? I mean we were on our own and he was so much bigger than me. I told him that I didn't want to get involved and he agreed and then just carried on. He obviously wasn't interested in what I wanted. I think that he is just a pervert, and I can imagine him taking prostitutes out and having sex with them all the time. That is all I can think of him really. Although, he said earlier in a conversation, that he hates slags. He must have thought that I was one if he imagined that I was going to have sex and everything with him on our 1*st* day out, I mean for fuck's sake I am fifteen years old. Actually, maybe that's why he thought that he would take me out, Oh Yeah; she's only a child, won't know what she's doing and is feeble anyway. Christ, I wonder if he did think that?

Eventually, he started on my jeans that I was wearing, trying to get inside them, and again took no notice of my refusals. He undid the zip and put his hand inside, making a horrible comment that I didn't want him to coz I haven't got any pubic hairs. That was nasty and once inside, he obviously found out that I had and said nothing more. He then started to push a finger up into me and it was very uncomfortable because my jeans were in the way (This is horrible coz I'm getting feelings down there that makes me want to cross my legs, you know what I mean, just thinking of his dirty hands being near there. I feel really dirty myself and I keep thinking that maybe it was my fault, but it wasn't, I'm just trying to make myself feel better). Anyway, I wasn't going to help, so he said that he would have to pull my jeans down, so I began to get really frightened that he might try everything on, I mean how could I stop him. So he started on my baseball boots, I knew what he was doing, but put on an act that I didn't, so I asked him what he was doing. He said that he'd have to take my jeans off coz he couldn't get inside properly. It was then that I knew he would put his dick up me and I felt like screaming. But I couldn't, who would hear anyway, and that would be silly anyway because he would of got nasty as well. So all I could do was put on an act that I suspected nothing and I was enjoying it, so that he might understand better if I said No, if he thought that I liked him and wanted to see him again. (maybe he would think that he might get IT another time) I thought it was the right thing to do, and I still do, so he got my jeans off and carried on with his hand, kissing me all the time. His dick was out all the time, but I kept letting go when I could and he didn't seem to realise, probably 'coz he was getting too carried away with me, and he was moving about all the time.

As I said, I was putting on an act, but he still knew that I didn't want him to do what he was doing. So, I was there on the floor without my jeans and he got up, pulling me with him as he went over to all the doors, shutting them, and the curtains, so that no-one could see in, and it was then that I realised that he was going to go all the way and I was getting really worried 'coz there was nothing that I could do.

He pulled out the sofa, making it into a bed on the floor, and he took me down onto it (Oh, before this he had also tried to get himself up me on the sofa, but I was making it difficult by being in the wrong position for it, plus I was pretty rigid because there was no way that I could relax). On the mattress on the floor, he spread my legs apart, so I was trying to keep them together as much as possible, so that he might go off the idea after all. He did actually attempt to lick me out, but he wanted sex more, I could tell. We kissed again (I had to respond because if I had fought, it might have ended up with full-blown RAPE, but it wasn't far from it anyway, 'coz I didn't want any of it all) Before I knew it he was positioning himself to go into me, so I told him that I had had enough and it had all gone too far, making excuses that he had no protection, which he hadn't, but he mentioned that he had been having sex with his previous girlfriend for four years without protection and nothing had happened (he was supposed to have chucked her 3 weeks previous, but I couldn't really believe a word he said, why should I?) Then with a quick jerk, he was up me before I knew it, it really did hurt and after 3 pumps I nearly screamed, but swallowed it instead. He asked if it hurt. Half paralysed I felt, I said yes and told him again to stop, and he did. Before I could be relieved, he started again saying that it would get better, but it didn't. I think that part of the reason that it hurt so much was because I was so tense that everything had gone tight. This may have been good, because after a little more pain, he quickly pulled it out and came all over my belly, it was disgusting (I remember him telling me that the withdrawal method was how he did it with his ex-girlfriend). That may be so, but I still have his dirty, horrible sperm up me, for Christ's sake I hope not. He picked up some tissues and wiped the spunk off me and went and flushed them down the loo. He came back and I got dressed.

He tidied up and we went to the car, he drove around and then took me home (I couldn't walk home, I was hurting. Also, I noticed on the loo that I was bleeding, enough to show on my knickers, but I didn't tell him that) He asked me if I wanted to go out with him to a club on Friday and I said yes probably and he believed me.

He then expected a goodbye kiss, so we did, but I hated to do it after everything. He said he would pick me up from school the next night.

I went in feeling horrible, needing a good old clean. I was still bleeding, but it didn't hurt anymore. I said nothing to anyone, and was as nice as I could be to everyone despite the happenings. My mum asked me if I enjoyed the day and I said yes and hated lying. I wanted to tell someone, but I couldn't so I stayed in my room most of the evening. I went to bed.

Got up for school the next morning, went to school and I was shitting myself in case he saw me. By the end of the day, I had told Susan about him, but only that he had suggested, not done. She wasn't impressed at any rate though. I wanted to tell her the whole truth, but I lied "No" when she asked me if we had done it. I couldn't tell her, not in school, so I bottled it up instead. This was in last lesson and after I met Jane and some mates. I told them that I wanted to avoid a man called Vinnie so we walked across the field. Then Jane and I turned back to see if he was there, so I could maybe tell him what to do, but we were 20 minutes late anyway and he wasn't there. I was glad 'coz thinking about it, if I had told him to piss off then he might have followed me or something, I was really ready to believe that there was nothing that he wouldn't do.

So, we walked home and I couldn't stop thinking about it all. When I got home, the phone rang, so answering it I could hear it was Susan (I was frightened it was going to be HIM, but he wouldn't have my number anyway). She said that she'd phoned Dave and that he said sorry, then I couldn't handle it. I told her the truth. She said she'd come round after phoning Dave back to tell him. Also, that I shouldn't answer the door. I didn't think that he would come anyway, so when there was a knock at the door, I answered it, thinking that it was my Mum, but it wasn't, it was him. I closed the door a little so that I could just talk to him and he could just see me, just in case he might try to get in or something. I was literally shaking, I was so shocked and frightened. Everyone was out. I didn't know what to say. He asked where I'd been 'coz he'd waited (too fucking right) so I said I was late out. Did I want to come out with him for a spin?

"No."

What was wrong?

"I've been thinking about yesterday..."

He blanked me out and said that it was just one of those things, so I started to really upset myself (though I hardly showed it) by having a right go. He said *"It takes two to tango."* (fucking cheeky bastard, I felt like crying)

I told him that he knew that I didn't want to do it from the start and he then began to agree saying *"Sorry"*

What good was that going to do me now?

He didn't know.

He said that if anything happened he would do anything, pay for anything, and that if I wanted to get him into trouble, he would carry all the blame and admit to everything by the laws (too right he would – but he seemed to think that he was being nice saying that).

That reminds me, back at his sisters, yesterday, after everything, he said that if I did get that way inclined (pregnant) it would be OK 'coz he's with 'Bupa' and an abortion would be free – he laughed like it was some kind of joke and I had felt ill at his behaviour.

He didn't mention that now though (Oh, he'd also said that no-one else would know – before it happened - 'coz he's not a big mouth). Then he actually had the front to ask me if I was still coming on Friday.

I said "You must be joking?"

But he wasn't. He'd bring Dave and Susan along and drop me off first to show me...

"Show me what?"

That it wasn't just a one off and that he did want to see me again.

Fucking cheek I tell you, I think he has got something wrong with him, he just cant face up to facts. I told him that I wasn't going to, and he said that if any trouble was caused, he would tell the truth. HUH, too right too. He said he was going round Dave's and left.

I shut the door, noticing how shaky I was, so I went and got a fag and the key to the phone and phoned Susan straight away. I told her everything and she said she'd phone Dave and come round to me.

She got here and we talked of HIM and she phoned Dave as he wasn't in before. He said that HE had been round to him and is shitting himself in case I phone the Police. He thinks that I'm going to for some reason. And he told Dave a bull story that we had both got carried away and it was both our faults. And he'd just been to me saying that he will tell the truth. Oh shit!!! Susan thinks that I should go to the Police, but although I want to see him punished, I don't want to get all the hassle as well.

Today, 5th October, Susan told me that he reckons I gave him a blow job and everything and Dave believes him, saying that if I did that, I've got nothing to moan about. He's obviously just looking for a good alibi 'coz he thinks I'm going to the police.

I didn't go to the police. I wrote about the day instead, as you've read here. Shortly after that, my memory of Vinnie disappeared as if it had never happened.

It was a whole seventeen years later, in 2006, I rediscovered the rape as I searched through my diaries while undergoing therapy for my depression. I felt uneasy about myself when I read about this incident with Vinnie, as if I were reading the diary of someone else, with her dirty little secrets and self destructive behaviours, not a fifteen-year-old version of myself. I wasn't a virgin when Vinnie raped me, but I didn't deserve that.

    Not long after that, I cut myself.

Chapter 9

Ho Ho Ho

1989/1990

Christmas has always been a time for celebration and family.

I remember Christmas 1989 very well, three months after I was raped but of course it couldn't hurt me then because I had pushed it to a place so deep I couldn't retrieve it. Not yet. I guess that's why I made the cuts. Of course I was only an amateur at that form of self-harm: not a real cutter with a few knife or compass flesh wounds and my measly thirteen holes – unlucky for some? Thirteen holes in my ears. I never questioned why I did it. Or why I did any of the things I did. I suppose I just did it. But when I think of it now it must've been a reaction to what happened. The memory of Vinnie I had shut away. He couldn't hurt me, but I could hurt myself.

Every time I made another cut I liked the way it felt

I got a small gold stud ready to put in the new hole in my flesh and placed it on my chest of drawers in my bedroom. I closed my bedroom door. Using a ball point pen, I made a small mark on my ear where I wanted the next piercing to be. I burnt the end of the needle with one of my collection of novelty lighters; the one shaped as a gun that my mum had bought me.

I pulled my ear lobe out with my fingers, to make it taut and ready for a new hole, watching in my bedroom mirror all the time. I placed the needle onto the pen mark and pushed onto it to pierce the skin, using fairly hard pressure. Once it pierced the skin, I jabbed it right through the thick flesh and took it out quickly, replacing it with the gold stud and fastening the back in place; finished with a good dab of surgical spirit.

I threw myself onto my bed. My little ritual didn't satisfy me. Twiddling with my thumbs and wiggling my toes, I stared at the ceiling, struggling with my brain to think of what to do next. I didn't have any more spare earrings to fill new holes with. Then, I had an idea. I leapt up, grabbed my pencil case out of my college bag and took out my compass. I burnt the compass point using one of my *Zippo* lighters, enjoying the smell of petrol it emitted. All ready.

Using the sharp compass point, I began to scratch the knuckle of my left index finger. One line down, about one centimetre in length. One line across, about half centimetre. An L shape. I had to scratch the same lines several times to make it bleed and clearly define the letter on my skin. Sharp, scratching, pain, self inflicted relief. It gave me relief – the enjoyment I was looking for. And it was something different. A word will soon be etched across the hand, and then I will be satisfied. Next knuckle, scratching, digging with the compass point. Circular. An O. Needed to be more careful with the O. Next knuckle, a V. The pain, very nice, scratching and digging, bright red blood and jagged edges to the letters. The taste, lovely, natural, as I sucked on the cuts. Next and last the knuckle of my little finger, an E. LOVE. Marvellous!

When I showed Mum she wasn't amused and nor was Dad. So after that instead of carving something they could see, I resorted to using the bread knife sawing little lines into my forearms – deep enough to bleed but not so deep they would scar, although a couple did very slightly.

I'd been going out with a guy called Zack for a week who didn't ring or come round and he said he would that evening. I phoned him and he said he was sorry. I felt dreadful, and grabbed the knife from the bread board in the kitchen and headed upstairs to my bedroom with it.

Everyone was out.

I rolled up the left sleeve of my sweater and with the knife in my right hand I rested the blade on my left forearm before pressing down and sliding the blade down. The serrated edges caught my skin and dragged it as it was partially blunt, so I had to saw up and down a couple of times before drawing blood. The cut, the blood, the soreness, all had the power of relief for me. I put cotton wool and plasters over it, after squeezing the luscious red liquid out for a moment and tasting it, then rolling my sleeve back down. Mum and Dad came home later and I stayed up with them and watched *Top Gun*.

I cut myself just a few times. I wanted to do far bigger cuts and bleed much more, fantasising about it regularly, but I resisted. I didn't want to ruin my looks too much and I was very much into how my body looked. I wanted to love my body. It was one good thing that I had and that men wanted.

The word love featured quite a lot in my life. Not because I was told I was loved by my parents, because I wasn't, only in birthday and Christmas cards, but because I wanted love. In my diary under miscellaneous I came across something I'd written. It said *please love me*.

When I think about it now I was shown love. I just didn't always feel it.

Mum, Dad and I would often go shopping and they'd buy me clothes and take me out for lunches and dinners. And on Fridays I'd go food shopping with Dad: he'd let me choose anything I liked more or less. He was also my 'taxi' service on many occasions. And when, in early December, I suffered a kind of breakdown at my café Saturday job, Mum and Dad were the first to come to my rescue. After spending the night at Julie's house, where her mum cooked me a roast dinner and a cooked breakfast, Dad came and picked me up and took me home instructing me get some rest, to go to bed. He even changed my bed and tucked me in. After five days recovery he took me out for a pre-Christmas lunch and some Christmas shopping.

Julie's mum was great too. She'd let me stay round whenever I wanted, and even gave me a key, because she knew I had a habit of missing the last bus home, and had a penchant for walking the streets alone scaring myself that I was being followed. I didn't want to be followed but I liked the adrenalin. She also fed me - not that I wanted to eat but she refused to have me in the house if I didn't.

And at that time I also had Auntie Agnes and Auntie Teresa who I'd visit often. Agnes would not let me leave any food.

It was a strange experience, the breakdown I had, if you can call it that; maybe the first real signs that something was wrong with Amanda G?

So another family Christmas followed.

One with just my brother, Ian Mum, Dad and myself. Ian and I had been down the local pub for a quick drink before our Turkey dinner at Mum and Dad's house where I still lived. It was nice to escape to a place of festive cheer and jolly people and we bumped into lots of people we knew. Thing was, I think we may have stayed down the pub a little too long.

Or maybe we didn't ...

We got home to find the Turkey on the table and the rest of the roast dinner trimmings going cold on four plates – two of which had been touched, but hardly eaten. Where were Mum and Dad? It was silent. Ian and I just looked at each other.

"Oh," whispered Ian, "Shall we go and see where they are?"

I told him to do it.

Ian crept upstairs and realised that Mum and Dad were indeed still in the house. They were both in bed, in their respective bedrooms. I imagined the whole scene that had most likely happened– shouting, screaming, slamming doors and all over nothing no doubt; Dad giving up for the day and seeking solace under the covers.

We panicked, for a minute or two, then burst into giggles for a short while and ate some turkey – just the two of us. I don't think I really knew whether to laugh or cry, but it was quite cute all the same, just my brother and I, peace and quiet.

After lunch, we decided to get the Chinchilla Ian had bought for his girlfriend Clare, out of its cage for a quick run around before she arrived.

Because it was a Christmas present, it was un-named. He had bought it a few days before, so I had been looking after it for him, at Mum and Dad's, to keep it a secret from her. I had enjoyed that of course, taking on the responsibility and enjoying the little animal. It was going to be a nice surprise.

I'd always loved animals.

After about half hour playing with him and letting him run free, Ian decided we had better get him back in his cage, as Clare would be turning up soon, and we didn't want it running out of the front door when she arrived. Thing was, it had gone behind the pine dresser by the lounge door, so we had a job on our hands. We came up with the idea for Ian to pull out the dresser, while I caught it as it ran out from underneath. As he edged the dresser out slowly, it did run out, and just as I was about to catch it, a heavy hardback book landed straight on its back.

"Oh shit!" I panicked, grabbing the book.

It retreated back under the dresser and we froze as all we could hear were tiny cries from the poor thing.

"Shit, if Mum didn't bloody clutter everywhere this wouldn't have happened!" I started. We hadn't thought about the pile of hardback cookery books teetering on top of the flimsy MFI pine effect dresser special! Bloody cookery books were never even used in our house anyway.

I felt sick, scared and shocked, and I could barely stand it. The cries only lasted about thirty seconds; then the silence was even worse. I told Ian it was his animal and he will have to deal with it. He pulled it out and it was dead.

Now what? Clare would be there soon!

Ian chose to wake Dad up and tell him the news. Dad would deal with it – he was good at things like that. Ho Ho Ho, and all that.

But of course Dad was not amused. In fact, he told us he was still angry with us for going down the pub and ruining the day as we weren't there to please *Mother*. But he did his fatherly duty and came down to sort our situation out. Since we thought it best for Clare to be oblivious to the fact that there ever was a chinchilla, it was decided that burying it was best. So Dad and Ian wrapped the little lifeless fluff ball up in cloth and quickly dug a hole in our side garden.

We were almost ready to lay the chinchilla to rest, when…

"Hello, Happy Christmas, what is that you've got there?" asked a jolly Clare from the other side of the garden wall to the hole, pointing at the tiny package in Ian's hands. Dad, Ian and I looked up simultaneously.

"Erm…" said Ian.

Poor Clare was in tears moments later when she realised that her present was so cute, but yet so dead. She held him for ages in the back garden, refusing to let them bury it for a good half hour or more. She named him Bob.

I couldn't tell you how the rest of the day went. It was probably a mixture of tension, pacifying *Mother* who'd been coaxed out of her bedroom, salad for tea, beers and plenty of laughter, I don't know, but this was not the worst, nor the best Christmas I remember.

It is, however, the one I remember the most.

Poor Bob. That night I prayed for him.

Maybe I should've prayed for myself.

Chapter 10

Sweet Sixteen

It was 1990; the start of a new decade. Maybe what I needed after what happened with Vinnie and then the saddest Christmas I could remember.

But it wasn't the best of starts.

My close friends had become increasingly worried about me losing my periods for what was now five months, so Jane had offered to come with me. Sitting in the waiting room, my nerves were frayed, my thoughts filled with horror, and I got more and more restless as each minute passed. I was just short of bursting into tears when the doctor called me in. I told Doctor Griffiths everything, five months, I've had no periods. He gave me a form to send to the local hospital for a referral.

Finally the hospital appointment came. I had the day off school to go and managed to get Mum to go with me, although she didn't like hospitals. The letter the specialist sent to my GP said…

This lady has secondary amenorrhoea, I am sure because she lost two stone in weight in three months last year and though she has gained some weight she is still only 7st 4lbs clothed at a height of 5ft 3 ins. She actually knew the reason and has spent some time dissuading some of her friends from dieting this year. I have told her that she has to be well over 7 ½ stone and I think she will probably achieve this. I don't think she is in a particularly anorectoid state. I have arranged to see her again.

A great start to the year that was. I was always good at dealing with these things with my happy, positive 'persona'. I temporarily didn't care about how I looked anymore and had my hair cut into a crop – back to my natural dark mousy blonde colour. I didn't want to look pretty anymore or attract any boys or men, although I did have a boyfriend of sorts, but I didn't really like him. I wanted to end that Amanda Green; take all her armour away. I didn't care. I felt shit. I wanted to be a child again and couldn't stop crying. I was an emotional wreck; nervous, inward, lacking confidence, dressing down in baggy clothes and had a real need for drink… So, it was no surprise when I went on my skiing trip in February that I had a few problems…

"I can't go down there, I can't do it."

I whimpered to the teacher. I was a child again – innocent, scared. When I think about it now perhaps that little girl came out because of what Vinnie did to me, taking control of my body and mind like that. But there were always those two sides to me. I was the little girl who didn't want the men to look. Maybe that's why at that time I'd had my hair cut off into a boyish crop and donned baggy tops and trousers. And then there was the Amanda G who wanted them to look. Who so wanted someone to see me.

And that day I wore my purple all in one child's ski suit, cheap sunglasses and factor thirty sun block.

The day was warm, with the most stunning Mediterranean blue skies, white melting clouds and blazing sun illuminating the pristine white snow, but the beauty of the environment made no difference to how I felt.

Shaking, I looked down the snowy piste, watching bodies in colourful suits traversing across and down the slope, in and out, passing each other, some going fast, others slow, all enjoying themselves. I watched my school friends grouped together near me, preparing to form a line, aided by Mr Gray. I wondered what they thought of me getting drunk the first night and crying so much on this holiday. I didn't even know what I was crying about, I couldn't work it out; I cried at home a lot too over anything, particularly when Dad went on his skiing holiday and left us at home; abandoned for a couple of weeks. I sat down on the crunchy, yet cushioning snow, my skies still fastened to my boots. I felt safe sitting. *Still, Nicky is being nice to me, he's a nice boy and they are mostly a pleasant group…*

"You can't sit there," said my teacher, jolting me out of my day dream. "You have to come down with us, there's no other way."

"Yes there is. Please don't make me ski down, I can't do it," I pleaded "It's too steep. It's a red run and I can't do it. I can walk down. I can't ski it, I'm too scared."

"There's nothing to be scared of," she replied "You can do it, and you are going to do it. Stop being silly, you skied well last year, and you can do it again."

My face screwed up. I started to weep. The teacher reassured me that I was capable, and that there was no choice. She organised my group so that I was at the end of the line.

"That way," she said, "you will stay in control of yourself – you just have to follow the line."

I was to stay at the end of the line and ski in line with my group, keeping behind them at all times. Mr Jarvis was talking to Miss Turner quietly a few feet away from me. They looked over at me in unison, Mr Jarvis frowning. They were fed up with me. They named me the 'mad skier of the holiday' and I even got a certificate saying so at the end of the holiday. One of my lesser appreciated accolades.

I didn't want to be a pain. I just felt scared and incapable of everything and my instincts told me not to go down this hill of snow attached to skies. But the teachers were giving me no choice.

With me last in line, we commenced a slow descent, sliding across the slope with our skies dug into the snow for balance in our long train of young humans. First turn – a careful wide snow plough turn with our skies pointed in at the front and out at the back. Everyone does it, one by one. All good. Then my turn. Lean into it. Nice and slow. Yes, that was OK. My legs were shaking though. I was not enjoying it one bit. We started across the slope again to the other side, ready for another turn. They all turned, one by one. All very neat. My turn. I began a turn. Halfway through it, whilst facing down the slope, I froze. I couldn't finish it. Oh no. Instead of swinging my body back into the slope, I was going down. I passed all my friends and teachers. I was going too fast to do anything. Just down and down. People were getting out of my way; and quick. Down and down, so fast, so out of control. Death, I saw death coming. I saw the end of the piste coming – rocks, trees, abyss at the bottom.

I saw the bottom coming closer. So fast. I've had it. I summoned up movement and threw myself into a skid stop. I was going too fast. I skidded. I skidded. I skidded. So fast. "Shiiiiiittttt!" That was the only word that came out of my mouth. After that, no more words. The slope finished. There was no more land to hold me down. I took off into the air. Oh quite spectacular it was! A couple of seconds... then thump, I landed.

I was hurt.

I remember being surrounded by people, I heard Mr Jarvis moaning about me. I was rescued by the emergency services who carefully packed me onto a stretcher on skis, and two men skied me down and down through the mountains, to the bottom, where I was transferred by ambulance to the local hospital, me crying all the time. I was alone because I was transferred faster than the teachers could accompany me and I found myself in a corridor of an Austrian hospital where no-one seemed to speak English, until I met the doctor. It was all a blur, waiting what seemed like an age, and all alone surrounded by the sounds of an alien language, and footsteps along the corridor. It didn't seem a busy place, so I couldn't work out why I was waiting in the corridor, but once I was seen and X-rays done, I was told my diagnosis. All I had with me was my hard massive clumpy ski boots, and no shoes to change into, so I couldn't put them back on for swelling in my leg, and I asked for crutches as it hurt so much to put pressure on the damaged leg, but because I didn't have any money for a deposit on me, they refused to give me any. Once all this was over, my PE teacher, Miss Brown, turned up.

Still, I was more fortunate than the best skier in our school group, Larissa, who was sharing my room – she fell over a suitcase in the room the first night and broke her leg!

Whenever I shave or moisturise my legs, I see the dents in my shin bone through my fair skin. I feel them occasionally, running my finger over them and I remember how lucky I was that day. Torn ligaments, cuts and bruises, that's what I got away with. I was meant to survive. It didn't stop me skiing either and I was never scared again.

I supposed the lesson learned was just do it. Face it. And if it goes wrong, don't be afraid to try again. *Get back on the horse.*

It's a pity not all lessons in life are that simple to face and overcome.

After the holiday, I started to find my alter ego again fuelled by drinking alcohol which took away my inhibitions and changed me from quiet to raucous and I was back to trying to find love from men, through shagging, but I was beginning to have more mood swings than usual, grumpy, angry, happy, like I had a chip on my shoulder

***

Summer of 1990

My brother, Peter, and Mel got married. My friend Debbie came to their wedding; my mum did not; no surprises there. But, by now, a couple of years on, they had moved to Australia – an emigration that had been well planned out.

Fly away Peter...

Sunday 22nd July – *After an evening of wandering about the streets of Woodgrove, my friend, Natalie and I bid each other farewell, as I got the late night bus home.*

The nearest stop to my house was up the top of the hill, a fifteen minute walk away, which I was quite happy to walk on my own, since I enjoyed the terror it would produce – walking, listening, watching shadows, imagining someone following me from behind. But, this night I had two companions – Rod and Andy who I'd been chatting idly to on the bus journey. They were nineteen and I was immediately attracted to Rod, with his short dark hair, tattoos and stubble; a typical rebel of the time.

Being that Mum and Dad were away on holiday, I was able to ask him round for coffee which he jumped at and we watched one of my favourite films, *American Werewolf in*

London. I gave him a massage and we were kissing etc on the floor when Mum and Dad walked in. Rod left.

Monday 23rd July - *Dad took me up the White Hart and I saw Rod. I went back to his house. Rod was pissed and we went up to his bedroom and had sex. He wanted it up the bum but I wouldn't. He used two condoms.*

Saturday 28th July – *Saw Rod tonight. The condom split so we couldn't have sex. We laid in each other's arms. How sweet, it's what I've always wanted to do.*

Monday 30th July – *When speaking to Rod and moaning coz he was going to sleep, he said not to bother coming round anymore.*

When I left school I wanted to be a secretary. I did well at my RSA typing in school. But when I did leave I continued working for my Saturday job at the café and ended up working in factories, temping, during the week – pill packing, hospital laundry centre, all sorts. I also canvassed for and collected money for a hospital fund regularly in the evenings. But then who really knows what they want at that age?

In the September, I started college at sixth form, doing French, Psychology and Law. It was OK but I was often late. When I think about that time I was too busy shagging men and getting drunk to really care about my career choices, or who I wanted to be.

There was plenty of time for all of that. Right then finding love was most important.

Chapter 11

The world was my lobster

August 1990 I went on holiday to Turkey with Natalie, my friend from the café. We told the manager we needed two weeks off for our holiday and she said no, so we both gave her our notice and went anyway; a fun experience of leaving a job that I was to repeat many times in my life.

The Gulf war had just started and Dad said I couldn't go, but I convinced him that we were going to the other side of Turkey to the war and he changed his mind.

Although I had some adverse experiences with the men in Turkey, (due mainly to the colour of my hair, my provocative clothes, my age and naivety) I was astounded by the diversity of culture, scenery and people. Sipping peppermint tea in *hubbly bubbly* shops, wandering the busy streets of Istanbul, with the smells of sticky sweet Baklava and rich meats wafting through the air, to the azure seas and rugged coastlines at Oludeniz, it was an experience I'll never forget. We'd just bought a flight and spent two weeks travelling about finding places as we went.

Sixteen and already too many notches on too many bed posts - but did I care? Of course not! I was young and free and I could do whatever I wanted.

I woke up one day after Turkey and decided I didn't want to go to college. I guess I was bored, (I don't 'do' bored very well) and I still didn't know who I really wanted to be. It only lasted three months. I left just before Christmas.

I wanted to get a job; earn money and be with older, more mature, people. Amanda G was ready for the world. Amanda G who'd worked different jobs for years, and had good feedback, Amanda G who'd dated loads of guys, Amanda G who needed to prove her worth, who'd got drunk, smoked, been abroad, related to adults… I wanted to be independent, have a career and get noticed; be an adult myself…

A confident adult.

I wanted to prove to everyone that I could have a career and get noticed, to be wanted and appreciated by employers, to get money so I could do as I pleased. I wanted to be responsible and show that I wasn't a fuck up, I was a useful person and could pay my keep to my dad. My brother, Ian, had told me I'd be better off getting a job and I was very easily encouraged.

But was the world ready for Amanda G?

Chapter 12

Go out and get it

1990/1991

Saturday 17th November – *met Gary, the guy from the Spanish holiday last year. We had sex (without a condom!)*

Monday 19th November – *Went to Woodgrove to get a job. Went to the Doctors with Dad about my depression as I keep crying and breaking down. Doctor Griffiths said that he'd arrange for me to have a counsellor.*

It was Dr Griffiths who first used the word depression. I don't think I knew what depression was then. I do remember the events that led me to a doctor though. How I broke down at in that café and how Julie didn't know what on earth to do. Until then I guess I always thought my emotional outbursts were typically hormone-driven and normal.

I wonder if things would've been different if I'd taken the doctor seriously back then? However, I was referred to a 'depression counsellor.' Merry Christmas.

Tuesday 18th December – *Dad gave me a lift to the mental health centre for my depression counselling. Whoopee doo. Not.*

I say in my diary that Christmas was 'peachy'. Well, it might have been peachy, but when I look at the photos of that Christmas time, all of us crammed into that bloody lounge at home, we look 'uncomfortable.' Aunt Agnes leaning forward on the settee, Ian perched on the arm of Mum's chair and David at the dining table. It just looks like too many people and bits of mismatched furniture in one room; the walls with that awful brown patterned wallpaper with a brown and orange patterned swirl carpet. Everyone (except Mum) has their shoes on and there's the pine effect furniture and some balloons but not much in the way of the usual glitzy, tacky, multi-coloured, Christmas decorations.

I guess there is some comfort from how life goes round, like a giant wheel that keeps on turning and we all get together at Christmas again like a roll-call. And the sense of melancholy that comes from knowing eventually everything changes.

And I couldn't help thinking that a year before Bob the chinchilla died under Mum's dresser.

This was an odd time when I think back on it; of no real direction or sense of purpose. Although I'd left college in December I'd made no real efforts to look for work and I had a skiing trip planned for January, in Romania which Dad had treated me to for getting eight GCSE C grade and 1 GCSE D grade (yes I could've done much better than that, as I was in mostly top classes at school, but I was always distracted). He told me well before my exams that he'd book it if I did well, to encourage me to concentrate and do well. I liked that he was taking notice of my exam results. I never really ate properly – a quarter of a sandwich and some crisps would fill me. And then there was the counselling; the lady there had said she would put me in touch with a qualified therapist in the New Year. A therapist? Come on?

It never happened and I never chased it up. Besides I had my therapy. I had alcohol.

And I had something else by then too – I had drugs.

January 1991 – aged 17

So the start of 1991 was much the same as 1990 – boys and clubbing, but this time with driving lessons and drugs thrown in. No wonder things started to spiral into chaos.

Friday 25th January -- *Smoked 3 spliffs with Frank* (my current boyfriend) *gave me 2 blow-backs from his spliff and I coughed my guts up.*

Saturday 26th January – *Left for Romania for a 2 week skiing holiday with Dad – met two guys on the coach who seem alright.*

I guess Romania wasn't so bad, as it was lovely to spend the two weeks with my dad skiing, meeting people, drinking and having fun without arguments, apart from my usual moments of acting like a spoilt child, but I found the poverty, begging children and crumbling buildings difficult to take in. It was all very humbling. And I think some of that stayed with me afterwards, but it didn't stop me floating around, although I made some efforts to look for work in the city. In the end I did find an office junior role in a firm of solicitors.

Wednesday 6th March – *First day at the new job. Got to work 20 mins late, but it didn't matter Typed a bit, loads of photocopying, filing and running around collecting and taking things and making drinks.*

Thursday 7th March – *Clubbing!*

I did a lot of clubbing on work nights, getting very drunk and usually surviving on less than three hours sleep before getting up for work again. That behaviour along with lack of nutrition meant that I was weak and confused most of the time – my concentration levels were very low at work. I sometimes wonder how I managed it.

I guess I didn't really – well not for long.

Sunday 17th March – *Stu really likes me, but he won't go out with me because I'm seeing his mate Frank. With Stu I really like him for him, I mean we've never made love and he respects me (the 1st) so it's a mental and physical (a bit) attraction, whereas, with Frank it's just physical I mean, I find that I only want to go round there when I can have sex*

Tuesday 2nd April – *Brother Peter and wife Mel are back for a visit from Australia and came round tonight. So good to see them.*

I have a photo of us, taken around that time in my life; on the sofa with the cat, Suds. Pete is hugging Mel and I and I have on my beige suit jacket, skirt and tights, so I have been to work. I look so skinny.

Friday 5th April – *Work – awful – really long and hard – got really pissed tonight. I dumped Frank.*

Monday 8th April – *I weigh 7 ½ stone*

Wednesday 15th May – *Work good today – best day in a long time! Had my hair up for a change, now it's long enough. I looked nice. I wore my crocheted white jumper and black skirt. Everyone was looking at me. I was confident. Went out lunchtime on my own. Met Jason. He gave me his number and said he'd take me out sometime. He lives in Woodgrove, just round the corner to me – what a coincidence. I didn't believe him at first. Phoned him* later on – he's taking me for a drink at lunch at 1 tomorrow. He's twenty six – nine years older than me!

Thursday 16th May – *Went for a drink with Jason. I'm going to Glitz's Nightclub over in Woodgrove tomorrow night with Julie. He'll be there.*

Friday 17th May – *Day off – went to Jason's house. He had a spliff. When we were alone (Jase and I) we sunbathed in the garden. He was quite close (touching me – arm round me and all that). I started getting a bit claustrophobic. Went clubbing later. Jason bought me and Julie a Pernod and Black and I started feeling really pissed. Had to go in the toilets. I couldn't get this grin off my face – then I was crying hysterically and my face wouldn't move. My legs went numb – my arms were moving uncontrollably and I felt faint and sick. Julie pulled me into a toilet and my back ached I could feel all the bones (I've lost weight again – I'm only 7 stone now – I just don't want to eat much lately – I haven't felt like it. My bones stick out everywhere again now) Anyway, I sat on the toilet and my arms and hands kept spasming and moving. I don't know why – I couldn't stop them. My stomach kept spasming and I felt sick and faint again.*

Things that could have provoked it:-

<u>Spliff</u> - 3 or 4 puffs

<u>Fags</u> – 2 or 3

<u>Alcohol</u> – 2 drinks

<u>No sleep much</u>

<u>No food much/weight loss</u>

Julie said I should see that Counsellor for depression I never went back to. Jason treats me like a kid, but I think I like him. Didn't kiss him – I think he wanted to kiss me but Julie was there.

It wasn't long before I was going round Jason's every night.

More smoking, drugs and rock n roll! Part of me was being good in trying to hold my job down, but clubbing at Glitz's or Cinderella's often on weekdays, and having two hours sleep and lots to drink and hardly anything to eat, was affecting this job, my energy levels and desire to work. In hindsight, I didn't really have a hope of keeping that job – I wasn't fit enough.

Wednesday 22nd May – *I'm feeling run down – no food or sleep.*

Thursday 23rd May – *Was totally fucked at work – and hated every minute of it!*

There's a photo of me in my bedroom, taken by Mum, with white lingerie on, and I look skinny and horrible, like I am trying to look older than I am. No shape at all…

Was that really me?

I guess, even though I never realised it, that was my life – no shape. What I thought was order was shaped by booze and drugs. And Jason – he felt like the one, or maybe he was just the one for now. But he was there. We had fun and our lives fitted each others at the time. We also rowed constantly, to the point of throwing stuff around and breaking things, screaming, shouting and numerous break ups. Yet, we still came back to each other for more.

He'd make me joints and hot chocolates when I couldn't sleep from the pain in my gut from my IBS. My periods had come back with a vengeance and I would bleed and bleed for days on end. He did look after me to a certain extent. We had lots of sex, I learnt to DJ on his decks, and we'd always be having people round his house to smoke joints or party in his decks room. I loved the attention I got when told how good at mixing I was. "You should be a professional girl DJ," Jase's mates would say. I liked that, I liked that a lot. I did DJ once on a family skiing holiday, and my brother Ian was really impressed. "That's my sister!" he told people proudly, pointing at me. I had *blagged* the set as I had no records with me, but the club had good records, so I mixed up all the ones I knew. Like a pro! People carried on dancing through my mixes. But I never did it again. That was the only time I had the balls.

The drugs get harder

I remember a time of rhythmic beats, hard baselines, bongos, and melodies.

It was a time when I would get lost in the music and, for a few hours, was in heaven (or ecstasy, like the name of the little pills we'd down with water). My body would be taken over, my ears more sensitive to the sounds, I'd feel euphoric; feel so happy and loving. The sensitivity of my skin and lips would be so enhanced and the slightest of Jase's touches would be heavenly. Or was it?

I've seen the photos I took, my pupils dilated so that my eyes appeared almost black – I thought I looked great. I thought those were happy days, happy times. But really – was it? In some photos, I just look completely trashed, gone, eyes rolling up into my head. Then, the come down and copious amounts of cannabis and skunk smoked just to stave off the miserable after effects. The come downs could be just awful: drained, pale, stomach upsets, feeling 'not normal' – wired – unable to sleep, paranoid.

And yet I was just waiting for the next party, and the next high.

Now I had a new list of favourite things; so different from those as a child where I thought about Aunt Agnes and cakes baking and...

Now it read:

- Ecstasy
- Speed
- Drinking
- Clubbing
- Dancing
- Acid (LSD)
- Cannabis
- Skunk
- Cocaine
- Jason.

Where had that little girl gone?

It had all started when Jason encouraged me to go out with his friends to night clubs, and while they were dancing 'til 6 am, I was knackered as I was much younger than his group. Was I trying to be like them? To fit in? It was Jason that gave me my first E, no wonder we had a tumultuous relationship, how quickly everything unravels. In the beginning he would go out without me, which was fine with me, I enjoyed cross stitch at his house waiting for him, but within weeks and with the introduction of drugs, I changed, I was jealous of his drug taking, wanting to take exactly what he did. We lived on the edge in more ways than one and we argued.

One of the most poignant memories is my dad coming to his house. Jason only lived a few minutes walk away, on the same block. I had been going mad at Jason, and he shut me out of his house (I once had a key but he took it back after a while to keep me out) so I was banging on the door and kicking it uncontrollably. He'd phoned my dad to come and get me. Imagine that! Dad remembers today, and will never forget, that people were watching him in the street as he pulled me away and told me sternly to 'pack it in' (his favourite words) and 'come home'. He will never forget it and nor will I.

I don't often look back on this time, I suppose many of the memories seem like I'm looking at someone else and I am not proud of some things. I wonder how much I realised what I was becoming.

Or maybe that was why, perhaps without knowing it, I always wanted to run away.

My brother had made a happy life in Oz... maybe it was my turn... but not that kind of Oz where all I needed was a twister and... a pair of ruby slippers.

Letters from Peter and Mel

Monday 1st July 1991:

Dear Amanda,

It seems like such a long time ago now when we were back in UK with you. The time has gone so quickly.

It was really great to see you. Do you still plan to come to Australia? If so, when? Please let us know. How is the job going?

Unfortunately Mel has not been too well since our return. She has been feeling increasingly short of energy, nauseous, sick and sometimes headaches, often tummy aches. She has been off work now for two weeks and is having extensive tests done as the specialist doctor suspects she has gall stones. Hopefully all will be revealed soon.

Take care and keep in touch.

Wednesday 7th August 1991

Dear Amanda,

Mel is fine. Thank God it is just a virus. But when are you coming?

We phoned you twice last week as soon as we received your letter. Dad and Mum answered both times and said you were out staying at your boyfriend's house. Who is he? Tell us all about him, if you want to.

Anyway holidays... Mel's sister is coming over in December and I am sure would greatly appreciate having you to travel with. What do you think? Fancy a travelling companion?

Perhaps Agnes could help with the cost of the tickets. What better time than now to travel, particularly while we are still here. We have not decided to definitely stay in Australia yet. We could probably help with the cost of your passage. Have a think about it and talk with the family to see how they feel (you could get a years work permit and get a temp job if you wanted).

We would be so pleased to have you for a while. Let us know soon.

I don't know if it was something I planned as an escape or not; that trip to Australia. I still lived with Mum and Dad, so I had the freedom to up and leave. And my brother was over there; urging me to go and visit. The only thing really holding me back after finally losing the job in the solicitor's and flitting between jobs I disliked, was that I'd finally found a job I liked; at the local petrol station of all places. I worked there a year believe it or not, did lots of overtime and got a very positive reference from my boss, before I did eventually go to visit my brother and his wife – and I paid for it all myself.

When I look back this was a relatively stable time in my life, well apart from Jason and the drugs. Maybe it was an escape, maybe it wasn't. But I did dream about a new life, a possibility of what?

Finding myself?

Chapter 13

August 2008

Treatment

Letter from Psychiatrist 14th August 2008

Thank you for asking me to see this patient. As you know, she is single and has no children. She attended the interview with her boyfriend, Chris; the couple live separately. Quite clearly, she has many unconscious conflicts from early childhood; she has abused drugs in the past and has had a series of co-dependent relationships. In 1999 a Great Aunt died and the patient was very close to her, this aunt acted like a mother to her. The patient bought a flat as she was left money in her aunt's will. However, she had to sell this flat as she couldn't take the responsibility of living there on her own... She has been living with her parents again for the last five years and finds it very difficult to trust people. She unconsciously chooses 'damaged' men and obviously feels very 'needy' and lonely. In 2005, she had to go through personal bankruptcy and she met her present boyfriend in July 2006, who was separated from his wife. During this time the patient was extremely jealous and possessive towards him and would telephone him up to forty times per day. She has seen four therapists in the past including counsellors, hypnotherapist/CBT therapist and a psychotherapist but she has never had any psychiatric treatment.

Her mother has Catatonic Schizophrenia and was an inpatient at Hinton Hall and Woodgrove Psychiatric hospital. She was admitted to hospital frequently when the patient and her brothers were children.

At the age of 14 years she developed an eating disorder, Anorexia Nervosa and during this period she had self induced vomiting and abuse of laxatives as well as exercising excessively. Her lowest weight was 6 stone and she developed amenorrhoea. She had this eating disorder for three years and she was frequently promiscuous from the age of 15 years. She was taking illegal drugs from the age of 17-24 years including Ecstasy, Amphetamines, Cocaine, Cannabis, LSD, Mescaline MDMA and methamphetamines; she used drugs to "blot out" her conflicts and for fun.

Quite clearly, she is going to need considerable psychiatric treatment and I will see her again in the near future to continue my assessment.

Chapter 14

The Land of Oz

1994

Everyone needs somewhere to go – somewhere where the grass grows greener.

I was young. I'd spent that last four years unwittingly looking for something other than the pink walls of my childhood bedroom or dancing in an ecstatic haze pretending it was real, pretending what I felt for Jason was real. There comes a point when there's been too much fighting. That's why I said yes. Yes I'd go to Australia; maybe even find a new life.

They'd asked me so many times, I suppose they knew one day I would say yes. Why not? Jason and I were forever splitting up. Auntie Agnes was always encouraging me to go. She loved travelling and so wanted me to have some fun and experiences too. She went to Australia for five weeks in 1990 when she was ninety years old and she had a ball.

Australia was my way to break away; to do something for myself. It wasn't hard to leave Jason behind; so I couldn't have loved him. *Not really.*

But in the end I didn't really leave him behind.

While I loved working at that petrol station and had been offered management training, I did ask for time off, to come back to it, but my boss said no. They couldn't do that. When I look at it now he was setting me free.

I'd saved hard that year before I went. In fact, in spite of those lost years I'd always managed to save money – from every little job when at school and then on. By the time I was ready to go I had £6,000 - a lot then. I loved having money. It only took me six months to spend it all though – you only live once and all that!

I booked a flight, applied for and got a working permit for one year and off I went. It was as if all the pieces fell into place – just like that

Almost.

I got back with Jason during that year's wait before the trip. He wanted to come, but he didn't have the money, so I told him to save. He never had any money despite his previous lucrative career in air conditioning, had been on the dole since the early 1990's recession, and had his mortgage to pay for. I was going anyway. That little bird in me was trying for freedom wasn't it? When I left for Australia Jason agreed to join me there later. But at least I spread my wings and I chose freedom.

That reminds me of a very important song that came out a few years later, *I'm like a bird* by Nelly Furtado – I said that that song encompassed what I felt and who I was at the time of its release in 2001. Yes I was like a bird, yes I always flew away, no I didn't really know where my soul or my home was… and no I couldn't commit to anyone.

Peter met me at the airport.

It didn't occur to me until I arrived at Sydney airport that I didn't really know my brother, odd as that sounds, and yet I was going to live in his little family home. But I soon settled in; lots of chores like cleaning, cooking, and my gorgeous and well behaved eighteen month old nephew, Jamie, to play with. So it was fun. I missed Jase within two days. I'd take the forty minute train into Sydney, meet my brother for lunch and embark on various day tours of the City's highlights by myself. Museums, the Bridge, Darling Harbour, Opera House, Botanical gardens and Kings Cross red light district; so different. I felt immediately comfortable and for once I didn't care how I looked on the outside as much. Although I had grown my hair into my long curly, bleached blonde, Amanda G bob before and during my relationship with Jason, I had cut all my hair off yet again to go on this trip – always what I've done, cut my hair off and be a new me. Or that's what I thought anyway. So, I looked quite boyish again. The atmosphere, the friendly people, hot sun, bright blue skies and slower pace of life; it was a new place and I felt like a new person. I walked round utilising all forms of public transport, taking photos of everything. I'd pause every so often to soak up my surroundings, to try to be in the moment and appreciate how lucky I was to be there. It was something that came naturally to me then, but I had to be trained to do when older, when I had forgotten how to be 'in the moment', using sound, touch, smell, sight and taste to be truly there.

Pete, Mel, Jamie and I all went out at weekends to places such as the Blue Mountains and a weekend away in Manly. We cooked, drank Baileys, watched Mr Bean videos and played scrabble, but I was distracted with thoughts of Jason.

Saturday 24th Sept 1994 – *Up at 6am to phone Jase… Stayed up on my own and watched TV. I really miss Jase. I wish he could join in on what I am doing. Pete and Mel are lovey dovey and I need a cuddle.*

Sunday 25th Sept – *Wrote some letters to Jase and to Mum and Dad. I miss them all!*

Monday 26th Sept – *Went to Sydney at 11 to George St shops and the Rocks centre. Posted my aerogrammes- a pre-paid air mail letter that folds and glued itself, so I didn't have to* *have paper, envelope and separate postage. I was convinced that the post people were going to steal them.*

This was one of the first bouts of paranoia I experienced.

Tuesday 27th Sept – *Jase rang me. I said something about his sister and he got all funny so it wasn't a nice call. Went out for dinner and phoned Jase to say that I miss him. He said to just 'get on with it and enjoy yourself!'* (He'd said that when I missed him and phoned him from one of my skiing holidays, leaving him behind a couple of years before.)

I wonder now if he was 'getting on' with it. I have since found out that he was indeed getting on with a few women during our four years together.

My photography obsession began in Australia and I took 1600 photos in the six months I was there – reels and reels of film.

Friday 7th October – *Got up at 8.30 to ring Jason but he wasn't in (he wasn't in last night either)*

Saturday 8th October – *Before I left Jason rang (2 o'clock am in England!). He said he loved me and he got us to say we could trust each other. He said he was coming in a couple of days!*

Yeah right. If only I knew what he was up to then - hindsight is a great thing. It's not the cheating that bothers me, but the possibility of sexually transmitted diseases.

It seems incredible now that I went from drug induced partying and doing as I please, straight into Christian family life, church on Sunday's, singing hymns, cooking, chores and 'getting on with people' (well, apart from a few moods when I had my period, but that's hormones and normal since I was on the pill). It showed a great ability to accept change and proof that drugs were not an addiction for me, but simply something to 'fill the void' in my life. Once I had other things to concentrate on, I was perfectly fine. Perfectly.

My diary excerpts were as detailed as ever, recording the time that I got up, what I ate and exactly what I did and what I watched on TV all outlined each and every day. An obsession, and one that was to be my saviour later.

You don't always see yourself the way another person sees you looking on from the outside. I may not have known it but that obsession of mine for writing it all down, in all that detail was like a dot-to-dot puzzle – a way to go back, to see who I really was. In my hand was the answer, but it was a few years yet before I was to see that.

Tuesday 11th October – *Met Jason at the airport... It was nice – we kept smiling!*

Thursday 13th October – *Up at 6.30 to go to Sydney with Peter and a ferry to Taronga zoo. Had a lovely day. All sorts of Australian, Indian, African animals etc of course, my favourites were the Orangutan. They were very funny. Pete and Mel cooked us a lovely Bar B Q then we packed ready for our big adventure! Got a bit stressed about packing a small rucksack and went to bed.*

I have always got stressed about packing no matter how much I have travelled

Saturday 15th October – *Tour of Ayres rock, then the Olgas at Sunset where we walked through the Valley. Very hot! (100 degrees) and the sunset had clouds over it so we didn't get to see the changing colours of the rock at sunset. (just our luck!) Spent our time dodging Aboriginal people in the evening because Jason upset them. They wanted him to buy them alcohol as it was against the law for them to buy it and he nearly got in loads of trouble with security as it's against the law to buy it for them as well.*

We had plenty of fun, and plenty of arguments, travelling round Australia.

We met lots of people, beat lots of people at pool doubles, and had a blast canoeing gorges, walking and experiencing amazing feelings, tastes, smells and sights. I have a vast journal from that trip, far too much to show. I challenged my fears and felt great for doing it even if it didn't solve them, such as my claustrophobia and fear of water, but I had so much more strength, energy and will to fight.

See how I only speak about what 'I' did and how proud of 'myself' I was – not about Jason - as if something was opening up between us. Maybe I could see it, maybe I couldn't.

On a horse riding trek, we learnt a lot about plants and trees.

There is a stinger tree which feels like an iron burning you and the *Acacia cuspidifolia* strings grow long and catch onto your clothes, so you cannot get away for a while until it releases its grip. That is why its nick name is *Wait a While* – I should know because when wandering off in the rainforest on my own to 'catch a photo of a possum' I was caught up by one. I had a slight panic attack, but Jason and I were reunited eventually, by calling each other through the trees.

When I phoned Mum and Dad later they seemed surprised to hear from me. I didn't ring often. I guess after years of me not phoning them to tell them what I was up to and disappearing to Julie's or elsewhere they were used to me being out of contact. I feel bad now that I was very selfish in that way, and must have worried my dad at times when I didn't get home on time or phone him. But guilt seemed to make me worse…

Mum had a cough, a cold and a septic toe and she sounded really old. I didn't say much. But I do remember one thing she said to me: "Have you been diving yet, Amanda?"

So I learned to dive. We decided to do a Pro-dive PADI diving course. We sat in the classroom for two days, learning the basics. Had a medical test (I didn't think I'd pass, but I did) and we learned quickly how to breathe underwater. Slowly we mastered how to fill our masks with water and clear them, easier than I thought. I could do it. I was learning a whole new way to breathe.

Sunday 6th November – *Pro Dive ON THE BOAT TODAY! The 'Kalinda' – shoes off for three days. We went down to 12m and sat on the sand at the bottom. Later I saw a shooting star.*

Monday 7th November – *Our 3rd dive and we all passed. Hooray! Now we can dive on our own. Went the wrong way, was watching my depth gauge all the time and getting freaked so was breathing quickly. I panicked and surfaced with Jase and we were quite a way from the boat but it was OK – we were OK. Later we did a night dive. The boat shone with light* *and we had torches. Swam through the coral alleyway and sat on the sand. We turned off our torches and waved our hands in the water so we could see fluorescent particles called plankton It was amazing, just how I imagined being in space would feel, weightless, dark and tiny stars shining...*

Tuesday 8th October – *We hired a diving camera today. Got up at 6 and in the water at 6.30am. Spent time mucking about taking pictures down there. Saw a black tip reef shark – what a result. It came right in front of us and swam away so I took photos, really excited. Much more relaxed now.*

I had lots of strange dreams.

But at least not the recurring disturbing dream I would have repeatedly throughout my childhood and young adult years where I was always being chased and never could run away fast enough, always my body slowing down and they are catching up and I become numb and my legs wont carry me – I am doomed… or dreams about being trapped in some way…Chased or trapped was the theme night after night.

What will happen to Mum when Dad passes? I asked it then, I ask it now.

What will happen when I get home?

What will happen…?

I made a list…

I should travel around the British Isles when I get the travel bug – by car – easy and cheap.

Do more cross stitch, it's relaxing

Theatre/cinema

Swimming/sewing machine

I don't want a baby

I don't want a 'nice' bloke

I need a reliable person

Every woman can moan, not just me

I need to be number one /respected/thought of

I need to trust people.

Everything we do becomes a memory so soon

Priorities –

1. *To see my family and enjoy them, especially Auntie Agnes*

2. *To see friends and go out and have fun*

3. *To see Jase – decide*

4. *To get a car*

5. *To sort out pension and money*

6. *To do a new CV*

7. *To get a job and enjoy it!*

8. *To get a place to live and to holiday!*

Our travels lasted two months and had an unfortunate ending.

We were going to Manta Ray Reef for two dives. First day was OK but the second day Jason and I had a row. That was the first day I had a sore throat. Next day – another row, it hurt to swallow. We boarded the boat separately for Whitehaven Beach on Whitsunday Island. The beach was beautiful white silica sand (like cornflour). My throat was worse and I found out that there was a kind of cyst. Jason and I played a game of pool and suddenly I got prickly heat on my back. I showered and cried; my throat and my ear were painful. Tropical Ear they called it.

Next day I left the cruise to go back to Airlie Beach with Jase (not that he wanted to). I needed a doctor. I was taking lots of painkillers. The doctor was English and friendly and as I explained and he looked, he decided it was 'Tropical ear' and 'Tonsillitis' both together and he syringed my ear.

Recovering, or trying to, the following day, Jase decided to get drunk with the guys. I got pissed off that I couldn't drink as I was on antibiotics and we had a huge row. I sat outside near the pool waiting for him to come back. When he did, I watched him realise I had disappeared from the chalet, and he went looking for me. Then I felt guilty. When he came back again we had a fight. Not just a row, a fight this time. He knocked my bad ear and grabbed my throat where my glands were already swollen.

In spite of what happened we decided we would finish the holiday together, but by then I think I knew it was over. I was fed up with him. We went to stay with some of his family in Gympie and although they were lots of fun, I'd had enough of Jase after a week.

I left one morning, alone, got the bus to Byron Bay and hung out at a Youth Hostel where I soon met some new friends. Being on my own did me so much good – in just three days I realised it was OK to be on my own. I felt immediately independent and I liked it, just myself to think about. I met Lilly and Anne there and was destined to see them again. I had also put on half a stone and was feeling very fit and well due to the lack of alcohol intake, a healthy diet and all the outdoor exercise. During my time in Australia, I learnt to form a healthy approach to, and enjoyment of, food again. I learnt to love food – the flavours, textures and smells of each ingredient. Chopping, preparing and cooking pastas, barbeques and vegetables. The food was so fresh it made me feel good on the inside and I stopped weighing myself constantly, becoming more relaxed as time went on. It was easy in Australia as I didn't have the same self consciousness as I did at home. One of the first things David said when I got home was that I looked 'healthier' and he was pleased. I have never 'dieted' again, never deprived myself of food again.

Wednesday 7th December – *I should be going home today, but I'm not. Jason is. He doesn't want to carry on our relationship. Got emotional at the bus stop so said a rapid goodbye and left when the airport bus arrived. Got on the wrong train and got home 2 ½ hours later. Jason rang from the airport which upset me even more, so I blurted out my story to Pete and Mel. They hadn't realised we had split up.*

Monday 12th December – *Decided to go to Orange on my own to be independent again. Felt very lonely on the coach and I miss Jase a lot. Got off the coach and straight into an old pub – met a few Ozzies and an English guy who took me down to the Canobolas Pub/Hotel to meet a load of Ozzies who were going out to dinner at Gumbo's restaurant. I had Cajun popcorn (prawns). I got offered a job waitressing by the manager.*

Tuesday 13th December – *Started work at Gumbo's restaurant.*

So there I was. Jason had gone and I was alone with new friends; a far cry from those days at the petrol station; those heady days, those drug-filled days, those good old days... what did the future hold? Would I stay – forever? What did I want? Did I even know?

    Maybe I would – soon.

Chapter 15

August 2008

She needs help

Letter from Psychiatrist: 19th August 2008

I reviewed this patient as an outpatient on the 18 August. As you know, I last saw her five days ago and she attended the interview with her boyfriend. She told me that she has seen her counsellor in Woodgrove for one year and she also had Cognitive Behavioural Therapy at her family doctors surgery weekly. She still gets mood swings and everything is magnified out of proportion. She tends to be unpredictable and has periods of anger, aggressions, violence and displaced this anger onto her boyfriend. She cannot form close relationships easily and has a chronic feeling of "emptiness" in her life. She is also extremely jealous. She is attention seeking and exhibits disturbed behaviour. Quite clearly, the patient has longstanding personality problems and has great difficulty trusting anybody. She drinks up to 42 units of alcohol per week which is obviously twice the safe level of drinking

She would benefit from 16 sessions of Cognitive Analytical Therapy and also Quetiapine as a mood stabiliser. The dosage of this medication could gradually be increased by 25mg BD up to 150mg BD if she had no side effects. She will consider these options and will let me know her decision in due course.

Chapter 16

Is the grass really greener?

1995

They were in their thirties with long, dark curly hair.

After a few games of pool they invited me round one of their houses for a smoke and off I went. I was greeted by a couple more guys when I got there, I felt a little uneasy; outnumbered somehow, although they *were* friendly. One brought out some silver foil and filled it with something. I was so caught up with what they were all doing, conversation and worry that I didn't even ask what it was. Burning the contents of the foil with a lighter, it started to smoke and he inhaled through the top of a pipe, as I watched the smoke being sucked up into his mouth. He paused before offering it to me. Always up for drugs, I sucked up the smoke next and within a moment I found myself lying on the lounge floor on my back.

I have no idea how long I was down there but I was aware at one point of one of the men coming to lie down next to me and I didn't like it, but I couldn't move, a bit like those recurring dreams I had. I think I drifted off and I came back to life much later so it seemed and took a look around. The man was still next to me, he was touching me. I woke up then and told him firmly to get off me. I got up gradually, and went over to the other men in the kitchen.

"I want to go home now," I said.

"We can't take you right now – we can go later."

"Oh no, I want to go now."

Anger took my sleepiness away

"We can't go now."

"Oh fuck, where am I? I don't even know where I am, you must take me home!"

"We can't."

"YOU MUST TAKE ME NOW!" I was screaming by this time and started hitting things. "GET ME A FUCKING TAXI THEN!"

I was aware there were four men and me and if they wanted to they could take me in any way they liked, but they were so shocked at my outrage and tantrum, they just stared at me aghast until one of them spoke.

"OK, OK, calm down, it's OK, I'll get you home."

"I want a taxi!"

"I'll take you, it will be fine."

I went with him. I *had* to. Anything was better than staying in that house with all of them. I got back to my hostel around 8am I think it was. I must have been out of my head for a while, and I am still not sure exactly what went on there, but it disturbed me.

Thursday 15th December – *Felt terrible all day. I've got a bad cold, last night was awful. Spoke to Pete on the phone and said that I want to go home to them as it's not safe on my own. Met three Scottish lads staying in the hostel. Blew out work tonight and stayed in watching TV with them and had a chat. All they talked about was how Scotland now had its own government and I felt a little sorry for myself.*

Friday 16th December – *Went to work at 7-11. It was OK, but there were four of us waitresses and they were a bit funny to me. Then some of us went for a smoke (pipe) of Ozzie weed. Got very stoned, went back to one of the guys houses and had a sausage sandwich. Stayed 'till 5 am.*

I didn't have a great time in Orange, and felt lonely, so left on the Sunday.

Sunday 18th December – *Phoned Peter, he picked me up and I was glad to be back (again!). At 7pm we went to their Baptist church for a Christmas service and carols (noel noel, while shepherds watched, oh come o ye faithful etc) It was quite nice. I wish I could sing better. Got back, chatted and had a 10 o'clock swim in the pool with Pete and Mel. I couldn't believe we were swimming around in the night time.*

I got myself a charity job. They sent me raffle tickets which I sold door to door for a Children's Leukaemia and Cancer fund. It took up a lot of my time and I enjoyed meeting people; doing something useful, as well as entertaining my nephew, Jamie.

Sunday 25th December: Christmas Day - *Got up at 7 for tea and stocking pressies, then Peter and Mel went to church with Jamie. I didn't go, but wished I had in a way. Went to Jim and Natasha's* (Peter and Mel's friends who we saw quite often) *at 10. Her mum and dad and brother were there, they were really nice. Well, it was quite a religious day and I realised that Christmas is actually all to do with religion. I think one tends to forget the real meaning. Anyway, I had quite a chat with Natasha's Dad about the world and he spoke about reading the testaments. Oh dear! Had a lovely cold buffet lunch which lasted all day, The day was raining and quite chilly which is unusual for Oz, so I wasn't chuffed – I had been looking forward to Xmas day in their pool. Anyway, we ate and played Pitt in the evening, which was good fun. I didn't have a drink all day. Left at about 11 quite sad the day was over.*

Peter and Mel talking about going to hell affected me more than I thought it would.

I was half convinced about Christianity but I could not believe in a God that would send me to hell and how could my family believe that? It halted my religious progress. What if I couldn't fully give myself to God?

Monday 26th December BOXING DAY - *Woke at 9 because the family were making a Christmas day call. Spoke to Mum first, apparently I have an admirer who wants to take me out and lots of post at home. She was happy on Christmas day! Unbelievably with David as well. I spoke to Agnes who is missing me and our chats, then Ian who said to stay out here with nothing much to go back for. Then David who briefly asked if I was having a good time. I don't like home phone calls much with time limits. I always say the wrong things. Phoned*

Dad as I never got to speak to him this morning. I said for him to send me £200 cheque and the money on the phone card ($10) ran out. How shit. I didn't even say happy Christmas to him. He'd just woken up. How sad. I hate home calls now, they are too rushed.

I started exercising every day as I felt I was getting a fat belly – swimming, aerobics and walking. Mel joined in sometimes as she liked my *get up and go.*

Friday 6th January – *Canvassed again for the children's charity – enjoying the work. I got caught in a thunder storm whilst talking to a Dutch middle aged man called Oliver. He offered me a cup of tea and a lift from his friend in an hour so we had a good chat. He is a tiler (Roofs) and fell 18ft into a rockery. He broke both arms, paralysed ½ his face, drinks through a straw and is partly blind. How awful. He was glad of someone to chat to. It was nice to talk to him and I think I might be good at social or voluntary work. How lucky am I to be OK at the moment. Stayed in on my own 'til nine and went out with a guy I've met from round the corner. We went to the movies with his cousin and boyfriend to see Highlander III. It was good. Went to the Catholic Club after for a drink and went home. It was nice to get out for a change. Jason rang earlier. He misses me, can't wait to see me and has sent me a letter – CONFUSING!*

Saturday 7th January – *Jason rang me again "just to hear my voice." Maybe he was pissed, but definitely wants me to ring him. I'm confused now!?! Went canvassing...*

Peter and Mel's friend, Natasha, suffered with severe depression. She had a young daughter but kept talking of wishing to die, to be in a better place and happy with God – in heaven. I didn't know it was depression at the time, I'd only heard of depression that one time when I was supposed to get counselling. What I couldn't understand was how she couldn't just happy with her life, her home, her family, her swimming pool. And she seemed so happy on Christmas Day. She told me all this when I went to stay with her, Jim and their daughter Rachel, for a few days to give Peter and Mel a break. It was only later, when I was older I was to realise what depression was all about...and to understand how she felt at that time.

Things aren't always what they seem.

Letter from Auntie Agnes when I was in Australia (one of many)

17th January 1995

Dear Amanda,

Many thanks for your lovely letter, which I was so pleased to have. I am so glad to hear you are having such a good holiday. You have done such a lot of travelling, it's nice to meet up with people out there and make new friends. You have seen more of Australia than all your family. I don't think Peter and Mel have seen as much as you. I hope you have good luck with your job and earn enough to keep you going. I would love to pay another visit to Australia but doubt I will be fit enough again. Have still got my chest trouble but am hoping I shall be better in the summer. Christmas wasn't the same without you, I kept feeling something was missing, there was an empty chair, but I am glad you stayed with Peter and Mel now you will always know and visualise their Christmas. We are all looking forward to your return to learn about all your travelling. Will write to you again soon, make the most of your time now as it will pass quickly. My love and best wishes see you sometime. Auntie Agnes XXXX

Travelling again… and Sophie who I met in Byron Bay came down from Brisbane to see me for a while.

Tuesday 24th January – *Went to Sydney today. Left my rucksack at Peter's work and met him for lunch (Sophie went off on her own) Peter and I had a good chat. Shopped with Sophie in the afternoon and took our rucksacks to North Bondi to Sophie's friend, Jazz, had a smoke and went to sleep.*

Wednesday 25th January – *Had a look round Bondi Beach today and back to Jazz's (they left the keys) then the contemporary arts museum. Went back at 2am and had got locked out, so slept at the Swiss hotel (really posh).*

I remember this hotel well.

We walked in, past the reception and went up in the glass lift a few floors. We got out of the lift, and found two nice comfy armchairs by the lift in the hall, with an ashtray beside them. We didn't smoke, but just settled down and went to sleep. Sometime later, I was woken by a man's voice. "Yes, two young ladies, sleeping in the corridor, what do I do?" Silence. I kept my eyes shut even though I was in shock and waited to hear the outcome. "OK, are you sure? Yeah, well they aren't harming anyone, they're sleeping." I heard him leave and opened my eyes, turning to look at Sophie. She was awake and had heard as much as me. We laughed it off and went back to sleep, waking again at 6am. Straightening ourselves, we decided on a plan – we'd find the back exit to the hotel and leave that way, to avoid embarrassment or trouble. So off we went, down the stairs we found and hunted for the exit, padding along quietly using sign language instead of talking at all. We found the exit and smiled at each other, until a man appeared in a formal looking uniform.

"Morning ladies, have a nice sleep?"

I recognised his very Australian voice. We were surprised, both the fact that he was there in front of us, catching us in our act of fleeing and that he was so nice to us. We were so hungry that we took a loaf of bread and a carton of milk from a pile in front of a shop from morning delivery on our way back. I'm really not into stealing but the shop wasn't open and we were desperate

After more adventures, micro lighting, wine tasting and staying with another friend in Geelong and Melbourne who I'd met in Byron Bay, I headed back to Peter and Mel's, but my money was running out fast. I'd had a great time but I didn't see me working in Sydney, so I decided it was time to make a decision; and I decided to go home.

Australia was great to visit but I felt more comfortable back home, more comfortable about getting a job and more comfortable living the kind of life I knew. Peter and Mel wanted me to stay as Billy Graham (American Christian evangelist) was coming to Sydney and they wanted me to give myself to God at the event. Maybe that just swayed me more to go home. Yes I believed in God but for me, that was taking it a step too far. So I did not meet Billy Graham or give myself to God.

After a few days I was saying my goodbyes at the airport and heading off home. But the Amanda G that came home from Oz, well she was a different one to the one that had left; more confident, a few pounds heavier, hadn't drunk or smoked much for months and above all she was OK. She was OK with herself and OK about being on her own.

But the only thing about going back to what was comfortable and, need I say, familiar was going back to the old me and that made me feel more uncertain. Amanda G back with the parents. Yes I'd missed them, but as soon as I was home the place seemed to suck my happiness out and all those good feelings I came back with, they just drained away...

Tuesday 7th March – *Popped into the petrol station to see my old boss and he offered me a job in Clinton.*

Friday 7th April – *Went to local job centre today. Am going for an interview at 3 (receptionist) in Woodgrove. One at 5 in the Texaco garage and one at 6 at the Clinton garage. Jason still hasn't rung me since Tuesday. I got ALL 3 JOBS! I'm so chuffed. Decision time!*

I've always been good at getting jobs, just not keeping them

I had charm, I knew what to say. Oh, I was great at starting things, just not finishing them. Like Jason and me. I saw him when I came home; spent time with him, never really knowing why I did that. Of course eventually we did split up for good. Coming home was like putting on old slippers; even if they were ones with holes. He said he wanted me back; no wonder I was confused. I told him that he was not committed enough.

Letter from Jason:

Mand,

I read your last letter tonight and realised how much of it was true. You know 3 months ago I never realised.

Now you have gone I know I have never wanted anything as much as I want you.

I have never written a letter like this before.

I think back to the times when went away by ourselves. We had a great time. I know I get tied up in too many other people but I was always thinking of you.

You never seemed to realise how much I did think of you.

Mand, I don't really know why I am writing this letter, maybe you will read it and laugh but I am missing you like crazy.

I know me and you can get on really well together, but why oh why did we argue to much, maybe the age gap. 9 year maybe to many. Anyway I am not going to go on and on. You know me, I haven't got to much to say but that doesn't mean that I don't think about things.

Amanda – I love you and there will always be a special place in my heart for you.

Phone me.

Jason x x x

I never phoned.

Jason phoned me and asked me to marry him – I said "Don't be so stupid!"

He found someone straight away and rang me to tell me that she had bigger tits than me.

But I had met a nice chap, Craig, at a nightclub and we hit it off straight away.

Within three months, Jason was engaged to the other woman. He has had sex with many women during said marriage – a lucky escape for me.

I got a new job in a bank call centre in Laytonhoe and I found happiness with Craig – we did drugs, drank, I stayed in his room at his mum's house with his sister and step-father, and we had fun. We loved each other. It was an easier relationship and perhaps a period of remission for me – that was until I fucked it all up.

Chapter 17

Why can't I get it right?

1996

It didn't even mean anything. It was one night.

Everyone says that, don't they? But it was true. I went on a skiing holiday to Bulgaria with Dad, David and Linda, spent three days in bed with a stomach upset and then came the argument. I was angry with Dad and it was because of that, it happened. Three days off skiing and a guy who I was a bit obsessed with and there it was – mistake number one. And in a corridor of all places! But being the strong changed person I was I couldn't deal with the guilt so a week after I came home I told Craig. He had been so wary and had been checking the negatives of my photos. Perhaps I just couldn't cover it up. Turns out that was mistake number two.

Of course he tried, but couldn't handle the idea that I could do such a thing to him after one year, as we were very close and had been talking about moving in together. It was Tuesday February 27th 1996 when we split up; over the phone. All that love and that's how it ended. And it was my fault. I learnt a lesson and never did it again, but it made me distrust men. I decided that if it was so easy for me to do - and I had no idea why I did it when I had someone I loved dearly - then anyone could do it. And I became pretty much convinced over time that most men would probably cheat on me. I even had to stop reading newspapers and women's magazines, as they further compounded my fears with their numerous stories of infidelity, a favourite theme of the media.

My life seems full of so many new beginnings. Although I guess after this it seemed OK, life went on and I survived.

I smoked more weed. I saw a lot of Ian, Agnes, Jane and Trace (one of the girls who used to taunt me at school), and I actually loved my job. I even did aerobics or yoga videos before work and had had plenty of energy for what life had to throw at me.

In March my brother Ian had an operation on his ear; to remove a pollop.

In March I asked Craig back. He said no.

And in March Agnes celebrated her 96th birthday.

So life was... well, life was moving along. With a little help.

"OK, I'll be there," I said to him.

I'd only met him once at a nightclub, when I was drunk. I wanted to go to Eastbury Country club and no-one else wanted to go out So I got ready – black leggings, white crop top, hair down, biker boots, touch of make-up. It was an hour's drive, so I played rocking beats in the car, getting in the mood for dancing. I didn't need anyone else. I was cool. And I didn't need Craig or Jason. I didn't need anyone.

I parked up, was searched by the bouncers, bought a ticket, in I went. I saw the guy after about fifteen minutes hunting.

"Hello."

"Hello, it's great music," I shouted at him.

"Yes, how are you?"

"Fine. Want some E's?"

"Yep. OK, come with me."

So I did.

Cash was exchanged for my little white pill. In my gob, water to wash it down. And I waited. He hung around for a bit then told me he was off to the toilet. I didn't see him for quite a long time. In that time, I nearly died.

I stood there, waiting for the pill to work. I tapped my feet to the thumping beats. I felt the vibrations of the baseline on the floor. People were dressed up, dressed down, skirts, trousers, dresses, lots of makeup, this was different; a different group of people to those I was used to from underground Soho, or local nightclubs. They seemed straighter. I waited and watched. I watched them dance. I tapped my feet.

I felt tired, so very tired. I needed to sit down. From the floor, I still watched people, but my eyesight was going. I felt ill. Not sick, but dying. There was something seriously wrong with me. I was going to die. I couldn't move, I couldn't see properly. Serious. Inside I was dying, soon it would reach my head, and it would be over. Sadness. Great sadness. I had no-one to ask, no-one to comfort me. Jason wasn't there. No Jason or Craig. They would've helped me, but they weren't there. I had no-one there. I couldn't say goodbye to anyone; my friends, my family. What would they think when they found out I was dead, in a nightclub and because of drugs? Dear God.

And I would be gone.

So tired, I still couldn't move. My mind carried on. I would be found dead. How long 'til someone realized? After I stopped breathing? *Please let this stop. I have learnt my lesson. I'll never do it again. Please God, please stop this. I will change, I will stop, please don't do this, I don't want to die. I want to live. I don't want to feel like this. It's too late, my body is already dead – it's stopped working - just my brain to go. Oh please get this over with quick, I can't take much more, I am going insane. Please hurry up. Please let me die quickly.*

Amanda? Amanda, are you OK? A voice came from close by. I knew that voice, it was the guy. I couldn't open my eyes, because I was almost gone. I couldn't use my arms. I couldn't move my mouth properly.

"I'm dying," I told him shakily.

"What? I can't hear you?" he said.

"I'm dying."

"No, Amanda, you're not dying. It's just the pills. I'm sorry, let's get you up."

Can't, Can't move. Dying.

I didn't die.

I don't know exactly what happened but I came to at some point in the night, my body became functional and the man helped me. No ambulance, because it was too dodgy. I vowed I would never go out doing drugs on my own again. Thank goodness the man had come back to find me. No-one else in the place had even noticed me on the floor. I was down there some time. Ketamin. There had been Ketamin in those pills. They were supposed to be ecstasy pills. Far from ecstatic, I was paralysed. Temporarily, thank goodness, but I didn't know that at the time. Why would anyone want to take that stuff? I went there to dance and felt I was going to die; an experience I will never forget.

We all make promises to ourselves, some we mean in that moment but sometimes the pull, the craving, the longing for the feeling of freedom takes over.

I could stop if I wanted to though. When that happened I decided I should. I could. But I didn't.

Chapter 18

Thai sweet chilli

1996

"Fancy going to Thailand?"

It was Helen from the bank who asked me that. She knew how unsettling it was for me coming home, how much I missed the travelling. Much as I liked my job in customer services without Craig or anyone else in my life, Thailand for a few months sounded perfect. I would go with Helen, her boyfriend Trevor and his mate. I'd met the mate a couple of times and I knew her boyfriend.

We went on Wednesday May 26th 1996. Helen's family saw the four of us off at the airport and we enjoyed the luxury of flying *Quantas*. We chatted excitably on the plane, looking at maps of where we were going to stay and how we'd get there – they had planned it all carefully in advance. When we landed, we were met by beautiful, friendly Thai people at the airport and the hustle bustle of all colours and creeds – a very multi-cultural mix of visitors, business people, brief cases, travellers, rucksacks, tourists, suitcases, all ages.

It was a long cab ride to Bangkok Eastern Bus Terminal. Although very hot in the cab, we had the windows closed as we headed into the visible fog – the 'smog' Bangkok is famous for. I'd never seen anything like it and I was glad we were only staying two days in the city. The first bus out of Bangkok broke down. The heat was all too much. Finally, we got a boat to Samet Island, followed by a Safari taxi directly to our accommodation – huts on a white beach, an azure sea and bright blue skies.

'This is OK,' I thought, smiling.

"This is your room, Mand," Helen said, showing me into the hut, which was basically just a wooden small room with two tiny beds in it. I was to share with her boyfriend's mate, Colin.

"What?" I said, and I know my face must've dropped. "You are joking? I'm not sharing with him. I thought I was sharing with you?

It turned out I wasn't sharing with her, and it had all been pre-arranged without my knowledge. I really couldn't stand the guy by then, quickly realising we had nothing in common.

Day one and I found myself alone. I'd lost them somehow out on a walk. But, I got on alright by myself as I had a lot of inner strength then, and met people straight away as I wandered along the islands coastline. I soon found the others' boring as they didn't have the drive and excitement that I had, but I got my hair braided and we headed off for a three-day trek.

We got to walk for hours in the hot, humid jungle near Chiang Mai, covered in green and black leeches amongst the biggest bugs I have ever seen. I wrote in my journal: '*Lost the group looking for leeches and shit myself, realised just how lost in the middle of the jungle I was. Went berserk and cried and luckily Papad, the guide, came back to find me.*'

'It stormed with torrential rain, so we were soaked through and the ground was saturated in mud and puddles and we were slipping everywhere It was really exciting, trekking in the rain. At last, we got to the elephant camp and had lunch (noodle soup – yum!) We were sitting on a platform sheltered from the rain and elephants were roaming around the place, some with chains around their legs. I was quite wary of them at first, then a baby and mother came along. How sweet. The men loaded four elephants up with seats and we got on them via a platform. I rode the smaller one with Colin for 2 hours along the river and through the jungle. Fantastic! We couldn't believe we were in the jungle on elephants. I think it was one of the best things I've ever experienced. Grew to really like the elephants. They ate, shit and pissed a lot! One of them liked to decorate his head with leaves. It was a really sunny afternoon. We got to the raft camp and our hut was excellent! A platform with blankets and a fire in the middle. It stormed again as we ate dinner. (had a shower down at a bamboo waterfall) dinner was stir fries and curry. Excellent food. We made a fire inside and sat round playing an animal noise game and chatted. There were lots of bugs – grasshoppers and a massive spider. Went to bed paranoid of bugs under my mossie net and hardly slept. Woke with tiny ants all over me and bites all over my back.'

In time I met Kenneth in Chiang Mai (a guy in his fifties from London who was long term travelling thanks to his redundancy money). He made me see things clearer, to gain some sense of direction. I got a Tuk Tuk to the Thai Massage hospital to enquire about a massage course and got a two week course booked up. 'Went downstairs for my first 1 ½ hours Thai massage and it was very strange, like gymnastics on the floor.' I then went straight to a Thai cookery school and booked a two day course with the very nice couple who ran it.

So, I bid my farewells to the others, who left for the rest of the planned trip, and I stayed in Chiang Mai where I hung out with Kenneth and lots of new friends. We saw the spectacle of the 'Rocket festival.' The Thai people believe that by firing rockets into the sky, they will burst the clouds, so the rain comes. The rockets were twenty-foot long but most of them didn't get more than fifty yards. We visited the Chiang Dao Elephant Training Centre, the Doi Suthep mountain (1668m) and went to the Wat Phar temple where we had to take our shoes off and wear a sarong to cover our knees. We visited the Golden Triangle where the mountains of Thailand, Burma, Vietnam and Laos meet and lots of Opium was, and maybe still is, produced. We watched monks, went to waterfalls, to the night market, played pool, got drunk and smoked joints. I learnt how to make Thai salads, curry pastes and Thai fishcakes on my cookery course and then my Thai massage course began…

Monday 17th June – *Feel like shit from being drunk last night. My morning telephone call woke me up at 7 and I got a Tuk Tuk to the Traditional Thai massage hospital to start my course today. We started the morning sitting in an open classroom. At 9 o'clock we pray to the father doctor (Om Namo) and then do 1 ½ hour theory. It was like being back at school. Then we go and watch Sutun practise the first section of massage moves. You must take notes whilst watching and then practise with a partner afterwards. The people in my group include Chris from Pensylvania, America, Tracey from Scotland, Simon from Liverpool, Bjork from Denmark, Ann from America, Majnu from Japan, Margaret from America, Francisca from France, someone from Ireland and Ulrich from Germany. Went for an Italian with Ann and Margaret across the road.*

Listening to peoples' travel stories, I got to learn about so many other places in the world. One guy told me all about Sumatra and as my plan was to go to Sumatra to see the Orangutan on my way back to Singapore airport at the end of my trip, I think that's what I looked forward to the most.

Chiang Mai, a large town surrounded by a moat all the way round, was magical, particularly at night when the huge street market opened, a myriad of delicious food smells wafted through the air from the street stalls and cafes – ducks hung in the doorways, noodles simmered in huge saucepans, and meat smoked from griddles. It would take months to try everything that was on offer.

Tuk Tuks and motorbikes whizzed about the town like fire flies, sometimes with children balancing on the back, doll-like. But the main thing that inspired me were the huge smiles Thai people wore on their faces – so friendly, calm and content. It wasn't about material wealth, most lived very simply in tiny basic homes and had to work so hard to keep food in their families mouths, yet it never dampened their optimistic spirit.

Giving or receiving Thai massage was so relaxing. It incorporates applied pressure to the energy lines of the body, and a form of applied yoga. It also incorporates meditation, owing to the gently rhythmic way it's conducted. It quietened my mind and I was to return to this when I really needed it, when I was trying to find myself again, a few years later.

Chiang Mai was great, I made many new friends and the atmosphere was so relaxed, but it was now time for partying again, so once I'd finished my courses and received my Thai massage certificate, I headed off on an overnight train back to Bangkok. I loved the trains, as we got a chair that folded up and made a little bed with a curtain across so no-one could see. I sat in there with the light on writing my diary until I felt able to sleep.

At Bangkok I got a River Taxi to the Grand Palace and Wat Po temple which were very touristy. Then I caught a 6.30pm train to Surat Thani overnight, where I got the ferry to Koh Pan Gnan – one of the group of Islands in South east Thailand. Hired a bungalow in 'Chad's place'. *'Had dinner, met a few people and went to the full moon party. It was massive. All the way along the beach at Hat Rin. Did loads of energy drinks and got drunk. Met Helen and Trevor (Colin went to Australia). Lost everyone.'* When I look back it doesn't seem like I was being looked after by anyone – not even myself! *'Got to know a couple of English lads, had a good dance and drank loads of Sang Thip. Had 1 ½ hours sleep and went back to my place at 10.30 am.'*

I met so many people on that trip and I even got myself a Thai boyfriend. I spent many a night out with him and all his friends, at bars, getting stoned, drunk and eating the most fabulous home cooked Thai food. Just amazing! Hot and spicy fish curry for breakfast and the freshest of scallops. And the fruit from the market – Rambutans, Longans, oh such lovely tropical fruits. And scenery like I'd never seen – the whitest sands, the biggest greenest palm trees, the bluest skies…

I'd lie in a hammock smoking a joint

My first 'hut' was just ten feet from the ocean. It didn't have a toilet. It was no more than a wooden hut on stilts, with a dirty old mattress but what did I expect for eighty pence a night? I was out most of the day, but if I was there people would bang on the door to wake me with a bong or a drink or an invite somewhere. I was never alone. For me it was paradise.

And best of all, I was free. Like that bird in the song.

I often think back to that time. On my return I'd see people, happy in their lives while I always wanted more. I always craved that sense of freedom while they seemed content with the mundane. Sometimes I even envied them. They didn't seem to mind the routine, while I always struggled to fit back in, get a job, to keep the job and all the while knowing how good life could really be. I'd spoilt myself and would never be the same again. Nothing would ever be 'quite good enough'.

I found myself eventually hanging out with Mafia club owners and their run-arounds, doing ecstasy with them and partying all night, dancing on the podium and gaining lots of attention. We'd also drink 'Sang Thip' (a very strong Thai whiskey that is banned from export) and do diet pills which were readily available at the pharmacies, basically amphetamines. I met a lovely couple of girls, Dawn and Sarah from Manchester, who told me all about hostessing in Japan. They'd work there for three months, save money, then go back to Thailand for a few months to spend it because it was cheap to live. That's when I made a new plan.

I find it hard now to take in how disjointed my life was then, and how it became more and more so. I went from feeling confused, scared, confident, angry or loving so quickly. If I felt depressed, my compulsion was to take drugs and party to feel different. If I felt that became too much I'd go back to Chiang Mai to be a meditative, reflect for a while.

But I couldn't trust everyone.

So many people from so many places and despite some silly mistakes, I managed to stay safe.

I had a few boyfriends. I find it hard to take that I was so quickly infatuated with these men – one after another, but always someone. It's like I couldn't be on my own.

Reading my diaries is like reading about a stranger – I remember what I want to remember, and my diaries tell the rest. I always said I wouldn't have regrets, but now I'm not too sure.

I seemed so forthright and sure that I wanted to be on my own and proud of it. I knew what I wanted and I did it. There were no consequences.

But it couldn't last forever.

It was soon time to go home.

It was a shame that I didn't make it to Sumatra to see the Orangutan – I just got stuck in Thailand – hooked and unable to leave until I had to. I'd even chosen to fly into Bangkok and out of Singapore was so I could travel through the tea plantations of Malaysia, and sail across to Sumatra to stay at Lake Toba and visit the rainforests to see the Orangutan. I had it all worked out, with my South East Asia *Rough Guide* in hand, but impulsivity, once again, got in the way of my well laid plans. I promised myself I'd get to the Orangutan one day.

But I did not regret the people I met there or the people I travelled with. One of those friends wrote me a poem she tucked into a letter for me to read on the way home. It was a poem about friendship, comparing an acorn to an Oak and two acorns, two Oaks entwined, and how much stronger that made it. I've never forgotten it.

Chapter 19

Am I nuts?

September 2009

18th September 2009 – Letter from Community Psychiatric Nurse:

Presenting Problems:

Feels desperation not being able to get on with her life and feels she has been down for several years. She has been going through old diaries looking at previous therapies she has received.

She sometimes feels she has to hide her emotions as her mother suffers from catatonic schizophrenia and she has to hide all her feelings. She saw a psychiatrist privately, but couldn't afford to continue with his therapy.

She stated she got to thirty-five and has no control over how she feels and her actions, never knows what will upset her or make her cry. She feels that this is stopping her having relationships. She blames everyone else for her own shortcomings.

As of late she feels she is going downhill with extremes of highs and lows.

Her moods are out of control punching things and hurting herself. She never wakes up happy. She has been diagnosed with borderline personality disorder.

Home circumstances:

Living with parents at present

Vulnerable people/dependants in the home:

None

Family History:

Mother has catatonic schizophrenia.

Significant life events:

Has been bankrupt in the past, said she was raped but never recalled it or reported it, recollected when going through her old diaries.

Mental Health History:

Has seen psychiatrist privately, diagnosed with borderline personality disorder

Medical History:

IBS through stress and anxiety, under active thyroid and back pain

Employment/Occupational History:

Has developed various web sites

Finance:

Declared bankrupt in 2005.

Social Networks:

Has a boyfriend who is very supportive.

Activities of Daily Living:

Writes and works from home on the computer

Current Medication:

None, has had medication (anti-depressants) prescribed but stopped taking them as they make her feel strange

Previous Therapy Provided:

Has had GP Counselling, Hypnotherapy, Psychotherapy, Cognitive Behavioural therapy, was advised to have Cognitive Analytic Therapy

History of Self Neglect/ Self Harm/Suicidal Ideation.

History of aggression/harm to others:

Hits objects, walls and things when angry. Very easily distracted can feel upset from 20 minutes to 2 hours, then gets over it.

History of substance misuse:

Has taken drugs in the past

Coping strategies:

She feels that it has got worse since going over old diaries that she had written

Sleep:

Poor, cannot stand any little noises uses ear plugs

Appetite:

When she is happy she is OK with eating, but when down or unhappy will not eat

Concentration:

Feels this is all over the place, can be creative or productive but doesn't know how ***Variation in mood:***

Can be generally up and down with her moods usually only lasts up to 2 hours but can last for 2 days.

Summary of needs: *(does the person want help, can they make use of therapy. Can their needs be met externally?)*

Wants help with her thoughts and feelings

Actions:

Referral for out- patient appointment – ***medium priority***

Chapter 20

Life back home

1996

Life went on.

I was home from Thailand and it was time to get a job again… this time in a different bank.

Thursday 29th August – *Can't concentrate at work as I'm still in Thailand in the head. Was on the computer again in the morning and listening to calls in the afternoon. How boring!*

I decided in my mind to go away again.

I was soon bored with the normalcy of home – getting a job, the same old landscape, same old roads, same old people. David and Linda were emigrating to Australia, leaving only Ian behind. And I had no man in my life. So, when I received a letter from my friend Sarah (recently home from Thailand) with details of her agent who was setting up work for her hostessing in Japan, that familiar surge of excitement was back. I decided I would do the same. Tempted by the idea of Japan, more parties, and making enough money from it for another trip to Thailand I got myself an agent too.

The woman at the agency asked me to send in photos of myself for evaluation, seemed simple enough. I still lived with Mum and Dad and told Dad that I had the opportunity, so we had a mini photo shoot in the garden. It was a warm, sunny late summer's day, so I wore a little black dress and posed standing and on a chair amongst the flowers in my dad's carefully kept garden, while ordering Dad to take various shots of me with my camera. I took the camera film straight into the photo processing shop and paid for them to be developed as fast as possible. I was not entirely happy with them, as they were not sexy enough, but I couldn't be all sexy in front of my dad.

My friend, Julie having recently split with her boyfriend asked if she could come too, dazzled by all my tales of the exotic life I'd led in Thailand. I reluctantly agreed. While I liked her a lot I had become pretty selfish and wanted to do things my way. But she sent her application off too, and after a few weeks not knowing whether to get excited, nervous or fed up, I found myself on a train, with Julie, going to the Agent's Manchester office to sign the paperwork.

They worked from a small room in a huge building. So where were we going? They would let us know just before we left and *Aeroflot* flights would be booked on our behalf at their cost. The contract was fairly long and laborious, with quite a few things to worry about: the main one being that if we did not work the whole of the three months, our return flight back to England would be taken away and we would not be paid. What with that, and the fact that we were just about to take up three months of cash paid illegal work in Japan on a tourist visa I had concerns. However, the draw of the money put paid to any worries and I enjoyed a risk or two.

It would be a vast culture difference, which I was always compelled towards when choosing destinations for myself. I had bought a book called 'culture shock, Japan' and a Japanese phrase book to help me along the way.

But could I Amanda G from Woodgrove, get these guys to buy me drinks, take me on dates and part with lots of money?

Chapter 21

Being hostess with the mostess

I initially started work in Fujiyoshida, a town one hour from Tokyo, surrounded by beautiful winter mountain scenery and the majestic snow topped Mount Fuji. The idea came from Dawn and Sarah – my friends on Koh Samui, Thailand – who had made plenty of money themselves working as hostesses in Japan. They said it was both enjoyable and paid well. Who could ask for more? It was irresistible.

I was reluctant at first about my best friend, Jane, coming with me. I had planned this on my own, had done most of my travelling on my own but in the end, once out in Japan, we were both happy to have each other.

Jane and I were met on arrival at Narita Airport, by Yamadasan – a friendly Japanese chappie, who sorted us out with a bus ticket for the journey into Shinjiku, Tokyo Centre. The next little helper was Simizu, who provided us with a noodle soup lunch, a beer, cigarettes and a throwaway camera. Huge modern buildings covered with brightly lit advertising towered over our heads, ten people wide zebra crossings, with maybe fifty or a hundred people plus rushing across them through the busy streets, and just the whole alien world of small Japanese people everywhere, was mesmerising. The lift experience to the restaurant in the department store was fantastic – a young pretty girl dressed in the cutest porter uniform pressed the buttons while everyone presumably told her where they wanted to go as they cramped themselves into the little arena. I never liked lifts. I always suffered hot flushes and palpitations, panic attacks, but as long as I wasn't thinking about it, I was fine. I was amused by reactions of those watching me as I tried not to think about it. They watched me. And I was distracted by them. Distractions have always helped me. I'd listen to them speak. The Japanese chitter-chatter like a tirade, yet softly spoken as if they sang the words. I wondered if I would ever be able to communicate with them, and with such fluidity. I was in another world.

We were transferred out of Tokyo to Fujiyoshida, beside the beautiful lakes surrounding Mount Fuji. We slept well.

The next day, we got the low down from Shelly (a fellow hostess) on the whole deal, and Papasan. Papasan means male owner of the club – Mamasan being the female owner of the club. He was a Korean man, had a fairly small build, wore strong lens glasses and was rather rushed in everything he did. At first I thought him rude, but we soon got to know the story. We then met some of the other girls in the flat next door but one. In the middle flat lived the Yakuza (Japanese Mafia). They were not high up in the rankings, more like the run-arounds - but still, they were the ones who kept a close eye on everything to do with the club where we'd work and the money absorbed from it on a regular basis for their bosses.

It took us a few days to get used to the strangeness of the place, getting to know the system. The Yakuza's presence never worried me – I felt protected. As long as they didn't 'want' anything from us female Gaijin (Japanese for Foreigners) directly and they lived next door, then who was going to cause problems for us? The Yakuza were not a secret society – in fact, they often had an office with a sign on the door openly showing their group name or emblem, so they were not hidden from the community or the police.

They were often involved in drug trafficking, particularly Methanphetamines (Ice), which I was to get to know more about. Much of their work has been in the 'protection racket' for shops, nightclubs and prostitution markets, partly due to the owners not seeking help from the police and the police not wanting to get involved, therefore they are left to their own devices. This is where Papasan was at with his nightclub and probably his other club. However, if they stayed for a drink after their collection, we would get very nice tips, so we were not complaining. It must have been hard for Papasan to stomach though.

We worked the clubs, got drunk, chatted to the men that came in, played games (usually drinking or clothes swapping entertainment), learnt or practiced our Japanese, sang karaoke and danced. Sometimes we went onto 'Jonathans' – a great American style all night restaurant that served alcohol – got more drunk, had more fun and went to bed to sleep all day.

The Fountain Club was a really tacky place. The black walls were covered in paper cartoon bubbles with Japanese writing in them. I'm not sure what Papasan was trying to achieve there for the customers, but I guess they were there to drink and have a laugh with us. The seating was old with a red and black stripy velvetine finish, and the stage area, complete with dance pole (which we occasionally swung around when very drunk) and mirrored walls, had the karaoke setup, which was naturally very popular with the locals. The layout was designed for small groups to sit together with their hostesses separate from other groups.

Hostessing was a fairly simple job. The men walked into the door and were greeted by Papasan and his large entry fees. They could either pick who they wanted to sit with, or Papasan would do it. Beckoned over to a table, our job was to entertain, talk, get them on the Karaoke, get them drunk, get them to buy us drinks (as we earned commission on every drink they bought us) and make sure they had a good time. Drinks we were bought were whiskey and mixer and Papasan decided how weak or strong they were depending on the circumstances. They got drunk easily – the Japanese cannot hold their drink like us Europeans. And they paid for us by the hour, so we would sometimes get through many tables in a night. Papasan would often swap us around too, so the clients got a good mixture of company.

Many clients came regularly, so we got to know them and go out with them on dates or days out. Others would visit from Tokyo or other neighbouring towns – a wedding group or business trip. Apart from getting drunk and mucking around, I did manage to practice my Japanese on them. The other way to earn money was to go on a 'Dohan' which is a date. We got to be taken out by the guys, bought lunch or dinner, go sightseeing and got paid for it – they had to pay Papasan for the privilege of our time and we took a commission out of that.

Within a week, challenge number one arrived, when Papasan asked me to sing. '*Oh no, I can't sing, no-one would want to hear me*' didn't work. '*But this is not in my contract, and no-one told me I would have to sing*' didn't work, and it was apparent that '*no*' was not an option and so I got up and did a rendition of the Bananarama track *Venus*, dutifully accompanied by my supportive friend, Jane. It turned out that I liked it a lot, the customers and Papasan liked it and so I repeated the experience on many occasions, usually singing a *Beatles* or a *Carpenters* song.

I quite liked Papasan, but he did have a temper. We were forbidden to have men round our apartments, and he would come round on the odd occasion to check on us.

Our apartment was a basic two-bedroom affair, shared by four girls – including myself – all English. We had futons for beds on the floor, a tiny deep square bath that you could just about sit up in with your legs crossed to wash, and a tiny kitchen. The one glorious thing about it was the view of Mount Fuji from the back window.

I never had sex for money. I was disgusted by the whole idea of it, but I did occasionally wake up to find that quite a sum of money had been left for me.

I knew that what I was doing was different, not what people normally do, but it was who I was then. My two favourite words were 'individuality' and 'spontaneity'.

But it wasn't all about the hostessing; we visited many places in Japan. Mount Fuji and Lake Saiko where we could see Lake Kawaguchiko. Fuji-Q Highland is a huge theme park right in the middle of stunning mountains, where I braved the then highest and fastest roller coaster in the world, *Fujiyama*, which only opened that year (1996) so it was all very new and exciting for the Japanese people. I would have probably liked it there in the Summer, but the Winter sun was just so pretty, shining on the mountains with shadows. Fujiyoshida itself is a large Town in the middle of the Mountains and surrounding lakes and villages. As you walk up the main road that runs through the Town, you can admire the clear view of Mount Fuji right in front of you, like a vast monument, overlooking the town with such grace. I have never seen such a pretty sight in all my travels since, and I feel privileged to have been there.

And then after another four months in Thailand I moved into Tokyo.

***

The nightclub was crowded.

Loud music: blaring, topless dancers: gyrating; me: sitting with yet another group of complete strangers.

There were men there, always men, who I pretended to be interested in, having conversations with them, eagerly encouraging them to get drunk and buy me drinks. Their very presence in the club meant money for me, and it was my job to get them to part with as much of it as possible, by being their *platonic girlfriend* for as long as they wished to pay for, by the hour. I was a nightclub hostess in Tokyo, Japan, in probably the most expensive, best paid club in Tokyo - a period of time that would change my life forever.

Tokyo was a huge city. Japan is a safe place – but the Roppongi area of Tokyo, where all the internationals, drugs, hostess nightclubs etc are situated, is a different matter, with drink spiking (Rohypnol), theft, assault, attacks, a huge sex industry, illegal working by foreigners with illegal 'employers' and contracts and other seedy affairs, it was another story and so were the clubs.

The clubs in Tokyo were varied, with some more flashy with dancers and others with dark and dingy rooms fitted out with tired old tacky furniture. Some were run by Yakuza – the Japanese Mafia, and one I worked in was managed by a freaky sixty-five year old cocaine addict who said I looked like a hippy and insisted I plaster makeup on like a clown. I only lasted one night there. But now I was in the best club in Tokyo run by an American guy who, as part of the 'induction' process, was to get me stoned after work, lie down on the club's dirty floor and get me to have sex with him. I did it because I wanted the job, but I hated him for it afterwards. He took advantage of me, while I was so fucked with the drink and smoke (whatever it was we did smoke) but I don't remember all the details. But I met a Jewish girl from New York, Bethany, there and we became very good friends, doing loads of things together during my six month stay.

We started at 9 pm and finished at 3 am, six nights a week. We were fined for lateness and earned four to five hundred pounds a week.

We were putting ourselves at risk every time we went out with a man but we did it anyway; it was our job. I was propositioned for sex many times and was offered money up front, which I refused every time. This was not a part of my job; I didn't need the extra money.

And then there were the drugs.

Ice is a form of Meths (Methamphetamine) so called as it is bought in crystal form. We smoked it from a small glass pipe, which had a thin funnel and a little ball on the end for burning the ice with a lighter or we burnt one of the little ice rocks in foil and sucked up the meth vapours through a straw. It felt smooth when inhaling, unlike cigarette smoke, and it hit me virtually straight away, lasting for many hours, suppressing my appetite and speeding up my system. Like Speed, I enjoyed it most when drinking huge amounts at the same time, so it suited my job. I got the effects of the drink without the dizziness or sickness due to the way the ice woke me up. It livened up my body so that I could stay awake for hours chatting or doing whatever I needed to do, but with it came paranoia and disrupted sleep. And for me that was dangerous.

Acid is quite another drug entirely. It usually made me hallucinate, feel more awake and sensitive to my surroundings and often brought with it paranoia and depression.

So we took drugs. We took drugs to go to work. We took drugs in work. We took drugs after work and stayed up all night long, sleeping all day. We took drugs in the day, or on the rare occasion of a day off. We took drugs in Yoyogi Park where families walked. We took drugs in the sun, rain, and on cloudy days. We took drugs at festivals where drums played all day long. We took drugs to wake up and we took them to go to sleep. Any time of the day we took drugs. There was a drug for everything. In Japan it was easy to get hold of methamphetamine and acid. Both of these drugs would never have been my first choice, as they didn't really match my personality, which was easily paranoid, but I took them anyway

– anything was better than nothing. We got drunk every day and that was never enough of a buzz to cope with the pressure. Not everyone turned to drugs but many of us did.

I was with a group of 'friends' in a nightclub; a grubby dark place where Techno beats and baselines filled the air. Strobe lights flashed and peoples' faces shone green, red and blue as they danced, eyes wide open, eyes closed, eyes vacant. Clothes bright or luminous with huge patterns, swirls, shapes of colour. Brightness, darkness. Thumping beats. Trance music. My head, so strange. Crying. Can't dance. Can't move. Everyone's looking at me. They hate me. My friends, they all hate me. Why is everyone looking at me? A statue. I look down. I cannot look up anymore. Sobbing. Wailing. Someone help me. Someone please help me. Someone must like me. Blurs. It's all a blur of colour, darkness, bright lights. I can't see properly, but I know they are all looking at me; I know they all hate me. I need to go. I need to get out of here. But I can't. I can't move. Please, please, what did I do to deserve this? Help me someone, help me. One of the Swedish girls I share my flat with is here… I beg her. She says something like get on with it. Is she going to help? No. Nicky, help me. She's English, she'll help. Fuck off crying. Get a grip. Come and dance. No, please. I can't take it, I can't do this. Give me my sight back. Give me Amanda back. Will she ever be back? Regret. What have I done? I can't stay like this. They all hate me. Someone, please help me… I hate acid. I'll never do it again – please let me come back and I'll never do it again. I can't see, help me …

The drugs are one of my biggest regrets, but I needed something to turn to, that could take some of the pain away and take me to another place – like travelling thousands of miles around the world, drugs gave me an escape; stupid really. I didn't have to stay there, but I felt compelled to, like I couldn't escape. What I didn't realise at the time, or until many years later, in writing this book, was that it was the alien situation I was keeping myself in, that particular vicious circle, was bringing out the worst in me. I was losing my inner strength as each day a higher hurdle was placed in my path and my happiness drained, but I still stayed. Maybe I was testing myself. But happy little Amanda couldn't even keep the façade up on top of it all, not all of the time; insecure, desolate Amanda was coming out, showing her weaknesses Drugs. They made me desperate, needy, more impulsive, lose my senses and intelligence, they made me incapable of conversing with the more normal people I lived with. I was soon snapping at people, they noticed changes in me.

Seeing adverse effects from the other side made it clearer in a way. So after a great night out at a rave, dancing and mucking about on Ecstasy and Acid, when my friend freaked out, I became responsible. Yes, responsible. I always have if I have really needed to. She became very paranoid of myself and my other mate, who was out of his head, and thought we were plotting against her. She wanted to wander off in a panic, which wasn't great since we were miles from home and I was the driver so I had to calm her down and ensure she realised we were her friends and there for her. It was unpleasant to experience.

People don't like me anymore

When I look at all the photos of these times we are laughing, smiling and having lots of fun but that's not the real truth. Although there were good times, times I remember. There was the drumming festival, the 'Fuji-Rainbow 2000' festival near Mount Fuji, the mud, the dancing, the freedom of it all. Eating noodles and sushi in the middle of the night in downtown Tokyo, chilling out in parks. We'd go to temples, morning fish markets and took in the culture.

It was a crazy place. Then there were all my Japanese friends. Lovely they were. And a bit crazy too. Some did drugs, others didn't, some were younger, some older. Their sometimes childish ways were enchanting, they were honest and more than anything they welcomed me. I'd be taken to their homes, on days out, driven round Tokyo on the back of a motorbike, taken out to try all the weird and wonderful foods of Japan and I even had a friend in his fifties who'd take me to Karaoke bars with his friends, to golf driving ranges, and even on a mini break to the beach where girls wore stilettos and makeup in the hot sunshine as they giggled, stumbling across the sand between the hundreds of occupied sun beds with identical rainbow umbrellas. I didn't have sex with him. I learnt conversational Japanese by the time I left, and this got me through. In the club, instead of being flirty, or dirty like the other girls, I would get away with chatting in Japanese and picking the quieter guys to sit with or just getting drunk and chatty.

I did have sex with quite a few guys – Japanese and English. I admit it. I still had a high sex drive. But never for money.

One night I was attacked in the street in Roppongi. An older American guy pounced on me and tried to sexually assault me. I was screaming and punching and kicking which I think stunned him and he backed off. There were a few people around and no-one tried to help me. Though I didn't see it at the time, a part of me must have remembered Vinnie. But it wasn't going to happen again.

Before I went home I went with some friends to get various things pierced – one guy had his foreskin pierced, one girl had her nipples pierced, one had her vagina pierced and I, not so brave, had my tongue pierced. It was done just how I would've done it. No anaesthetic. A cork under the tongue. A metal tube with a very sharp end was forced through the tongue, meeting the cork at the bottom and a tongue bar was inserted secured with a ball at the top. Short and sharp. I was presented with said tubular spear and cork in a little bag as a souvenir. It made me think of that string of my tongue the tube had cut out – where did they put it? I dread to think about my friends' piercings, as mine got very infected and my tongue swelled to nearly double its size. Even when it went down it seemed to make my lisp even worse. I also had a 1 hour Shiatsu. She told me that I had a bad liver (alcohol) and bad stomach and lower back.

Maybe it was time to go home.

Chapter 22

Holding it together - am I happy now?

So I did go home but I decided that my next move should be to work with Japanese people in the Leisure Industry.

And would you believe I got a stall on a market trading in Thai wares. But it didn't last long. I decided I was more suited to the leisure industry and got myself a job in a hotel. This time, at least I wasn't full of drugs. But I was back in Mum and Dad's house. Same house; same room; same me? Funny how a place absorbs you into it, Australia, Thailand, Japan... but then you come back as if home is a place attached to invisible elastic and somehow you end up in the same place; like Japan was now another world, a parallel universe – but are you the same? Was I the same? After all those drugs and experiences?

Wednesday 14th January 1998 – *Started my job at the hotel today. Just for a taster. It was all a bit much to start with and I thought that I wouldn't be able to do it.*

I realise, when I think about this time, how much my life has changed and if that was the same person. As you read you may ask the same question.

Many people stay in the same home, get married, have children. Their lives change too, as their children grow up.

I didn't have those stable things in my life, not then and not now.

Maybe I forced my own change by moving around, travelling to far flung places on holiday (and often), changing jobs, getting bored, trying out lots of self-employed projects but the best thing is not to regret it. Better to have done things than to regret never doing them. Like love – it is better to have loved and lost it than to never have known love at all. That's what they say, and I agree.

However, I did get to meet Ian's girlfriend, Michelle, who he'd met while I was away for thirteen months. She'd moved into his maisonette already. So, I was then the 'new' sister on the scene. But we gradually became very good friends.

Living at home again seemed OK – if I was in the right frame of mind – if I felt *normal*. So far, normal was getting ready to go travelling and settling down after travelling. And when I think about those times after Japan it was staying in the same place – for now. Just being normal. I seemed to bounce off problems and emotions then.

I remember a long chat I had with Dad at that time, and I did spend more time in his company. We spoke about Mum and mental health a lot. I always wanted to understand why four children were born to a schizophrenic woman and I was never satisfied with the answer as it was just 'the doctors said it would be good for her.' Like we were born to serve a purpose – I always resented that. We should have been born as we were wanted as children, not to satisfy a woman with serious mental health issues, to pass on her tainted genes to us, with a husband who doesn't know what else to do. But this only left me confused. I felt angry. I felt I was born just to please my mum. What about me? Innocent me? I never asked to be born. Another little pin to stick in my ever growing cushion of resentment.

I started a new college course – the first of many – doing what I loved: photography.

So I *was* doing normal things. The madness of that time in Thailand and Japan was behind me so fast and I had my full time hotel job. They loved me there. I'd be left in charge most of the time.

I was seeing Ian and Michelle and Ian's mates at his home, I was seeing Jane and had a pretty full life.

Dad set up with the internet. I'd had no internet or mobile phone when travelling. I remember Dad taking me to a conference showing the future of the internet, the world wide web, when I was sixteen and me thinking what the hell is that? Like that would catch on!

Of course, my normal life wouldn't have been normal without smoking and partying and drugs. But being back home, this seemed more controlled. I had a normal job to start with.

I'd smoke out my bedroom window at home, stinky skunk – madness. As well as the thirteen holes in my ears at this time I also had my nose and belly button pierced. Oh yes, and a tattoo of a large gecko crawling up my back with the Japanese symbols next to it meaning 'individuality.' It encapsulated my travels in Thailand and Japan. I felt those two places moulded me as a person at the time. And I realised just how individual we all are – not one person the same – and it should be celebrated.

I worked with loads of ex-servicemen as guests at the hotel and enjoyed the attention. I was good at my job and wanted a career in hotels so that I could work with Japanese people later on. I also started having private lessons with an old English guy teaching me Japanese written and spoken language. I thought I might even do tourist trips for Japanese people. I guess what I was doing was creating some of what I'd left behind, but without all the madness. It was nice to have goals.

I treated my boyfriends like shit at times.

If I didn't have one I wanted one. If I had one, I didn't. In reality I was more relaxed without one. Even when I worked in the hotels and I had a string of *boyfriends*, I felt lost. I needed something but I didn't know what. So I placated myself seeking new pastures for my hotel skills, I had been trawling numerous hotel chains across England, eighteen in London alone in case I wanted to relocate south, but in the end I found a position seventy miles from home, in Crompton, as a trainee manager (or rather 'general assistant' giving me the skills to become a manager they said), and moved there to live with a wonderfully interesting family of four in their huge converted barn. I had a massive room of my own with my own entrance and was even invited to join the family for a glass of wine or a meal sometimes. Work was great too. One minute I was behind the reception desk checking people in and out, next I was housekeeping and changing beds, next I might be in the bar or delivering room service or waiting in the restaurant or I might be in the kitchen learning the basics of being a chef. Hard work, but it suited me well and I was appreciated by staff and customers. I was gaining back some of the control – wasn't I?

Chapter 23

Old for New

On the 2nd April 1999 Ian and Michelle came to visit me, and to tell me that Michelle was pregnant with their first child – I would be an aunt again. I was so thrilled. But this news was thwarted by news that my aunt, my lovely Agnes, was ill.

Funny how good and bad news can come together like this.

Monday 5th April – *Dad phoned saying that Agnes is going downhill, so I decided to try to see her tomorrow. This is quite an event as Dad does NOT phone anyone!*

Tuesday 6th April – *Went with Ian to see Agnes in hospital. She had tubes out of her nose and drips into her wrist and she'd lost so much weight as she hadn't eaten for more than a week. Her stomach was a balloon. Bless her. She's contracted bronchial pneumonia since she's been in hospital, so could hardly talk, but she tried to chat all the time and seemed very bright considering. We left at 8.45pm and I basically said my goodbyes then. Went home to mum and dads, ate and stayed the night.*

The next day Dad went to see Agnes with Mum and she was in a terrible state, so they could not stay more than 15 minutes.

Thursday 8th April – *Agnes died.*

So, I was told of a birth on the 2nd and a death on the 8th. It just shows how life cycles; people being born and dying every second of the day. I was glad to hear that Ian had whispered in Agnes's ear about his forthcoming fatherhood. She heard him, and so she knew before she passed away. David and Linda decided to make a last minute trip from Australia to come for the funeral.

Chapter 24

Endings are new beginnings

Agnes's death changed everything.

It was a slow process, but one that helped me ruin my life within a few years. I thought I was getting 'happier' but it just couldn't last.

The funeral marked an ending, and maybe a beginning. April 20th 1999.

It was a nice church; a nice service. Nice. Like she was. People say it's a nothing word, a syrupy meaningless word but Agnes was nice. That's how I remember her. Peter had sent over a recording of a prayer to be played, which we couldn't hear properly. David and Linda were there, as were Ian and Michelle, and Dad of course. Mum was not. Agnes was laid to rest with Albert. She had lots of flowers. Just as she'd had when she was alive.

We all went back to Agnes's bungalow and had snacks, tea, drinks. A time to remember; a time for Agnes. We stayed the evening in Agnes's lounge where we reminisced about her caring manner and her superb ability to cook. We had a Chinese takeaway and the evening was just the way it ought to be, pleasant albeit tinged with sadness.

Within days, when we found ourselves routing round Agnes's house, unearthing her personal defects and getting the house ready to be emptied – to sell or decide to keep her things, it became much more difficult. To make it fair, we all decided that if we wanted to keep things, if they had particular monetary value, then we would buy them. So, when I decided to keep two of her rings, I staked my claim and purchased them. A beautiful star gold ring with diamonds and a blue stone in the middle, and a Victorian style band with ruby and diamonds. I felt that jewellery was the single most personal thing I could keep, after photos, letters etc, as she had worn them close to her skin. I kept more than that, but those were the most special items. Pulling everything else apart, getting things valued and selling them was very upsetting. We talked about how hard it was to pull Agnes's life apart, and decide what to do with her life's worth of items now that she was gone. She spent a lifetime collecting these materials, some of which she used daily, others just an ornament of her choice. They had an importance to Agnes in her lifetime, just like my clothes, my personal affects are important to me in my life – my car, my shoes, my memorabilia, my diaries… And now, much of this stuff had no real importance, but it was hard to sell or get rid of things. I realised that when I am gone I will leave all my personal affects behind and I will have no use for them anymore. Life is the important thing, not the material items, but we all have them, some being greedier for them than others, like me sometimes, but we all have them, even a homeless person will have a bag of things.

And when we are gone, they will be pulled apart and disposed of by others. Meaningless.

When I am gone, what will happen to my things?

With Agnes, I kept her letters, photos, everything. They tell a story of her travels abroad and life with her husband and us as her family. Her story is still there for me to see. Irreplaceable. Even if I can't discuss them with her – even if there are unanswered questions. I'd always thought this way about my things and it is, perhaps, why my whole life is logged.

Many times I have thought about mortality. I have asked God to take my life in order to give it to someone more worthy. These thoughts only come with the guilt and loneliness that depression brings but they do come.

When I'm gone, will anyone bother to come to my funeral?

When I'm gone, will anyone be bothered to read about my life?

When I'm gone what will people say about me? Will they say I was a good, kind hearted person, or that I was a moaning, problematic adult?

When I'm dead, will any of this matter?

Agnes's house had to be sold and her life's worth of carefully managed money would be distributed in the family. She had been so careful, always scrimping and saving telling myself and my brothers that she wanted to leave us as much as she could, but I never wanted to hear it. All for us. So unselfish. What a lovely woman. But I didn't deserve her money. I just wanted her to be alive.

I seemed to have so much energy at this time, in spite of what was happening around me and with Agnes being gone. Maybe it was the way I coped: *don't think about it, keep busy*. Then it's not really there – is it? And I would work all hours, do yoga before work, to relax, and socialised. My job was very varied – a hotel management training course that really was a cheap way of getting lots of work done – but working in all the different departments, among one hundred and sixty staff, kept me from boredom I loved the diversity somehow. Control, order in the chaos... was there chaos? Wasn't everything normal now? Apart from Agnes being gone?

And no boyfriend either... but stable. It all felt stable and I had lots of friends. I was a popular girl.

I planned a trip to Italy to see one of my fellow hostess' from Fujiyoshida, Maria, and did a static line parachute jump with Jane to raise money for Cancer Research UK in memory of her mother who died of cancer the year before. It felt good to help others.

I was OK then – accepted because I was behaving pleasingly. I had more zest, willpower, optimism and patience. I was quite normal after all – wasn't I?

I was so independent – I went to pubs for a drink by myself just because I wanted one and didn't feel strange or alone, and went out and treated myself to stuff. I seemed in control... together...

I decided that I wasn't earning enough at my job and worked far too hard for it, to pay for my rent and food and my lifestyle so I asked to move back to my parents at Woodgrove and got a transfer to a more local hotel within the chain, in Clinton.

So, it was all change again – but this time, instead of running away, I was back at Mum and Dad's. I was always running from and running back to – a pattern that had me moving constantly. I couldn't cope with responsibility. Everyone always questioned my reasons for moving and why I couldn't seem to settle or realise what I had was good, but they didn't know about my illness or my need for excitement and change to enable me to cope with it. And excitement and change worked for me – albeit for a short time. My family didn't realise that my outer personality wasn't quite who I was.

I'd had such a secret life of sex and attention seeking – my family never knew.

My life at this time was pretty full and exciting – interesting and satisfying. I thought nothing of travelling to see people and made a lot of effort in the name of socialising – stoking the fire of friendships.

I tried to continue with parachuting as the lessons for the charity jump had been so much fun, but the weather always got in the way of jumping, so after three five hour round trips I gave up.

Monday 11th October – *Message from Ian on my mobile that Michelle had a baby girl at 8am. They named her Elsa and she weighted 8lb exactly. Blonde hair, blue eyes.*

Friday 22nd October – *Rang the solicitors to hurry them up for my inheritance from Aunt Agnes and got stressed about money.*

I was rubbish with money. I was the same when the inheritance money finally came through.

I bought a maisonette. It was Ian's old place in Woodgrove. I had always wanted to live in Clinton since I was fourteen years old, but my brother's flat was less risky – he'd lived there for twelve years. He'd just had a daughter and was house hunting so it was perfect. I bought their flat and they rented it from me, loosening their property ties and I had some breathing space before I had to move in. Fantastic, I had done something good with Agnes's money. If she were looking down at me, she'd be happy with that – Amanda being responsible with her hard earned assets. Although, knowing Agnes, she would've been happy for me to enjoy myself travelling round the world with it, as she always encouraged me to travel. Still, for me, the big worry of doing the right things with her money was over and a decision had been made – it was all put in the maisonette so I couldn't spend any of it on anything else.

All very well, and the maisonette for me was security and my own home, with a very small mortgage of £230 per month to pay, and I appreciated it, but I didn't really want it, I wanted Agnes back. I didn't want her back to suffer the way she had in the last couple of years of her life, but a healthy Agnes, the one I knew for most of my life. I remember the doctor phoning her to make sure she was still alive years back, as she hadn't been to the doctor's for years and years. Until she got Diverticulitis, she was a very well woman – no doubt helped by her diet of home grown organic vegetables and the shot of whiskey in her tea in the morning. The person who told me I was loved, the person who wrote I was loved, the person who showed me I was loved; she was gone.

I don't think I grieved properly, shutting it away, but the pain was there all the time, I just didn't realise it

I was drinking but not doing drugs anymore, but when I drank it could be fairly large amounts but not every day. Self-medicating?

1999 ended with a Boxing Day working at the hotel in Clinton; with a disco for the guests, and we all joined in and danced to the tacky disco beats, and one even got his top off. The staff there were nice and many photos were taken by me. I liked wrapping my arms around people for a photo and I never failed to have my camera with me to record all life events. Always with the perfect smile for every photo.

My looks have been my downfall for getting into trouble and not getting help from doctors – they all say "You look alright" and so don't help. Looking 'alright' has helped me to feel confident at times, but it is very misleading as to what is going on in my head and life… my demons within… and had delayed me getting the help I needed.

Chapter 25

A New Millennium

After a relaxed and fairly 'normal' 1999 for a twenty something, 2000 followed in the same vein and one could be fooled into thinking that I was normal, but this was probably me giving myself a break and enjoying life. I drank alcohol, but not excessively. Still no drugs. I saw my family a lot and did normal things like going to work and pursuing a 'proper' career. Peter and Mel came back from Australia with Jamie, and bought a house over a hundred miles away, although I didn't see them much and our relationship continued in that vein. We hadn't had an argument or anything, but we had very different lives.

When the Millennium arrived, I met up with Lee James; a guy I'd first met Christmas Eve. We watched the fireworks and celebrations. He soon became my next 'boyfriend' and I spent a year with him until a prostitute in Amsterdam got in the way.

I continued to work at the hotel throughout the first half of the relationship, and progressed to a supervisor, working nearly every weekend, which got on Lee's nerves. I enjoyed my work though and it didn't bother me. I could stay over in a hotel room, work late Saturday, be back on a 6am start on Sunday and I still had loads of energy for it. I was pretty fit. Lee and I also got to enjoy some of my work benefits, such as getting hotel rooms all over the country for

£20 – particularly good when we stayed at the Waldorf, London which should have cost £250 a night. It was the start of my desire for quality.

I had fun and that was good. Lee worked for a major bank, played the Saxophone and had a recording deck, so he was really into music, which was great. I took my record box round there to listen to all the vinyls I'd bought when with Jason which brought back memories of drugs and dancing in underground clubs. I'd buy loads of clothes: I became a smart budget dresser – changing my dress and look yet again. So far, I'd dressed like a floozy when fifteen, a hippy in Thailand in Thai tye dye pants and long flowing dresses, in suits for work, in psychedelic clothes in Japan for my trance parties teamed with girly dresses for my job, I'd gone through many stages, many changes, hair and clothes. All in a search to find out who I really was.

In January I went skiing in Sauze d'oulx, Italy, with Dad. We had booked it quite a while before, in 1999, which showed how strong our relationship was at that time. I wore my long lasting children's purple all in one ski suit which still fitted OK, matching bobble hat and pink goggles. The first night was a memorable one, as we met some guys, including a BA pilot and went out drinking, clubbing and ended up eating pizza at 5am in a restaurant, still drinking! Dad knew the lady at the guesthouse, as he'd stayed there before on his own, so when we got back at 6am, she thought we were up early for breakfast and Dad was really embarrassed to tell her the truth. We didn't ski that first day, so it was a bit of a waste but really good fun – a memory me or my dad will never forget.

I shared a twin room with Dad, as usual, and it was in such a mess because of me – I am so messy and it shows in all the pictures of the times.

It was the best resort I have been to – good snow, fabulous food (unlike the delights we'd had in Romania and Bulgaria) and great *après ski*. We hung around with the British airways pilot and his mates the first week and the second week, three young guys (one with bleached blonde hair) and they were really good fun. We had the *après ski* drinking and dancing sessions large!

I had long hair then and didn't wear much makeup, but then I never really have. And I didn't have sex with anyone. Apart from that time when I was with Keith, I have never had sex with anyone else if I am in a 'relationship', including Jason and I still have the same ethics. I remember warning Chris when I met him that if he had sex with anyone else whilst with me, then he MUST tell me despite the outcome. I explained that what I felt was the worst thing about having sex with others when in a sexual relationship with me is that they could catch sexually transmitted diseases, transfer them to me and I wouldn't know. And that is NOT FAIR! I had regular sexual health checkups at the hospital so I knew I was OK.

Back home, I had days out with Lee, stayed in more hotels around England and visited Agnes's grave with flowers often, some things you need to hang onto, for how long will people really remember us? I was glad she was buried and that I had a grave to visit.

My bedroom at this time at Mum and Dad's was the bigger one that used to be shared between my three brothers, and had been for a few years by now. It was full of plants, *nicnacs,* mirrors, pictures and that funny poem my dad wrote for me when I went to Japan. It was given to me as a send off to my new job as hostess.

I then left the hotel industry, with Lee's support, and started my training as a recruitment consultant with a large company. It was a big change, but I realised that Hotel management didn't get paid enough – at least I thought they didn't. Lee was pleased that I would now do a 9 –5 so he could see me more.

The two week in-house course at head office was tough but with perseverance, I got excellent grades in my recruitment exams while having lots of fun since there were around thirty five of us on the course. I was placed in a branch twenty miles from home and went from being a nervous beginner to making the branch the most profitable in the area, even with my boss off sick. My confidence soared, as I, single handed, brought in loads of new business and employed a large group of temporary staff who were very loyal to me. I loved interviewing people and working out who to employ and where to send them. I'd feel important in my little suits, making appointments with Businesses and convincing them that I could supply their staff, permanent or temporary and doing health and safety checks of their premises with my clipboard. Most of my business was with warehouses and manufacturing, so I'd don a hard hat on visits and take the company bosses out for lunches.

The admin lady was nice and helpful, and when given targets from head office, I'd reach them in a couple of weeks, but the commission structure kept changing. I got a new client as requested by Head office, won loads of prizes for reaching targets, and then my useless boss hired a blonde long-legged cow that knew nothing about recruitment and gave half my clients and commissions to her! I felt sick! I had worked so hard to make that branch work, had proved myself, and that is what I got for it. To top it off, on returning from a holiday, I found he had placed her photo in the paper as the 'face of the branch' in my absence.

I loved that job and commuted quite a distance for it (although I was often late!), ate my sandwiches on the go and loved interviewing people and going out and getting clients. It was easy and I was professional and had a good database of working temps and perms in office and industrial, to fork lift drivers and builders work, to warehouses and post offices. I couldn't believe I had been taken for a ride like that, and started to file my case with the Union. What next?

When I think about this, I realise this marked the beginning of the changes in me; my decline in self worth and newly formed bitterness.

The holiday had been to Greece with Lee for his birthday. I was really slim with long blonde hair and I dressed nicely - cropped tops and leggings and funky hippy tops and shorts and I remember playing bat and ball on the water's edge of the busy beach with just a black thong on, everyone looking at me. I could never do that now. It was so hot that I slept on the balcony as there was no bloody air conditioning. We argued and I was grumpy and Lee said that the happiest he saw me the whole holiday was when I was on the plane going home.

We hung around with some English girls for a part of the time, and hired a fiat panda for a day trip, we had coach trips but they all went wrong one way or another – not booked on one, a romantic restaurant trip we were cancelled off, and much more shit. I also didn't like the food. We went to Olympic stadium in Athens, but it was so hot (over 100 degrees) and sweaty, we just wanted to shelter. One man died at our apartments. Lee also wanted to sunbathe and read his book and I was bored so was always trying to get him to play ball or something.

Despite all this negative stuff, Ian and Michelle found a new house at last, so I moved into my maisonette once they moved out and got a kitten, (who I named Aggie after Agnes even though she had never liked cats) and I enjoyed having my own home and my own freedom. I did a two-year evening interior design course and had friends round for dinner quite a lot.

My cat, Aggie, was gorgeous. A tortoiseshell kitten. She was so timid though and I had to work hard to get her outside and dealing with my friends and family coming round. I was covered in scratches for ages, but I loved her and fainted when I had to take her to the vet's for a cut in her paw, and she shit on the table. The vet came back in the room to find me on the floor still gripping Aggie! She adored me and clawed up the carpet outside my bedroom door if I didn't leave it open so that she could be near me. I even took her to visit friends out of town and she would mingle with the local cats and come back to me at the end of the day for the drive back home. I fed her *Iams* and salmon which she loved, showered her in the bath for fun and generally treated her more like a dog than a cat, but she did get out and about on her own.

I had a big mole on my face, which was growing all the time and worried me; I'd spent so much time sunbathing over the years. The doctors wouldn't take it off as they saw it as a cosmetic reason. Was it again my looks that stopped me getting medical support? I wasn't asking for it for beauty purposes at all!

My flat was decorated with a mix of stuff I'd collected from Thailand and Japan, had an orange and blue Mediterranean feel kitchen, a white main bedroom, a Japanese themed spare bedroom, a green bathroom as it had been left and eventually, when David and Linda came over from Australia for Christmas, they helped me paint it on Boxing Day - pale green and pale pink; an Asian themed lounge. It was homely. I also painted the garage door green and for once in my life, I kept it tidy

My birthday was celebrated with a few days in Amsterdam with Lee.

I got some lovely Levi's, a white Levi t-shirt and we went to the red light district and nearly got Lee a blow job but she wouldn't let me be involved as she didn't 'do ladies' so we went home. However, Lee had gotten wound up about it and wanted to call a prostitute to the room. I got upset, he sulked on the bed and I reminded him that it was my birthday and he shouldn't behave like that. That was basically the end of the relationship for me, as I didn't like it that he wanted someone else sexually so much. We had a great sex life already as I did with all my boyfriends. We also went to a sex show and it was like a small theatre, they brought beers to your seat and people on the stage really were having sex - *quite surreal*.

We had been together for one year when it ended like that.

After my birthday I threw a housewarming, birthday, Christmas party, toasted new beginnings. A party of my own – my first since my sixth birthday – and apart from worrying that people wouldn't turn up, which they did, it was fantastic being the hostess. Music was played on my Sony stereo system and Bose speakers and I felt that my home looked really good for my age; like I was doing well.

Chapter 26

Like a Bird

Early in the year, Mum won first prize in a competition with the local coach company she always used for her coach trips and holidays, for an all inclusive trip to London, with overnight stay in the Thistle Kensington Hotel and theatre tickets for two. We were chauffeured all the way to and from home and loved it. Mum has always enjoyed hanging out and staying out with me. We shopped, wandered through Kensington Gardens and had dinner – a lovely time had by all.

Even through all that has happened in the past with Mum and Dad, I still felt compassion for them and if I felt annoyance at one of my mum's moods, it would melt with either guilt or feeling sorry for her or both. I wanted to love my mum – to have a happy family - and so made all efforts to achieve this feeling. With Dad, I just felt sorry for him and respected him at the time, so I found it easy to ignore the past when he might have neglected me and my safety. I saw him having a hard time with Mum and didn't want to make things any worse, so my 'face' would go on and happy I would be. Being settled and happier anyway, this was not difficult for me at all.

I still regularly visited the cemetery where Agnes's and my nanna's graves stand, taking them both flowers and a few words. It would be a relaxing experience, snipping flowers with scissors to just the right length, fetching the watering can and soaking up the peace of the cemetery. It is a lovely place and I would like to be buried there. Although sometimes my worries of being buried alive, paralysed, or burnt alive, make me flit between the choices of burial and cremation. I always figured that if you have a grave, then people will come to see it and place flowers on it, like I visit Agnes and Nanna, but it depends only whether you have people left behind and alive that loved you and can be bothered to visit you, so I am not sure if I would have anyone at times…?

I continued to go out with friends and have weekends away while studying Interior design.

Later on I had an 'Italian night' at my flat with old school friends. We had Italian music and the wine cask of delicious Chianti I'd saved from my Italian holiday with Maria, my fellow hostess and friend from Fujiyoshida. It was really nice to share the evening with them in my newly painted flat and we hung out after, chatting and drinking on my recently purchased gorgeous second hand dusky pink sofas. It felt so normal, entertaining in my own home. Unfortunately it was not to be for very long and looking at the photos now a few years later, it is one regret in my life where I wish I had of kept with it. It was my home and I had my cat and a life then…

I spent a lot of time with Steve, a friend I'd known since my days as a general assistant at the hotel in Crompton. I naively thought we were just friends which did cause me some problems, as I recall around that time. He was not my *type* as a boyfriend (well his personality and fun aspect were, but his looks and physical ways were not) but everyone thought we should be together as we got on so well. He thought we were going somewhere but all the time I didn't know and he was seeing his mate's girlfriend anyway, so he was rather a user and a cheat! Anyway, we had lots of fun, and whenever he touched me in a friendly way on the leg or something, I told him to keep his distance.

He was such a laugh though and always drove the hour down to see me on week nights and stay the night in my spare room, and get drunk and muck about.

I wore my leather crop top that ties round the neck with my black leggings when we'd go clubbing with his friends all over England. I sound like a right tart, but I wasn't. I didn't wear much make up or high heels. I did fancy one of Steve's friends, but there was no point in pursuing it as he lived too far away, although I did consider buying a house close to him at the time too as they were cheap – always looking for change. Steve had a habit of flinging his arms about and his thumb and index finger up in the air, which made him look awkward, but he was such fun.

My self confidence was still reeling from being the victim of *constructive dismissal* at the recruitment company but I was too upset about it to pursue the claim through the union, as it would have meant I had to stay another month as you cannot claim unless you have been employed for a minimum of one year, so I left on my own accord after eleven months. I ran away.

I changed jobs to work for another recruitment firm in Woodgrove, but it was really different to what I was used to and the female boss was a nightmare to work with. She would do her best to belittle me in front of everyone. I had done well in recruitment, by myself, but I dreaded going to work there, as she hindered my progress and then told me I wasn't any good. I made business plans for working there and made quite a bit of effort, but she didn't allow me to go and visit clients or interview candidates – I had to work with existing clients and existing candidates just using these bloody cards and photos as intros to them. So I had to work blindly by telephone and internet only, but I was a people person and felt claustrophobic in that office. It was an archaic way to work and a bit like setting up blind dates except it was recommending someone I don't know work for someone else I don't know, and asking them to pay me commission for it. I know many do work like this, but I couldn't.

I lasted just about three months there, and the day I left I was so relieved and nervous, that when I got back home I sat on the sofa with the cat and drank three cups of tea and started shaking. I had my second panic attack - possibly fuelled by the caffeine - since having my first one after my *Thyphoid i*njection before my first trip to Thailand. It felt the same – sweating, shaking, paranoia, panic... It suddenly occurred to me that I still had a mortgage and bills to pay. I had already borrowed £10k and added it to my mortgage within that year, for home improvements, but I spent it all going away for weekends with Steve and enjoying myself or getting myself out of sticky situations. All I was really doing was spending Agnes's money that had been put down as the deposit.

I soon found another job in recruitment, and worked in an all women office. They were OK but a certain 'sort' and not my cup of tea. Again, I was not able to work in the ways that I was used to, ie. exactly how I wanted to, so soon felt fed up and my confidence waned.

I'd started seeing a guy called Ed who I met in a club in Laytonhoe. He was eight years older than me and had a son, fourteen years old, who he had sole custody of as the mother wasn't fit. I didn't mind. It wasn't a serious relationship anyway. We went clubbing, drank, took drugs and enjoyed ourselves camping at the V festival. Oh yes, back to drugs.

I took Dad, Ian, Michelle, Pete and Mel out for dinner for Dad's 70th Birthday. Ed came too. Mum didn't come of course, so we took the opportunity to go to *Andres* - Dad's favourite restaurant. I got him a cake made with candles and pictures of him when he was younger printed onto the icing on top with a 'Happy 70th Birthday Dad'. It was really nice. The bill was £270 but it was a real pleasure to treat everyone. It is funny looking at the picture the waiter took of our group, as everyone has finished their main meals, apart from Ian and I who had nearly a whole plateful in front of us.

We were, and I still always am, too busy talking to eat quickly.

I really took care as much as possible over my flat, keeping it tidy, but it was a bit cluttered; full of things I'd bought from around the world.

All the while, I was with Ed, and Steve would still come down and visit. I felt so low about everything, and then the garage started leaking which was not covered on the insurance and for some reason I just took it as a big deal and started panicking about the responsibility of living alone. At this time, David would phone me from Australia a lot and tried to convince me to keep the flat, and maybe rent it out as a second option. Even Peter had a go at stopping me from selling my home. I looked into renting it, but would have to re-mortgage as I couldn't rent it on my current personal mortgage. Many people would rent it out anyway, but my desire and fear to keep in line with the law and conditions, meant that I blew that idea out too. I could have got £475 in rent per month, and it was only a £45k mortgage at about £300 per month at the time, including my extra £10k I'd borrowed, but I got cold feet and sold up.

It was to be the start of many mistakes.

Steve suggested that I move in with him as a lodger and it felt good – I had a fun option so the decision of selling my flat was made easier. However, his current lodger was an ex of mine, Glen, and he said he would move out if I moved in, because I had just dumped him suddenly and that had understandably pissed him off… So Steve decided to keep with Glen and I felt let down, right or wrong. Also, this was around the time that Steve came on to me and asked me to be with him. I said I wouldn't go out with him and he accused me of leading him on 'all this time' which was not true as far as I was concerned.

So I was stuck.

Ed offered me to move in with him instead and I accepted. *Stupid, silly girl.* I moved EVERYTHING in that I owned, and that is a lot of stuff! Into the spare room, his loft and conservatory, boxes and piles of my things – my whole life! I had to buy a washing machine, as his Mum did all his washing for him and he didn't own one. He started going down the pub on his own, leaving me indoors and I thought he was a bit rude to his son. I taught his son to make pizza and we got on OK, but Ed and I were shit. His sister was always coming round and was used to it so didn't stop on my account. His mum also had a key so she came anytime she fancied, and sometimes I was there on my own and she would turn up. I felt claustrophobic. I didn't know anyone in his town. I didn't enjoy my job in Laytonhoe either.

Very quickly I became really depressed, walking the streets in tears a couple of evenings. I felt imprisoned and empty inside. I had lost my sense of independence and was panicking as my personality and self worth slowly disintegrated.

Jane had been seeing a psychotherapist and gave me her details. She lived near Clinton but I took her on and went over there regularly for counselling sessions. She was OK. I have had better therapy since then, more relevant to my issues, but at least I had someone to talk to, and she was able to trace certain difficulties back to my childhood, which is what psychotherapists concentrate on, investigating possible events or circumstances that might have led to my emotional turmoil as an adult – which got me thinking about my past a little bit. It was good - until I couldn't afford her anymore at £30 per hour.

Needless to say, I didn't last long at Ed's – seven weeks in total, start to finish.

I had to get out of his home as we were not getting on at all, so I asked my brother, Ian, my dad and Jane to come and help me to get all my bloody stuff out of there. How shit! And off back to Mum and Dad's I went! Even more shit. Still, I did it all myself, so I could not blame anyone else.

There was that invisible elastic again.

Back at Mum and Dad's events distressed me more and more – Dad wouldn't let me keep my beautiful cat, Aggie, and I was back in the tiny bedroom of my childhood, which dad had been in until I moved out. Shit! I advertised Aggie for free and spent a lot of time visiting people in their homes who wanted her as their pet, but I wouldn't let just anyone have her. After lots of visits and questioning, I found someone in Clinton - a divorced guy whose children were used to cats. Before I took her there, I took lots of photos and it was really sad to leave her with him. I was really fed up again. All these life events and small things just crushed me until I was full of negativity and woe. I couldn't even commit to keeping my cat! What would my future hold when I had such a low threshold of responsibility?

So what did I do? Rather than face my fears - I jetted off again.

Back to the Magical Land of Oz.

Chapter 27

Just keep running

I went in November.

Back to Australia.

I booked my ticket, via San Francisco, during the horrific aftermath of America's devastating 9/11 terrorist attack, so I got a very cheap deal on United Airlines. I had been talking to David on the phone about pursuing a new career in IT and he suggested that I go out there and he could show me some basic skills and I could see if I liked it, without spending thousands of pounds on training first. I stopped in San Francisco for three days on the way out and the plane was half empty so I could stretch out and have a line of seats to myself but the emptiness echoed of the 9/11 horrors and sadness as many people avoided travel to America.

San Francisco was fun though. I booked a few trips out and befriended a girl from Singapore Airlines (stewardess) who I met on the Muir woods trip. She came on the boat trip with me to see Alcatraz prison, and we also had a burger and chips and malt in the Johnny Rockets diner. I went shopping in Macy's and couldn't believe the service and level of shopping offered by Americans and the Christmas decorations were magnificent.

David and Linda were waiting at Sydney airport and it was lovely to see them, even though I was moaning about the flight and the fact that David was videoing it all. "Turn that bloody thing off," I said. Thing was, it was great he took the effort and he carried on videoing and I now have a wonderful five hours of footage to watch of my two months there with them, which has been very interesting for personal purposes and shows the true beauty of Australia. I have not really changed since then. I still throw my head back when I laugh, joke and skip around! I do an awful lot of laughing. At first I thought it looked like a nervous laugh like my mum and dad do sometimes, but it isn't and I am genuinely just finding things funny and joke around a lot.

David named the video 'Big Pants Productions' - *Mandy pants down under*. And he superimposes words and titles in it every so often. It is so nice that he took so much time to take photos and videos of me and for me; it is yet another example of him thinking of others and making a lot of effort

On my 28th Birthday, David filmed me asleep in bed and he was laughing and saying "do you have anything to say, Amanda?"... They gave me lovely presents, including flower shape placemats and coasters, and dark blue mule slippers with silver stars on. We had balloons too.

I did a tandem parachute with a nutty Ozzie guy, and I look like Ronald MacDonald in my flying suit – you can see that my laugh is a nervous one then! I bought the video which was great, but David came along too, videoing me and taking photos which was lovely.

When I was out there I had a Black Christmas.

This was a real eye opener as we were surrounded by bush fires on Christmas day. We had breakfast late on the patio, and had a look at the small fires in the local area. We had some presents (I got David a bottle cooler, Linda 'Celestine Prophecy' book and I got an inspirational calendar). We went to Bullai beach for a picnic, but while we ate, we could see fires and smoke billowing over the mountain that we had driven over, so we didn't know how we would get back to the house. The fires started two days before in Leona in the Blue Mountains. The escarpment was on fire. Black ash fell like rain and filled the air all around us, and the blue sunny sky became black with smoke filling the air, as if it were night time. We left, a little concerned about getting home and whether the house was still OK, but we joined huge traffic jams as the roads were rapidly being closed all around us. The fires raged as 90km per hour winds blew through the area and it was intensely hot and dry, which fuelled the fires to spread like wild fire as they say! Over five thousand fire fighters were on the scenes across the wide open lands; many were volunteers in orange jackets.

On the radio, as it took hours to get home, they mentioned fires all round my brother's home in Mount Annan and things got worse down at Woolongong where we were earlier in the day. We were getting worried that we would not have a house to go back to. Fire alert news took over the radio, as it was reported as some of the worst bush fires in Australia, and in New South Wales, since 1993. We had smoke and flames up ahead and smoke and flames behind us. What a Christmas Day! We videoed the whole thing – from the beach at Woolongong and all the way home in the car, reporting on everything, which is great to watch again, as it is very detailed and 'on the scene'. Those fires burnt for almost three weeks.

David and Linda did have a home when we eventually got back and on Boxing Day, we went to the Camden Valley inn which was local as we couldn't go anywhere else, due to the roads being closed all around us. We had a good laugh, raisin toast for breakfast on the patio, me saying 'I'm still here!' as I was supposed to be going home but had changed my flight to stay longer. For dinner, we had rib steaks with tomato, veggie kebabs, wine and sweet corn and there is me skipping around with excitement!

The trip remains a happy memory. All that time with my brother to chat, and boy does he like to chat! He was equally engrossed in getting me up at 7 am with tea in bed to get me at it with my IT classes. He did a marvellous job and is a great teacher in fact. He taught me how computers work, the computer diagnostic process, how to pull a computer apart and put it back together, upgrade components, the basics of MSDOS and much more.

But when we chatted, we discussed the ins and outs of our family, our emotions and feelings, and we got to the bottom of every good and bad part of our pasts - or should I say 'my' past, since David never says much about himself, even if you want him to. He wants to know about 'you' and everything about you, but never him. We also talked of our wonderful Auntie Agnes and how she kept our family together. In this respect, he did tell me about his childhood experiences of her and my family. It was lovely to have these memories uprooted again – happy times. Unfortunately, the negatives about people and events that I had not indulged in or thought about before, I took home with me, back to England, and they were to play on my mind for a very long time, changing my relationships with others when I got home. I was always easily influenced and began having 'black and white thinking'.

I was comfortable with David and Linda. I never felt like a spare part or that I was unwelcome as they are not emotional or loving outwardly to each other. This always kept jealousy or loneliness away – being a 'gooseberry'. I have that with all my brothers though. Their partners have always made me feel welcome and although I have had many boyfriends, I have been on my own a lot of time too, particularly when seeing my brothers and travelling. David and I had had a blow up two weeks after I arrived in Sydney, which hit me so hard I said I would go home. Uncomfortable situations always made me want to flee and I was always able to then, money wise, so I said I was going home and luckily David and I worked things out and I stayed not for the planned one, but two months.

I did my usual adventurous stuff too – the tandem parachute jump at 10,000 feet, white water rafting with Linda and climbing the magnificent Sydney Bridge with her, all with David videoing the action, since he wasn't up for these types of experiences, apart from skiing. But, we all joined in with trekking round the Blue Mountains and picnicking on beaches with wild kangaroos.

Inevitably, the time to go home came and we had a nice photo shoot of us all at their home, followed by a sad journey and goodbye at the airport which involved a few tears. As with all these trips to my brothers, the great thing is that we spend 'quality time' together. As David said to me, if we all lived in the same country, we would see each other every so often for a few hours and catch up, but not much more, but when we have a month, two months or more together, we get to talk much more and share our lives living together, getting past all the catch up chit chat. So this was the second visit to Australia to see my two brothers – Peter had come home by now and Ian was still at home.

Chapter 28

There's No Place Like Home

So, I was back to my tiny bedroom in Woodgrove, I didn't even have a wardrobe.

Dad had taken over the bigger room when I lived in my maisonette and so I was back to my childhood room, just without the pink walls. I remember hanging out the back door in the freezing cold, having a cigarette and listening to Mum and Dad arguing and just wishing I was back with David and Linda in the warm climes of Australia. They had their problems too, which I had seen up close and personal, as I had with Peter and Mel, just like many families or couples, but this was too much the 'same'. I felt claustrophobic again, but I was soon starting my IT course, I needed something to look forward to.

I bought a cheap computer, set up a network and went to college, doing my *Comptia A+ Professional* and *City and Guilds* hardware/software course. It was hard and the books very thick and boring – I'd often fall asleep mid study on my bed - but I passed the exams with flying colours and got a job in Internet Support where I met Laura.

At this time, I also went to a Spanish property exhibition and found a company to do a 'free trip' to the Costa Blanca to view property for sale. I promised everyone I wouldn't buy straight away on that trip, and I went out there with that carefully in mind, but their skills in selling won me over and I found myself putting a £3K deposit down on an apartment, which would be built within eighteen months. It was probably helped by the sunshine, warmth and stunning views from the hotel they put me in, which excited me (not difficult). This is another example of the impulsive buying and actions of a BPD sufferer. I should have just looked and returned home and trusted my instincts which were telling me not to, particularly as I had just written out the cheque and was enjoying some lunch on Torrevieja promenade with the Estate agent when suddenly some beggars were pleading for money round the outside terrace tables. I complained as I thought it wrong to beg when people were eating, and the next minute, a middle aged woman got up and was shouting in my direction "Your bag, they've taken your bag!" and she started running up the promenade after a couple of guys. I looked down to find that my bag was missing from beside me on the floor, and panicked. All in a whiz, the woman returned with my bag, as they had taken flight but dropped the bag as the woman chased them... I was in shock but thanked the lady wholeheartedly. Of course, the estate agent didn't make a big deal of it, so as not to put me off the area and my property, and I was too startled to talk about it, but that bag contained my passport, cheque book, camera, credit and debit cards and money.

Still, I didn't learn until more than a year and an awful lot of stress later.

The internet job was telephone support for dial up internet, but they put me on the broadband section without proper training and I didn't have a clue what I was talking about, since I didn't even have broadband in those days myself. Imagine if you were a customer, business or personal, and you had a problem with your internet, you had been waiting on the telephone in a queue for an hour (our queues were often that long!) and then the person you finally got through to simply couldn't help you. Because of my high standards in Customer Service, I hated the job. I wanted to help. I wanted to be good – a star employee with good references as usual. The supervisor (a contradictory idiot) was listening to my calls as well, and pulled me in the office to rip my recorded calls to shreds. Instead of helping me he just made me feel incapable. The people there were mixed, but OK I suppose, but the working environment and lack of support was dreadful. I left within about three months (even though this was not a good career move) as I didn't feel up to the job and was probably not interested enough anyway. I wrote to HR and explained what it was like on that floor and my reasons for leaving. They tried to get me to stay (as they lose a lot of staff and they were pleased that I had taken the time to tell them why I'd left) but I couldn't stay after complaining.

I met Louis on a night out in Clinton, in April, when I was out with my friend Laura. Though he wasn't my type, I found him unusual. He was in Sales and was used to driving Mercedes and BMW company cars and earned lots of money selling commercial car hire contracts. He was full of himself, yet had self esteem issues which I later worked out stemmed from his dad's disfavour and disappointment of him and also the child sexual abuse he had suffered. So, I felt for him and we had fun going down the 'duck pub' as we called it in Laytonhoe, watching ducks quack on the pond as we sipped our drinks in the beer garden during warm May and June evenings. We also went away for a weekend in a Travel Inn in his sports car and were playing our favourite tune *Scooter -Ramp*! (*The Logical Song*). We played it really loud with the roof down and were singing on the way past the Wymouth Pavilion and gaining quite a bit of attention – I was very embarrassed! We also went down to meet his mum who lived a few miles away from Wymouth. I liked her and the feeling was mutual. She was quite *mumsy* and we played card games. She wasn't a prude and just as well with a way out son like Louis. She bought me a notepad with a chimpanzee on the front, which was so sweet as she knew I liked primates. But it was obvious, even then, that I wasn't that committed to Louis and I was planning to move away.

I went to Spain a few times to research the area and see the progression (or lack of) of my flat being built. One time, Ian, Michelle and Elsa came too, as they were thinking of moving out there and were already learning Spanish by private home tutoring. I can see the photos on Campoamor Beach; Ian, slim with his green shorts and short hair, Michelle looking healthy with her lovely long blonde hair and Elsa a very cute, blonde two year old with her face painted orange with visible sun cream. I had found a lady local to us in Woodgrove, with a couple of apartments. We had visited her, got chatting about buying and living out there and got booked up for two weeks. Her apartment was quiet and on a complex like a ghost town, with most properties locked up and uninhabited. It was neither cosy nor holiday like. Ian sat on the roof terrace and counted over eighty cranes from all the new builds in the area, so that rather spoilt the view. Properties were being built at a tremendous rate, since the mayor had given a certain timescale in which new properties could be built, so all the builders went crazy. I just remained blinkered to it all, wanting to believe it was a better area than it was and thought that he was being very negative since I was buying there, when Ian told me the area was doomed. He was not impressed with this part of Spain at all, being such a concrete jungle (even worse than where we live) and having no greenery, that he decided not to move to Spain after all, and put me off my apartment. Still, that only fed my desire to go against what other people wanted me to do, and further inclined me to keep it, although I did see what he meant and worried a bit about how I would rent it and keep it secure since I learnt more and more about burglaries in the area when asking why all the properties had iron bars on the windows and doors. We also went to see the show flat for my builder, and Ian didn't like that either, picking holes in everything. I also did my own little trips out with our shared car, to photograph the golf courses and have a drive about. Elsa was under three years old and could be out of control at times as toddlers are. One evening, at a Thai restaurant where

Ian was complaining about the cost of the meal, Elsa was playing up big time, and I commented that it was a nightmare to concentrate on talking or eating and was a bit peeved at how she could take over the evening like she did and get away with it, when Ian turned to me.

"Amanda," he said, "you must never have children – you couldn't cope with being a mother!"

I will never forget that comment. It has haunted me in a way I never imagined. I have questioned myself time and time again if he was right. *I couldn't even keep my cat.*

I attempted to cook a pasta dinner in the apartment once, but the electric kept tripping out, and I was down to one or two rings and one light, so it messed up my meal completely. They were getting fidgety because they were hungry but it wasn't my fault. But I think that's when I decided I wanted to move out, like right in that moment. I phoned Louis to see if he would come out for the second week. I arranged another apartment and a cute smart car and he flew over.

The apartment was small and on a complex with not many people, and I still didn't take notice of this flaw in my plans, that there were not many holidaymakers for the amount of rental properties. Louis got completely drunk one day when we were due to go on the tourist promenade train at Benidorm, and I was furious with him. We had stayed in Benidorm just for one night and he spent the afternoon asleep on the bed of our room with a view of the beach.

We also went to Benidorm for a day trip with Ian, Michelle and Elsa and sunbathed on the beach one day. Louis went to get us all some beers with Ian and they took ages, as they were having a beer up there before bringing our beers back – I was furious and made a bit of a scene which they were not impressed with.

Ian and Michelle liked Louis but thought him strange, especially his constant pulling his t-shirt down over his belly, as if he was nervous.

On leaving the Internet Support company, I felt more inclined towards doing temporary work and I landed myself in the sexual health department of Laytonhoe Hospital and was there for about three months. I temped there as a medical secretary for the consultant. He welcomed my hard work and involved me in all his meetings in the end when he knew I was dedicated to the job. I learnt all about Syphilis, genital warts, Gonorrhoea and everything in between to Chlamydia and HIV/AIDS as I wrote letters and notes concerning the unfortunate patients the consultant was treating for such STD's. I felt so sorry for some patients, particularly when I would read about one who was given HIV by someone who knew they had it and couldn't be bothered to be careful.

At first, the job was really interesting and I was engrossed in the patient's stories, but it soon made me feel depressed, as it was so sad that people's behaviour should be so bad, (affairs being found out, shagging people in high risk HIV areas of Africa) and I realised just how lucky I'd been not catching anything despite sleeping with people all over the world.

In the end the consultant wanted me to work for him on a permanent basis, but the money was not enough at £11K a year, so I left as I had decided to leave Mum and Dad's again; this time to stay temporarily with friends in Molton, and look for a new house and a new housemate.

I just never figured on finding one that reminded me of that film *Single White Female.*

But it happened.

It was as if I could never stay in the same place for too long. Or sane.

Chapter 29

Single White Female

2004

I would travel home from work scared. Not scared of travelling, not scared of the roads, just scared of going home – back to *her*. My new house mate. SWF.

Just a few months before, I had moved to Molton to make a big change in my life; once again. It was becoming the norm to pack up and move – always chasing the dream in the hope that I would encompass, and one day manage to pin down and keep, that ambiguous feeling called inner happiness and have it all for myself.

I had found a new friend, Lynne, and I just could not work out what was wrong with her. But just one trip up to her home in Molton was all it took. If only I had known what was going to happen I would never have gone.

I'd seen an advert for a cottage just outside of Molton. Lynne already lived there. I called straight away and drove to meet her that same night.

All I wanted was to settle down in a nice new home. The people are pleasant in that area and I just wanted a happy home away from the concrete, the arguing, my home town – an escape.

Lynne had a dog called Happy, a Lurcher of some kind (a good omen?). She was an artist in watercolour and oils, and loved horses. I could tell she was the horsy type. I thought that was good, as I like animals, and someone who likes animals must be nice, mustn't they?

So, she offered me a glass of wine and we chatted for over an hour. It was such effortless conversation that we both decided we would be good friends and get on just fine. I trusted my instincts. So, without looking at any other properties I made arrangements to move in the following week. We would share the council tax, oil for heating and electric bills.

I was so excited – at last a home with no arguments, no guilt and no black moods. I could leave all the past behind and make a new start – put my belongings where I wanted, and sleep at night. I loved my family and I intended to visit them regularly but I needed to be me.

One night during the first week Lynne and I decided to go on a pub crawl round Molton. I opted to drive so that I wouldn't drink. Lynne decided to take advantage of this and got very drunk within the first hour, knocking back beers and shots as fast as she could. Although the last pub we went in was full of friendly, country people, I was upset that Lynne was chatting up various men and basically ignoring me, so I lost my patience and I decided it was time to leave. However, Lynne took my car keys and refused to give them back saying she didn't want to leave 'just yet'. Eventually, we made the trip back home on the premise that we would have a drink at the local village pub. Lynne went straight there and I met her a few minutes later. I found her downing brandies by herself and I realized she was incredibly drunk, slurring and staggering. We were the only people in the pub and she began harassing the bar maid who was wearing a pink and white striped rugby style shirt.

"You look like a lesbian," she said looking straight at her, glassy eyed.

She repeated it, laughing this time. I cringed, not knowing what to say or do. The woman stared at her and then went to get the landlady from upstairs – a stocky woman with bleached blonde hair. We were evicted from the pub and told not to come back.

I had never been banned from anywhere before, so I was hurt – particularly as this was the only local pub in walking distance that we had, and I'd done nothing but be nice to everyone.

Anyway, having lived for years in my family, particularly with my mum, I was used to pandering to peoples' needs, calming situations and occasionally being the one who took responsibility for others, so this was no problem I thought – at the time.

I did the usual rounds of applying to job agencies in the area. I had become very capable at interviews and applications. I found a temporary role of 'Drugs Strategy Co-ordinator' at a male prison. Different? I took the job. When I started, I was told I would receive training for self defence, as I was working directly inside a cell block full of male prisoners – all with drug problems.

The job was to provide administrative support to the Drug Rehabilitation Counsellors, whose role it was to support the male prisoners with drug addictions. The idea was to help get them off drugs in a supportive way in the hope that it would help to cut re-offences, such as burglary and muggings to get drug money – their vicious cycle. So, my personal history was checked out via the Criminal Records Bureau and I started.

I was given a set of huge bulky keys for which I had a leather key pouch strapped to my waist. They would open virtually all the doors within the cell block and prison internal gates and jangled loudly as I walked – giving me the slight sense of responsibility and authority.

Our shared office was situated in the middle of a cell block and although it was bigger than a cell, it had the same barred small windows and double locked heavy doors which had to be locked at all times, so it wasn't what you would call a pleasant office environment. However, I was shown how to do the job by the helpful counsellors. It was straightforward administration and typing, so nothing too taxing. I was given a whistle and told that I would receive a mobile phone in case of emergencies, but in the meantime, I should blow the whistle three times if there was an emergency, such as being attacked.

I was shown how to get in and out of the cell block and my cell like office. The main front gates to get completely out of the confines of the prison were security manned and one had to sign in and out. I had my photo taken and a security pass made up which had to be shown too.

I soon had to go shopping for new frumpy clothes - long flowing black skirt, baggy top, flat shoes - wear no makeup and leave my hair messy, as I realised one break time that it didn't pay to look good. It was difficult to cover up as it was a hot summer while I was there, but necessary.

I had left the cell block that day at the wrong time – break/exercise time for the prisoners – and there were about sixty guys hanging about in the cell block outer garden, and loads more leaning through the bars of their cell windows. As soon as they saw me a tirade of "Miss, Miss" started. Miss this, Miss that. That is what they were told to call a woman in the prison, as we didn't get involved with real names. Whistling, shouting, coming up to me close. I had never felt so uncomfortable - it was intimidating. At the end of the day, these people are humans of course, but it was the amount of them that un-nerved me; one piece of attention I didn't want for a change.

After that, I tended to avoid those times of day, so if I wanted to go to the Mess for lunch, I would go before or after the prisoners exercise time. Lots of them didn't have jobs, so you would hear them in neighbouring cells, bored, shouting at each other conversations of a sort – mostly undignified at times, about women being this and that, people they knew, who they'd beaten up, shagged and such like.

I had no problem making my own lunches, but to be honest, I wanted to get out of that office. I wanted to get some fresh summer air and talk to someone else. It was difficult though, as the people who work in prisons can be a certain type, and it could be 'cliquey'. Many family members work there so you had to be careful who you talked to about anyone else, as it may be their wife, dad or sister! I try not to do that at all now due to my new idea of karma and that bitching doesn't help anyone, but I have certainly involved myself in gossip in the past unfortunately, although not to a vicious degree.

The 'Mess' food was OK but not cheap. Human Relations were also at that end of the prison (my cell block was quite a walk into the prison), where I frequented with my grievances and to get my time sheets put in at the end of the week. In the Mess, I met quite a few people and they were mostly alright, although they are not the types you would find in an office – much rawer, serious and army like. The stories they told could be entertaining at times too.

The counsellors offered talking therapies to the prisoners, and I looked after the office filing system, which gave me access to all prisoner records. Unlike a person's general prison file which may contain general details and the crime(s) they had committed, these therapy files were personal, with details of their personal stories, as told to the counsellors, so they were very interesting. It was part of my job to look up records and keep all the new data up to date in their files, so I wasn't just being nosy! Not at first anyway! They might write poems or stories too, outlining their torture of drug taking or being in prison. They liked the counselling, and needed it. I also found a poem about heroin addiction, written by someone who had since died of a drug overdose.

They were mainly thieves and burglars, but there was a rapist too, who I met later on. It was bearable and interesting enough, albeit rather depressing to be in that cell office in the extreme heat of the summer, with the sun shining outside. But I thought it more a shame there was such a lack of jobs for the prisoners, as I couldn't see how boredom is going to help someone come off drugs. It may lead to even more use, and if they are doing nothing, and costing the tax payer and government lots of money (about £21k per year each prisoner at the time) then we should utilise them to put back some of that money for their time, doing something useful for society.

Suddenly there was an atmosphere between the counsellors and they were sacked First one person, then the whole team lost the prison contract for their charity. The head counsellor had sadly been having sexual intercourse with the prisoners, and had been caught out. So, I was left on my own for a few weeks, since I was a temp for the prison directly, not the charity, and it was so lonely and miserable I got quite bored and felt down. And I don't 'do' bored very well as we know… I had no real job to do. I proactively went through the office files and got some jobs done and the head of the cell block made use of me as a temporary secretary to keep me in work, but he was a dirty sod and came onto me with verbal sexual innuendos and offers. I felt trapped.

Sometimes I would go to sleep in my office in the afternoon, after listening to the verbal diarrhoea that came out of the prisoners' mouths. Sometimes they would come to the door and beg me to help them with counselling. "When are we gonna get counselling, Miss?" "What has happened to the counsellors, Miss?" I spent a lot of time, though, reading their stories, getting to know what it was like to be them – to do bad things like them and why - and reading their poems and stuff. It was sad, but interesting and I built empathy with many of them since they'd had a rough ride as children and had suffered greatly in their lives clearly causing mental health issues for some. Two wrongs don't make a right though, as they say.

I didn't believe that all the people who do bad things were born bad, and it seems that I was right to some degree – there's only so much abuse and neglect some children can take before their personality changes, particularly if they have low self esteem or are very emotional to start with. And if a child is shown by their adult carers that it is normal to take drugs, to steal, to hurt people, how can a child know better? Yes, they should learn better as they become adults, but it isn't that easy. They often continue to grow up as adults in areas rife with problems, crime and sometimes poverty as well. Not that I condone any bad or unlawful doings – empathy is an understanding of a person, being able to see things from their perspective, not to say what they do is OK or have sympathy.

One day, the fire alarm went off, and I didn't have a clue what to do, as I hadn't been told. I had to ask some prisoners where to go! I never got my self defence course, nor my mobile, so at all times it was just little old blonde me, the prisoners, the keys to the prison and my whistle.

I did go walkabouts too, to see who I could talk to and I would chat to the prison officers and find out what they did – all guys of course, so I was quite popular! I also got a tour of the prison blocks – the 'lifer's' cell block was the most interesting where they wore slippers and dressing gowns and watched TV. Now I know why some call prison a 'hotel'. All were a far cry from the block I was in though - which was the worst one and nothing like a hotel – foul smelling food and bare. One time, I had to go over to the female side, which I was excited about, to sort out some expenses, but it was awful – the female officers were hard looking, and the atmosphere was bitchy. Whenever I've felt like doing something really bad, I think about that female prison and it puts things into perspective. If I went to prison, I would kill myself. I couldn't hack it.

Eventually, a new group of counsellors started, and I stayed on to show them the ropes of the office, and left shortly after.

On leaving I outlined the sexual misconduct of the Officer, the lack of training, self defence training and mobile phone and all the other issues I had come across since working there for just three months. They replied thanking me for my support and hard work in 'such difficult times'. I still have that reference letter. It is one of many as I usually got a good one from each job I did.

Too many of my jobs lasted three months...

My family ridicule me for all my job changes. I've even had a job that only lasted half a day! This, I later found out, is a symptom of BPD; to keep changing, like a butterfly who needs to morph. What was I looking for? Was I still looking for the real me?

I didn't leave the prison until I had somewhere else to go though, as I needed to work for money, and I had done two things since I felt ready again to get back into a career and commit myself to permanent work. Firstly, I'd taken up Career Counselling locally, with a lady who worked from home. She'd carried out a psychological test so that we could work out what I was good and bad at. We'd also utilised various techniques and homework to look at what I liked doing and disliked doing. I'd also worked from the book *What colour is your parachute?* on a similar vein. It was very thorough with tests and grids to fill in as to personal choices and cost me quite a bit of money as all these counselling/therapy sessions did, so I had been committed to trying to help myself even if I wasn't ready.

I was suffering stress for one reason or another (living with Lynne didn't help) so we'd completed a stress management course as well, where we concentrated on certain things such as: If I was getting stressed in traffic and running late, not to sit there fuming and swearing, but to accept that there is nothing I can do about the situation and would not get there any sooner by shouting and getting angry with myself and others and hurting myself hitting the steering wheel. I was taught that the best thing would be to sit there, put music on, listen to birds, whatever, but to enjoy the present moment with my five senses. We worked on creating awareness of those senses, so to listen very carefully to all the sounds, to be aware of the taste in my mouth, to really see everything that is in front of me, to feel and be aware of my body's feelings, and lastly to smell – to be aware of all aromas around me . When you are stressed you are not aware of your senses, so concentrating on bringing them back to the forefront will take you away from the problems in your mind and help you to relax. I also used this technique for relaxation. So, to sit or lie, and go through my five senses one by one, being aware of all of them in turn and appreciating them. It is similar to the 'mindfulness' techniques of DBT (Dialectical Behavioural Therapy) which has been used widely to treat Borderline Personality Disorder sufferers. Mindfulness is being mindful of the present moment, and either paying attention to each moment in a particular way and non-judgementally, or present centred thoughts or feelings that arise are accepted as they are, without judgement. Mindfulness comes from the Buddhist ways of meditation. It worked a treat, but it was keeping it up that was the real problem…

At this time I was seeing a guy called Adrian even though he had a long journey to Molton to see me. He drove up to see me every couple of weeks. The first time he visited the cottage, Lynne made quite a fuss. Sitting down on a chair, flirtatiously, in the middle of the room, she launched into a flurry of abuse aimed at Adrian undermining his abilities as a carpenter and as a boyfriend to me, before demanding he go to his van to get her some weed and to the pub to get her some condoms from the toilet vending machine.

The signs were there, but I guess I tried to ignore them. But I wouldn't be able to for much longer.

She was a busy woman, but I still could not work her out.

She would get up at 4.30 am to walk the dog, go feed, muck out and ride the racehorses at the stables, and set off to her job to start at 9 am. She was an art teacher, yet 'a bit crazy'. However, I did befriend her, and although I did not like much of what she did, I relied on the relationship working, as all I wanted was a genial, relaxed home life.

We decided to go to belly dancing classes in Crompton which was only fourteen miles away. Lynne insisted on getting very stoned on weed beforehand, and her efforts were fruitful. I didn't smoke with her, and drove us there. She couldn't get the hang of the belly movements and within only twenty minutes, it became very embarrassing when she began slurring garbled abuse at the tutor and danced around the room in her own manic style, waving her arms about, skipping and spinning in circles. I got her to leave the room and drove her home immediately and I never went back to the classes that I had paid for.

After the career and stress management counselling I went to an agency specialising in management roles and they introduced me to a guy called Mark Harris, who interviewed me for a management position in his new business and gave me the job. He even said he would set up our office nearer my home for ease. I started there in October and it was a really varied role, taking up a lot of my skills – IT, recruitment, office and health and safety. It was a brand new telephone answering company, taking calls and messages on behalf of customers who needed it. All we had at the beginning was an office, the hardware and a load of ideas. Ian and Michelle still laugh their heads off now when I mention that job as Ian had asked me how many staff I looked after as an office manager and I had told him 'none' and they burst into hysterics. Anyway, I basically set up the office, the telephone answering switch, and got our first telesales member of staff, Tina. Gradually, I helped build the branding, advertising and customer services team, and we were doing alright for a start up business with a handful of staff.

It was around that time events span out of control with Lynne.

During a night out at the local nightclub, Lynne decided to throw a drink over the man she was talking to, and got kicked out of the club. I tried to hide, as I was having a nice time talking with a guy a few feet away, but the bouncers grabbed my arm and threw me out too, as they had seen us together earlier on. Wailing led to screaming as Lynne flew into a fit of anger at the humiliation, and she shared her abusive thoughts with the entire queue of people outside the club. "He said he wanted to shag me up the arse!" she kept wailing. I was in shock. I again made sure she got home safe, before police could be called. Then, I started to go downhill mentally myself.

Instead of dealing with Lynne's strange and abusive ways, I became insular and withdrawn when around her. I felt she had gotten a hold of me and was sucking the life out of me; overpowering me so that I felt I was going down a hole and couldn't breathe. I felt scared of her and what she might do next. I felt paranoid of her, and alone. This was very odd since I was used to conflict, but nevertheless, I couldn't stop it.

She seemed incredibly jealous of my bright spirit and did all she could to deplete it. My friend, Jane, also stopped visiting, as she said she didn't like my behaviour, as I was becoming more aggressive towards her and needy. She wouldn't listen to me! For some reason, I could not get her to believe what was going on with Lynne. Lynne was always out when Jane would visit me and she thought that I was kind of making it up about her as I wasn't always balanced myself which Jane had experienced before, particularly in Japan. But Adrian didn't seem to believe me either. *How come you stay there if it's that bad? She can't be that bad.*

I was so upset and alone, yet I couldn't seem to break the chain and leave. I couldn't get Lynne to leave me alone either – she just seemed to enjoy upsetting me and getting me to do things I didn't want to do. I had no strength past doing my job and paying the bills. Gradually my work suffered too, and I started getting drunk with Lynne in the week on her 'good days' or just going to bed straight from work to blot it all out. Somehow I had managed to take on a couple of new employees and train them to answer telephones on behalf of our customers, but cracks were appearing.

One day, Lynne and I decided to drink some flaming sambucas at home and video ourselves dancing. It started off fine, but we ended up drinking the whole bottle between us – on a work night! We did have a right laugh though, and I made the most of her high spirits that day, dancing to Abba and other such songs, and knocking back that hot sweet aniseed delight. Next morning, of course, I had a hangover from hell. I have no idea how, but Lynne was up and went to work. She woke me and I said there is no way I could go to work, so she kindly telephoned my boss and told him I was sick. I felt bad as it wasn't the sort of thing I would do, taking sickies, but what could I do, I couldn't drive or work or anything and I was the bloody manager!

As it happened though, the sun was shining and it was one of those beautiful crisp, cold winter days, with perfect visibility and bright blue skies, so by the afternoon, I was up for taking the dog for a walk. And did I walk. I videoed some of it. It was so peaceful out in the countryside, by myself. Happy loved it and we walked for miles.

Lynne had started leaving me horrid letters accusing me of being unclean, mental, nasty, abusive and unhelpful to name but a few words, and yet she was sometimes nice to me. What did I do to deserve this? Why was she accusing me of doing the things she was actually doing to me?

Winter set in with snow, and the cottage became almost unbearable to live in; it was so cold. Being a detached, old stone building, and the fact that Lynne refused to have the heating on most of the time (it cost too much apparently, even though I paid half) I ended up wearing a scarf, gloves, t-shirt, jumper and socks in bed just to keep warm. In fact, I would get back from work and go straight to bed sometimes to avoid her and chill blains. Sometimes, when Lynne did allow heating, she would barge into my bedroom at 4.30 am, pull my bedcovers off me and shout right into my face viciously; accusing me of turning the heating off to spite her and various taunts. The heating dial was in my room, but I wouldn't dream of turning it off. This happened quite a bit. Locking her out didn't work for long either.

One time, she came in my bedroom in the evening, telling me off. I told her to get out since it was my only little bit of space apart from my car I had. She refused. I asked her again. No. So, I tried to push her out, and do you know I couldn't budge her one step. Now, I am not Miss wrestler or anything, but I am strong for my build, due to all the wrestling I'd had to do with Ian as a child when he wanted to *play* and teach me how to *look after* myself. But, she didn't move an inch. She had a strong mind alright.

I am not the tidiest person in the world, but I do like cleanliness and our cottage was not clean. The basics were OK, like the kitchen and my bedroom, but the rest was different. When Happy came on heat, Lynne let her bleed all over the lounge – the carpet, the sofa, everywhere. She thought it was fine and her dog slept with her every night in her futon.

I went home for my birthday, after working during the day (I cannot believe I actually worked on my birthday as I wouldn't normally) and went out with Ian, Michelle, David and Linda (they were over visiting from Australia), Adrian and Dad. Maybe we went to *Andre's*, I am not sure, but the video is quite funny with Ian doing a happy birthday song, Adrian not knowing what to say and David with longish hair. Dad was of course being his usual self and talking about sticking his fingers up at the camera when David last videoed him. And no Mum, of course.

During David and Linda's visit from Australia, they came up to see me too. I had spent ages trying to find them somewhere to stay. Originally, I invited them to the cottage, but I decided against it because of Lynne and the cleanliness issues. So, I tried everywhere to find them somewhere, but it was horse sales week in Molton, so most of the accommodation was booked up. I got somewhere in the end. They came up, and on arrival at the place, we found it dirty, with toothpaste on the taps, uncovered butter for breakfast service in the fridge in the bathroom, and terribly uncomfortable beds, with stained bedclothes. Yuk! I tried to cover it, whilst Linda was not bothered and David 'went into one', but then I had to agree with him and we left without paying. I think we phoned them or something. So, they had to stay with me. We all loved our food and eating out. That night we got back to the cottage after a meal in my favourite local pub, and Lynne said hello and we went to bed, but as she had kept the dog in as punishment for killing a rabbit (so she said) it shat on the floor of the bathroom and of course, David had to come down at 6am for a pee and found it on the floor in the entrance to the bathroom. I don't know anyone who hates dog poo being anywhere as much as David.

Pink - Don't Let Me Get Me

Eventually I found the strength to sort the situation out. It was time to move out.

I begged Jane and Adrian to believe how awful it really was, and invited them to help me move out, where they could see for themselves just how bad Lynne had actually got.

Lynne had shown me some pills she was taking to apparently 'give up smoking'. I looked them (*Zyban*) up on the internet and found out they were also anti-depressants. Knowing what I know now, they wouldn't mix too well with cannabis and alcohol together, which might now explain some of those weird moods she went into. Although it had become clear that her mother and sister had quite serious mental health problems.

Jane came round the night before to help me move out. Lynne stood over us as we tried to have a conversation in the lounge and went on and on about my leaving, nastily, her face just a few inches from ours. We went out for dinner. When we got back, Lynne was already in bed. My room was tiny; just room for my dressing table and a single bed, with a small floor space running down the side of it. Jane insisted I have the bed, and get a good night's sleep for a change, and she took the floor. I stuffed towels under the door and we barricaded ourselves in with one of the dressing table drawers lodged between the bed and the door frame. We had to because Lynne had torn the lock of the door off ages before when desperate to get in my room when I locked her out as she was having one of her 'mid morning turns'. She'd barged and barged the door until it broke and came away from the doorframe.

Anyway, our barricade didn't work and when Lynne went mad later on, she managed to bash the door so much she got in and trod all over Jane on the floor, again accusing us of turning off the heating. It was like watching a predator in a horror movie.

Jane and I had a huge argument.

Adrian arrived the next day with his van. Lynne sat on a chair in the middle of the room we were trying to get through to get my stuff out the door, and read a book, whilst humming and singing. She also took my landline phone and wouldn't give it back just in case I wanted to ring my brother in Australia before I left, on *her* bill. She then phoned her sister and told her how nasty I was and how pleased she was to be finally getting rid of me. It's funny because I met her sister and her mum. Her sister was in trouble where she lived in London for smashing a neighbour's window because they were 'making too much noise'. And her mum couldn't even look at me or speak when I met her, just looking down the whole time – I think she suffered with depression.

My boss was great about it once I explained my situation and he supported me in having time off to find a new place to live. In fact, even with these problems on the domestic front, at least work went well, and I was given a substantial pay rise. We even organised a stand at the Business Start Up Exhibition in Birmingham. I met a web company there and took their details, as I already had an idea for a website of my own for renting my Spanish apartment.

I found a new home, a three-bed terraced house in Molton, and I treated myself to private Spanish and golf lessons. I also joined a Wine Club, adorning my wine rack with good wine, I ordered cable TV, broadband internet, and bought Tesco *finest* or Waitrose foods and products. I figured that if I worked hard and earned well, I would reward myself and had fresh flowers around the house. To all who might've looked on from the outside I was doing so well, I had got myself together, so maybe I did have a mental illness, but I was coping and I was coping well. And what's more, unlike Mum, no one could see it.

Nelly's *Dilemma,* featuring Kelly Rowland, became my song at that time, it made me think of Adrian, and I even recorded it for him, although I don't think I ever gave it to him… I could not stop playing it. *I loved him, I needed him, no matter what I did, all I thought about was him…*

With Adrian the sex was great.

We had some great times altogether; lots of meals out, bottles of his favourite *Chateuaneuf du pape* and even a fabulous sex filled holiday to the Algarve, Portugal, where we didn't get out of the hotel room for the first two days. Adrian met all my family, he came round for family meals and Christmas; he was a properly accepted boyfriend and my mum loved him, and still talks about him now. But even he had issues. He lacked in confidence, mainly it seemed because of the horrible way his ex had treated him, but my dissatisfaction at his lack of drive in life, for a home, a family, a marriage, didn't help. He was quite content to stay living at his mum and dad's house. But when things turned sour between us, and I went to his house his mother decided *for him* that he didn't want to see me. I sobbed and begged her to let me in like a young child and I hated her afterwards for letting me embarrass myself like that. So, when I asked Adrian about it, he was on his mother's side, and that was no good for me. I had to be number one. I guess I learnt that everyone had to choose *sides* from my mum. We had a break from each other, which was supposed to be permanent.

In an effort to make more friends and not rely on old ones visiting me, I answered an ad in the local paper (the making friends column), and met Karen – she was four years younger than me. We got on so well, we spent a lot of time together, clubbing, pubbing and staying round each other's houses. She lived in Crompton. During a night out once we met some RAF guys and I started seeing one of them. We would have the odd party at mine or I would go to their barracks and sneak around, fly around on their motorbikes and attend music festivals.

I continued my trips to the Costa Blanca in Spain, where I would meet up with a male friend, Jake, chill out with long lunches on the sunny promenade, visit my builder, building sites, and drove round taking photos, researching the area for holidaymakers. I loved it and felt Spain was my natural home. Jane came out with me in July. The more I researched owners' efforts to rent their properties, the more I realised that lots of people didn't have a clue how to market their holiday rentals. I also realised just how many properties in the South Costa Blanca there were for holiday rental, and that it would be difficult to get enough bookings to cover the mortgage on my flat. Increasingly worried about it, I would take more trips out there, asking more questions of anyone I could find. Stress took over, and started to affect my work as well. If anyone came to visit me (Jane, Ian and Michelle and Elsa or Karen or anyone) I would sob for hours after they left, feeling abandoned and alone. It seemed that Lynne really had sucked the life out of me.

I went to see my doctor this time and told him how lonely and down I felt. Luckily, he was very understanding and referred me for in house Adlerian Psychological Therapy (APT) which deals with how our own perception of self, inferior feelings for example, can shape emotional experience and the therapy is to change our perception and thus our behaviour. I am sure this kept me going when suicidal thoughts swept over me every morning. It would take so long to get out of bed; I was late for work every day. I couldn't be bothered to dress, wash or look nice. I began to hate work, paranoia set in, as I was letting my staff down, which were now a team of four, and 'Management' just didn't seem to suit me anymore.

But I actually liked Adlerian therapy. It helped me look into my childhood as the key to understanding myself, what I expected in life and hence why I behaved the way I did, i.e. child experiences = beliefs. Although some of this had been covered in my previous psychotherapy this was looking at it in a slightly different way.

On top of that, it was free and supplied by the NHS at my local doctor's, and it was regular every week. I really liked and trusted the therapist, and I could see that she was unfolding some very poignant issues from my past.

I would close my eyes and concentrate and tell the therapist the first memory that came to mind. She would ask me questions about it (who was there? What were my surroundings? What was happening?) and she would get me to talk about the event and bring out how I felt about it. What was significant?

We worked on memories about my family, what had shaped me, what was negative/positive, and how to then change negative self-belief into positive feelings; empowering, self-confidence.

For me one of the best things that came out of it, apart from restored self-confidence, was forgiving my mum.

In my mind, I visualised meeting Mum and telling her I forgave her for her illness

The result was an understanding, an acceptance of what my mum had been through and how she had affected me, and naturally that led to a better relationship with her, which makes me still believe in that therapy. We'd also search for truths by taking me back in time in my mind to find slices of memories which would come to me naturally. I found it very cleansing; a mindful liberation from my struggles. The new self-confidence also led me to the decision to finally give up my job and start my own business. So overall, APT was a positive experience for me.

But some of what I unlocked was not so positive.

In truth we start to see ourselves

My boss supported me in having time off for this therapy: off I'd go on a Wednesday afternoon, leaving work early, my staff no doubt wondering about my early darts. But they could never have known that what they saw, their manager, the confidence I wore like my suit, was nothing more than a crumbling facade. I had become so depressed, unable to cope with work or home life and the therapy was making me delve so deep into my memories and my childhood I was beginning to wonder if I would ever find my way out.

To put myself back together I needed to fall apart

Jane would occasionally visit, but I would wear her out with my woes, and cry for hours when she left. The same occurred with my RAF boyfriend – I became rude and needy to him, until he decided he didn't want to see me anymore. Can you blame him?

I had arranged a meeting with Jane, Julie and Debbie, but I got flu and was off work and couldn't make it. I had never had flu before and realised it wasn't just a bad cold. I felt so alone and realised that there was no-one around to look after me. Back at work I felt self conscious around my staff at work and started breaking down in front of them. I would cry all the time and contemplate suicide. I felt so empty. I felt so lost.

So what did I do? I found another man.

His name was James, and I met him in a nightclub when out on my own. He was a lorry driver and gym fitter. We were looking for places to live together within two months and he said he really liked me. He cheered me up.

Somehow, amid all of this distress, I was working on my new Spanish website, which I was preparing to advertise my own apartment, for when it was ready, and also other peoples' rental properties. I would charge a fee to the other owners to advertise their properties on my website and would offer flyer services too, so that they could have something professional to send out to their prospective holidaymakers.

I gave up my life to return home to Woodgrove, with promise of fulfilling my dreams. I left my job at the end of August and moved back home to Mum and Dad's *again* – hiring yet another van. I had the task of selling everything again too – sofas, washing machine etc.

If I kept moving it couldn't get me

I was still seeing James who lived in Macclesfield and I decided to go visit him. He didn't seem so keen and told me that he had a lodger. I said that they wouldn't mind me coming. He then told me it was a woman. After a half hour questioning, I found out that he was cheating on his girlfriend, with me. He also had a two-year old son, and lived with both of them. I was so angry; with him for lying and myself for trusting him. Unable to abide lies, I found it hard to get over this deceit. How dare he do that to me! OK, I kind of told a dirty lie to Craig for a week ... but never again.

I think with all of the change this is what finally broke me. I recall how I trawled the doctor's surgeries in my hometown by foot. I felt a strong urge to die and desperate to get help, and yet no-one would take me on as a patient and help me.

I walked from surgery to surgery and begged them, in tears to help me. Some receptionists told me straight away that their patient list was full, but others did let me see a doctor, which was only a temporary relief, since, after speaking with me for a couple of minutes, they all stated that they were full and unable to take on any more patients. This, I will never forget.

Doctors turned me away in my home town.

Doctors turned me away point blank.

Doctors wouldn't help me.

I am sure I am not the only one and will not be the last. What if I had died – killed myself? Did they care? I understand that there are discrepancies on when they can take people on, but with me in that state why didn't they refer me to hospital A&E or someone who could help? Anyone?

But they did nothing, they just told me "Sorry." I felt incredibly let down by the system, but it wasn't the only time I'd received no support from the system. I am not sure what I did next, as I was in a haze, but I do remember calling the *Samaritans* to ask them for help. The call didn't go well, as I couldn't seem to tell them just how suicidal I felt. It was hard to break down like that; to expose my weakness.

No matter how desperate we feel we hold some of it in

Thankfully, I came out of the darkness shortly after, for just long enough to find the strength to walk back into the surgery that I had left years before because of a disagreement with Dr Griffiths, the GP. But I finally found someone who would listen. And he'd known me since I was in my teens – my depressions, bad periods, everything.

Little did I know at the time that those GPs who had refused me should have given me reasons in writing.

Had I known that, I might have pursued it.

Rules like this change all the time; I did find official information pertaining to this but I urge anyone who might be in a similar situation to seek official guidance. I guess what I'm saying is- never suffer alone. There is always someone who can help you. *Always.* And don't be put off by what happened to me, the Samaritans might just be the lifeline you need when all else fails. But don't do what I did; **make sure they understand how bad you feel. And the NHS primary care trust must help you to find a doctor, so do contact them for assistance.**

My doctor suggested I contact the Woodgrove open door service for free counselling, and before I knew it I was seeing a male counsellor every Tuesday evening and all I had to do was put a donation in the box. I saw him for about a year, and there was never any pressure to stop. However, and in keeping with what I said about really saying how bad you feel, I think I had him fooled some of the time. I mean, we spoke of desperate times and he was very helpful, but I don't think I ever got across the severity of my problems, how I truly felt on the inside. At first I didn't want a male counsellor, but he suggested that, because most of my issues were related to men letting me down, using me etc, that he might be able to bring something to the table that a female counsellor might not – I could tap into his male mind. We worked out that the internal critic in my mind was 'male' maybe because of dad and boyfriends being critical of me throughout my life.

All the while, my brother, Ian, had definitely *gone off* the idea of moving to Spain since the two week trip he, Michelle, Elsa, myself and my ex boyfriend Louis, took the previous summer. He hadn't liked the concrete and the fact it was full of British people. So he was in the process of making an application to live in Australia and join David and Linda. Seemed I wasn't the only one trying to escape. And all three brothers had chosen a country on the other side of the world – you couldn't get much further than that. I tried not to see them too much towards their departure, so that it wouldn't hurt me as much when they left, but I would still baby-sit on occasion and see them regularly, hanging out at theirs, doing paintball or eating out. And I adored Elsa – she was four and we got on really well.

I celebrated my 30th birthday in Paris with Jane – a night at the Moulin Rouge and delicious lunches and following this had my last Christmas with Ian, Michelle and Elsa.

Being single again, and feeling abandoned by my brother, I put my energies into my new website, a business plan and network meetings and money started flowing out of my account, as I took on the web developer I met at the exhibition earlier in the year and started signing contracts and personal guarantees that made me feel uncomfortable.

On the outside I looked like I was regaining control; that strong confident business woman was back.

But on the inside I had already come undone. I just didn't realise it.

Chapter 30

Open your eyes...

I love buying flowers. I love buying presents. I love buying cards.

Occasionally I buy things for people adhoc, and others I make lists for. I love shopping; from browsing aimlessly, to buying new clothes or home wares, to buying new technologies in computers, and I especially like shopping for things for other people.

Mainly, I like physical shopping in shopping malls or Town's High streets, as I like to be able to see the items, touch them, try them. But you cannot get everything in the high street shops. Sometimes, the internet is the only place for inspiration or the right product at the right price. From my wanted list in Amazon, to using Google to find ideas for presents for people, I like to keep lists of present ideas for each person, so that I don't end up with last minute thoughtless presents that don't mean much. I like to think of things that the person will really appreciate, would perhaps never buy for themselves, but something they would love to receive, or perhaps staple goods for the odd staid person. But even if it is merely drink or chocolates, I try to get the best I can find – a fabulous brand they have never tried. A treat; the whole point of a present I believe. Something that will amuse the senses.

It is most fun buying presents when the cost is not an issue, but buying on a budget can be just as good, as I just have to think and search a little harder for an assortment of ideas within a price range. Saving money is a buzz and if I do, then I can buy another small present with the saving, so it all becomes a project almost.

Things to do, experiences to be had, things to wear, jewellery to dazzle, electrical goods, furniture, paintings and pictures, home stuff, music, film – it's all fun. And it's not about what I want, it's about thinking of what the other person would love. What would make their eyes light up when they open their gift? What would be memorable? What would be used and not just shoved in a cupboard?

And it doesn't stop there.

There are also presents bought from holiday destinations – silver spoons for Mums collection, cannons and beer mats from around the world for Dad, perhaps something for a friend. Postcards written and sent from holidays. Then there's something when someone doesn't feel well; flowers, chocolates, something to brighten their day. Moving in presents – flowers and home gifts. Presents for a baby – little tops or outfits, or tiny toys, getting bigger as they get older. There are thank you presents and good luck presents. Then there are the presents that don't have a reason, other than the obvious fact I must like the person and the gesture of giving it. Because I like you, because I love you, because you are my friend, I saw it and thought of you, or just because...

Cards too are also carefully chosen – the size, the pictures, the words, saying and showing just what I want them to. If I can't find what I want, then I get one made. Local shops will offer a selection of styles to choose from, and I can add an age, or a message of my choice. I don't use the internet for these, as I like to hand write my own words inside – along with my little drawn pictures of balloons, champagne glasses or Santa Claus and holly which I love to do. It comes back to my love of individuality as my tattoo depicts.

Receiving presents is also lots of fun. If they are on show before I am allowed to have them, I might touch them, pick them up, ask questions about them, want to know what they are. The excitement builds as I jump about the room or play guessing games, but if I were to know what they are before being given them, it would spoil the surprise, so I don't try too hard. Maybe I am eight again.

And I think of how I entertain my mum.

And the excitement of going on holiday; jumping round the room, singing, joking, only tainted by packing my suitcase, which, despite my using a detailed checklist to help me, still brings the onset of stress and depressive thoughts.

Packing is not my thing.

In November I started a new job in a publishing company, but I was so obsessed with my own company and my abilities, I couldn't concentrate on the job. So I joined a gym to help myself feel better. My diary became a sea of words, across, down, diagonal on the pages – a mess of hundreds of things to do, and stress took over again.

So I turned my business into a limited company and took advice from people I shouldn't have. The year became a haze; a blur of problems, trust issues and paranoia in my mind, as I worked harder and harder whilst being taken for a ride. By the end of the year, I was in debt, tied up in all sorts of guarantees, and found myself challenged with a situation that topped my stress levels. I'd got my company known, had clients, got featured in magazines easily, but I wasn't earning what I was spending, including what the website company was charging, £20K.

Bankruptcy doesn't just happen they say.

Maybe that's like mental illness.

Or losing weight, or being addicted to drugs or drink or...

I guess we all run away. Close our eyes. If we can't see it, it's not there.

Open your eyes, Amanda, I said.

Look at what's happening to you.

Chapter 31

In the sand

It was November 2005 and the Spanish holiday rentals website company I had put my heart, soul and money went into liquidation.

Actually, I had put it into liquidation since I had wrapped myself up so tight in debt and ridiculous contracts with my web developers, I was drowning. I had seen the warning signs but hadn't reacted quickly enough because I was so obsessed with the company, that advice I should've heeded, I didn't. My eyes were closed. It had meant everything to me. I had planned to make a million pounds and give lots of money away to my family and Orangutan charities.

Big, grandiose ideas is a symptom of my condition

It seems that once it started, it was like a snowball rolling, faster and faster until I didn't know how to stop it.

I had sold my flat in the UK, left a good job and put all my money into that business - twenty five thousand pounds. The money was what Aunt Agnes had left, which is why to lose it was even harder. Having made so many mistakes in the past, I was set on being a success and becoming a failure was not supposed to happen.

But it did.

I'd loved all the trips to Spain: photographing properties, compiling holidaymaker resort information; it made me feel important. I even had t-shirts printed with my business name and logo.

Hundreds of pounds expenditure turned into thousands and when my apartment in Spain came near to completion, just eighteen months after putting the deposit down, I didn't have enough money left to buy it and couldn't get a mortgage to cover it. As the costs of the website came to twenty thousand pounds alone, and I was relying on credit cards to pay for things, it became very clear indeed. I was spinning into the path of a hurricane. Luckily, I got my deposit back on the apartment, but that didn't help in the end.

I felt let down by everyone around me

With all of that going on, you start to wonder who to trust. But at the same it's easy to be seduced into thinking you have what you don't. And when I saw my face and name in some of the most prestigious Spanish magazines sold in the UK I truly believed I was becoming the success I wanted to be. Everyone says you make losses to start with. You need to speculate to accumulate... but everyone's not always right. Are they? Maybe I should've started listening to that inner voice.

But ... I was so encouraged by the exciting stuff; I was failing to take notice of the warning signs – however blatant they were. My instincts were screaming at me that something was wrong but my therapy taught me to look at the positive, not to dwell on the bad stuff. But that didn't mean close your eyes and pretend it wasn't happening.

I was even a runner up in two categories in the local Business Awards and my friends came to support me. I had customers and agents. I was so proud of myself.

And so was Dad.

That meant the most.

Amid all the turmoil I was also trying to find Mr Right, but I didn't realize that I wasn't quite Little Miss Right and was far from capable of having anything stable in my life – friends, boyfriends or even family relationships. The only thing that got my full attention was the business.

And Adrian was back on the scene, from time to time, amongst others, but it had always been erratic and I was always getting annoyed or obsessive with him, but the sex was still great. He was a nice guy, and I took advantage of it.

But somehow my depression closed in on me again and took me to the doctor's who prescribed me *Prozac* (*Fluoxetine*), which I only took for two weeks – I was too scared to continue once I felt *my brain changing*.

I had fun with Adrian but it all went wrong too fast and paranoia led to my texting… this shows you what we were like together:

14th August 2005 – Text from me to Adrian – *I get let down by everyone, and I don't want to be used*

Adrian's reply – *snap out of it and enjoy your life think about no one but yourself- if ur used, use back, u only get one life – do what u want wen u want and wiv who u want*

More Paranoid hate messages to Adrian followed and all I kept thinking was:

I am going to lose everything.

It was a time of change for us all; Ian and Michelle finally moved to Australia with Elsa although Ian was also diagnosed with nocturnal epilepsy caused by a rare side-effect to antibiotics and found to be deaf in one ear by now due to repetitive polyps that had to be cut out of his head. My friend Laura had moved to San Francisco, and Karen gave up on me as she said that I never made any effort to see her.

First Auntie Agnes left me. Then everyone was leaving me one by one.

How could they leave me like this? Abandoned. And why all at once?

All I had left to keep was Agnes's rings – I wore one on each hand and admired them constantly.

Text from another of my conquests: Big Dave, another that failed.

It went from: *I had a lovely evening again Amanda, you are a very special girl*

To...

Y don't u go boil ur fucking head, u ain't the full ticket, no wonder u can't keep a relationship wen u think everyone's lying to you

One day I stumbled upon a new temporary fix for my depression since I couldn't afford to or deal with running away – Internet dating. I got the email stating *'Need to find love? Thousands of men and women are looking for the right person – it could be you! Sign up today for two weeks free trial!'* I was about to close the message but decided to take a few minutes off work which was stressing me out that day, and have a look at this dating site, just out of interest. I was never going to find a man on the internet – *how ridiculous, how sad* – but I could look. I started looking at a few of the adverts and even did a search for my geographical area. There were loads of guys within a ten mile radius of my home – I could not believe it.

I got back to my work, but those words kept niggling in the back of my mind. 'Need to find love?'

Yes, I did need to find love. That would make everything else alright.

Open your eyes, Amanda...

I fantasised about a perfect caring and loving relationship, where I was deliriously happy, and it gave me the push to do something.

I typed the web address back in, registered as a new member, and got to work on writing a profile. The most important points, I accentuated, were my desire to find someone to look after me and that I would move to Spain if I didn't find 'the one' soon. The shenanigans of my dodgy property agent in Spain, I'd since found out about, had not put me off my long felt desire to live in their lovely country.

Two days later, I received an email to advise me that my profile was accepted and I was now live on the website.

Ok, so what next? I thought. *Shall I send a message to someone? No. Let them come to me – that's what I would do if I were out, so that is what I will do whilst I'm staying in.*

I had uploaded three complimentary photos and my profile was interesting enough, so I soon got floods of messages. Work can wait I thought, as I sifted through them.

I did not want a long distance relationship or someone with baggage – no children and exes on the scene and I made these points perfectly clear in my profile, but there were a lot of time wasters.

It suited me down to the ground – I could get lots of attention from men and didn't even have to leave the house until I had fixed dates with guys.

Some of the unwanted men just would not take no for an answer sometimes, much to my dismay… one had three children. Children – *no way*, I don't need to play happy families.

'Hi thanks for your mail, but as you will see on my profile, I am looking for someone who has not had children yet.'

'Amanda, I think you are making a mistake. Men with children are more responsible and caring than men without – think about it.'

'Since you clearly do not live with your children and are on a dating site looking for a new partner, I would say you are clearly NOT so responsible for them, or you might not have left them and your family home in the first place.'

I also got the 'copy and paste' deal, where the guys would send huge messages, outlining their autobiographies in short – clearly the same message would go to each and every female target.

There were also the very rude ones who clearly advertised the desire for just one thing out of a woman. They were all without photos, so who knows where that got them!

I found I was becoming a very busy girl. Messages would be coming in faster than I could reply and I eventually had to make a spreadsheet of prospective males that I liked, as I could not remember them all. This was so exciting – a spreadsheet of twenty six prospective males, whoopee! And I still hadn't been outside the house.

On dates, I found some were boring and I had to take charge of conversation, another didn't look a bit like his photo in a bad way…

Thanks for the meal. Maybe we could be friends? I texted after one unimpressive date.

No he replied *you are too good looking to b friends wiv.*

I persevered for six months, chasing dates, messages and phone calls like my life depended on it.

All I want is a nice man to take care of me

I would end up typing really badly as I was so drunk as my home drinking was getting out of hand…

Then I met Paul, and we went clubbing on our first night out – a very drunken affair, but he could dance, so I was impressed and started to see him regularly after that. I informed everyone I was in contact with on dating direct that I had found someone, and paused my paid membership. He loved walking along the seafront and we could top ten miles at times. He also cooked. But, there were problems from the start …

In the meantime I had Adrian texting too…

2nd July – *I want ur mouth*

Amid a flurry of internet dates and Adrian I'd still put every effort into trying to save my company but liquidation and filing for personal bankruptcy really were the only options.

For all those involved who had been a part of my downfall, including myself, I felt a belly of hate. I then found out that the web developers had transferred my website domain name to themselves months before. And since I didn't have ownership of the domain name anymore, and the website was the whole business, I didn't have a *proverbial* leg to stand on. And they had sat there as directors of my company by now, pretending to be applying to get me business funding through all the government and bank channels, charging me 20k for my website and letting me run out of funds and into debt. It was all a plan. Then came the biggest blow – they offered me one pound to buy me out. I couldn't. Yes it would buy me out of my personal guarantees with them, but I couldn't let them have my two years of work and everything I owned, for one measly pound so that they could go forth and make money out of it. But I still had those personal guarantees – twenty four thousand pounds of them to be paid to my two directors, just for giving up on the company. Why oh why did I sign that stupid thirty page agreement, in the beginning, when my solicitor had clearly warned me not to?

Sometimes you run out of places to go

By September 2005, when I realised that bankruptcy was my only fate, I still wanted to work in the same field and contacted every Spanish holiday agency on my database to find out if they had work for me in Spain or the UK, marketing Spanish holiday rentals.

Up in the loft, I took down my antique vases and put them into an auction. I delivered Yellow pages books to homes in my area. I borrowed money. That way I found the £2500 for the liquidation of the company and £500 to go bankrupt. I later thought how much more fun buying an Audi TT with my money would've been, or travelling with the £25k. Now I'd never own a house again – I was well off the property ladder and wouldn't even get a loan or a mobile phone contract for at least six years due to my now blackened credit rating. And my name would be listed in the local newspaper under the insolvency notifications. Humiliation.

I had a huge business support system to lean on – Citizen's Advice, debt recovery and debt management helplines, accountants and solicitors and business managers from my network meetings all helped me as much as they could. But they couldn't save me, because of the personal guarantees I'd signed and the loss of my domain name. And the web developer who was acting as my director, I later found out, was not only a disqualified director for ripping off the tax man, but he also was an ex-accountant, so he knew the ropes well and had covered everything in his plan to corner me and take everything from me. He began calling me, threatening me that I couldn't go bankrupt. I recorded one of the calls and he stopped his abuse advising me nastily that I couldn't use the recorded phone call as he hadn't been aware it was being recorded at the time. I was scared. Needless to say, waves of resentment surged through my belly daily, together with an incredible fear of my fate and self hate for letting myself down and being so stupid. But I had to do everything right, lawfully and right.

I had to write *hold off creditors* letter to the banks, and everyone I dealt with in the business. I was so ashamed, but I couldn't pay.

In hindsight, I should not have put 'all my eggs in one basket' – I should have been more careful.

At the time, it was crippling for me. I could not think straight, I was scared, I felt suicidal, and it certainly made my mental problems worse, but of course at the time I didn't have an up to date diagnosis. I felt worthless and a failure – particularly to Aunt Agnes for leaving me the money in her will. Now it was all gone, and I had nothing to show for it. No big holidays, just self depravation and hard work for two years, and a loss of friends. I'd become a hermit unless I was on a 'date'. I gazed up to the sky asking Agnes to forgive me and I prayed to God and Jesus for help.

And this time when it all went wrong; I couldn't fly away.

When I opened my eyes I finally saw it all.

Looking up at the judge, I fought back tears. "This is a sad day for you, Amanda," she said gently as she put the final authorisation on my bankruptcy application. She seemed genuinely sorry for me, as my case showed I had no way out, no choice, and that I was not entirely at fault. But I knew I should take responsibility for my actions – of course it was my fault, I couldn't blame it on others, but of course in the commotion of it all, I blamed everyone but myself.

And I was very sorry.

Chapter 32

I've got something to tell you...

He was painting the windows in my bedroom. My dad. There he was with the paintbrush in his hand, smiling, happy. Normal.

"I've got something to tell you," I said, sobbing.

He lifted his head.

"I'm bankrupt," I said. "End of the line," I said.

He glanced at me, face folded in disgust. Then he carried on painting.

"Yes," is all he said.

I would never trust anyone again

That's when I really started to write about my life. I found myself involved completely in the past. It was time to *really* find my way back to me. And I bought some domain names and used what I knew about the internet to start another website business, on my own. But always small steps, I had been burned already.

From now on things were going to be better.

They had to be.

I carried on dating various men. And I got a new temping job in property management five days a week. I was also still seeing my counsellor at this time.

What with my job, my dating, my website business and my new obsession with writing I really didn't have time to wallow in the misery of my bankruptcy for long. Although I couldn't run away at least I was distracted. I wrote twenty three thousand words, about my childhood, in three months and found myself quite motivated, until I came across something in my diary. Four A4 sheets of paper of typed writing. I had typed it at home and I froze, because there it was – Vinnie taking advantage of me when I was fifteen. The rape.

Dissociation is a strange experience and many people's brains do it as an automatic form of escape from trauma if an event is too much to bear, or people may experience it when indulging in drugs. I have experienced both forms but reading that rape scene, it really made me see there was something I had been hiding away in my *Pandora's Box* of my past.

And it wasn't the only thing.

But, true to the Amanda philosophy I decided all I really needed was my knight in shining armour; someone who would take me away from all that despair. Maybe that was easier than really facing up to all the things my writing was unearthing.

Chapter 33

Rescue yourself first

I met Chris through the internet dating site. There was just one thing in the way of him being my knight in shining armour – *his wife*.

It was the 19th July 2006 when I first saw Chris, in person. I was thirty-two. Our first date was interesting. He picked me up from home and I slowly opened the front door in anticipation. But I felt disappointed – he was not my type and far too old (I knew he wasn't forty-five as he'd said – he looked more like fifty) and his pale beige linen suit jacket was, as I told him later, 'not my cup of tea', even if it was 'Boss.' I immediately decided he wasn't for me and fancied closing the door quickly and bidding him goodnight. I didn't. I couldn't be that rude.

What did it for me was his passionate tongue action outside the restaurant as we sipped our after dessert coffee and smoked our first cigarette of the night. No sooner had we gone outside on the sea view terrace, he'd bent in and pulled me to him and his tongue was down my throat. I thought he might well reach my stomach with such a forceful tongue lapping round my mouth! After coming up for air, and resting my aching tongue for a minute, I told him "You are very vigorous." He was. The evening was full of laughter and chat, dining and drinking, and we had a fondle in the car when he dropped me home.

It wasn't just his luscious tongue that hooked me – his charm, intelligent conversation and excitable, loud, high pitched laugh that would turn any head, were just as much a pull. It's one of those laughs that could send me into hysteria myself, no matter what the pun or occasion – just one step down from Amadeus' laugh in that brilliant film. As the evening unfolded, his charm, wit and forward ways got the better of me. Dinner was had at a trendy, smart restaurant in Laytonhoe. A pre-dinner drink at their central bar established very quickly that we got on very well.

He was once dark haired, so I learnt, but I just couldn't imagine him any other way than with his short white and silver hair with dark low lights running through the textured longer section on top. It matched his ice blue enigmatic eyes beautifully. His mannerisms and body language exuded confidence. He wasn't quiet, but also not too loud. He was chatty, but a great listener too, and he had a fun sense of humour. He liked fine wines, beers from around the World and good food and wasn't short of a bob or two. What more could a girl, sorry (wishful thinking), woman, want? Well, nothing at the time, apart from the fact that I was bankrupt, suffered depression and acute loneliness, had a job in admin I hated and had been missing a partner for life for longer that I liked to admit.

It only took about three hours to find out he was separated, rather than divorced, about four hours to find out there were children involved (albeit step grand children, not his own, although he had been their Father figure) that he loved and were directly involved with his wife. It took four days to find out he was in fact fifty years old and not forty five, as advertised; altogether a huge big lie of a profile on the internet dating site. I was annoyed and made this known very quickly - too quickly in fact. I wasn't on that site to muck about and my profile said so, but when he asked if I would have met up or been interested in him if he had told the truth about these things, I had to say, 'No, I wouldn't; fifty is too old for me and I'm not interested in baggage'. His baggage was his wife he had not yet divorced from, her two daughters who he'd brought up from eleven and twelve, who were now adults, and one of the daughters' three children who he'd lived with and helped bring up as well.

He just smiled.

But, by this time, I had fallen in love.

This was very strange for me, as I never just 'fell in love' with anyone, and certainly wouldn't tell them for a long time if I did, but I told him so, kind of, on our second date I think it was, and little did I know he did not feel the same; not anywhere near the same.

'I think I could fall in love with you.' I'd whimpered in the car as he dropped me off. *What was I thinking?*

I didn't keep it up for long though. I began threatening and blackmailing him. Blackmail, manipulation and arguments – I am not proud of this accolade of bad feeling, but it is not all my fault.

I wish I knew then that it would take two years for the divorce to actually occur, as this caused lot of problems for me – and him.

Our evenings were filled with Chris and I smoking cigarettes, cooking and having fun in his flat or out at restaurants, intermingled with arguments, hate and great sex.

We'd dance round the lounge/kitchen area to Scissor Sister's *I don't feel like dancing* or Justin Timberlake's *Sexy back* and Nelly Furtado's *Promiscuous boy* and *Maneater*. Chris and I laughed so much. We even tried belly dancing to Shakira.

We both had our own lives – I had work mates by now, who I would have dinners with or go clubbing with. I also had Mum and Dad. I'd watch the odd film with Dad, like our favourites 'Pirates of the Caribbean' or 'Master and Commander' and have serious life chats with him too. I'd go for lunches with Mum and she'd leave me little notes all the time, telling me that she's washed my tops, or wishing me a nice day, or telling me that Orangutan are on the telly tonight, or leaving me magazines open on pages of fashion and beauty that I might like.

Chris had his mum to look after, as her health was faltering, but he still didn't let me meet her, or his friends, or any of his family. I felt left out. He had his best friends and his step grandchildren but I wasn't allowed to meet any of them. Partly due to all my threats and blackmailing and badmouthing of them all, but he also wanted to protect his wife from more hurt, which I can understand from her point of view. He had had an affair with another woman a few years back whilst with her, and she had stayed with him, just for him to leave her in the end anyway - so he said. His friends were their joint friends, and his wife saw his Mum quite a bit, and lived with her daughter and the children, so it was impossible for him but also impossible for me to deal with the secrecy. But he had abandoned them all, saying he didn't fancy his older wife anymore, so what did that say to me?

Chris had his own Cessna 172 and had been a private pilot for some time as well as a director of an established company. He hadn't told me for two weeks though to make sure that I liked him not just as a pilot or for the money he obviously had.

6th **August 2006** – *We went on our first day trip in Chris's plane to Le Touquet. Since his driving was terrible thus far, I was worried that he would crash the car and dreamt about it the night before, and he did crash the car, on the way to the airport – right in the back of* *someone at a roundabout. We had a nice day though.* I remember that Chris wanted to hold me and kiss in the street and I didn't like it, as I felt everyone was watching and talking about our age gap; something which happened a lot.

Chris often shouted at me, and became frustrated with my erratic moods and jealousy.

It was push and pull and we will 'see' each other from both sides. Chris was also showing signs of being down, and told me his wife was causing problems for him. He wanted to split up with me.

But I couldn't let him go.

I couldn't be abandoned again.

Could I even see what I was doing?

The build up to Christmas 2006 was horrendous.

"I am going to spend Christmas with the kids," said Chris.

"What?" I shouted.

"I am going down to spend Christmas with the kids."

"What, and your fucking wife?"

"No,"

"You fucking bastard, you don't want to spend it with me. You can get fucked!"

In no time though, he was hooked on me too – our chemistry grew through the arguments and great sex.

Texts are a mess. A bombardment of anger. And emails are a mess, and full of abuse. Although it isn't always rosy when we see each other either, we are as close as two people can get; our cuddles so tight I feel like climbing inside of his body, kisses so tender, and smiles so wide. We click. We work. We are in love. We laugh, cry, bathe and do almost everything together.

The love, hate relationship continued…

Chris and I had known each other only a few months when he came up with the idea. Although a tumultuous relationship had formed between us, we were bonded from deep inside. We knew what the other was thinking before they said it, we thought of each other at the same moment, about to call each other when one pipped the other to the post.

He announced, that day, that we should cut our fingers and mix our blood together as a bond to each other. He was serious and looked at me to conform. I wasn't sure I wanted to mix my blood with him. What if he had a disease that I didn't want in my blood system?

"Well?" he said "I thought you'd jump at it. Don't you want to?"

"Yes, um, what if you or I have a disease? You wouldn't want to catch it would you?"

"I don't care, I want you, and I want to mix our blood, so we're bonded forever."

I made my decision quickly, as I didn't want to disappoint him or make him think I wasn't committed to him, as I was, just as much as he.

"OK," I said.

"Good, OK. I'll go and get a knife."

"You'll have to burn it first, to avoid any infections."

"Yeah, yeah."

I waited, lying on the bed, thinking how nice it was that he was so into me he'd thought of this intimate ritual. He came back in the bedroom shortly after, brandishing a small knife from the kitchen set and a big smile. Lying back down next to me, he giggled. He held out his right hand and made a small half centimetre cut into the underside of his index finger. He asked me to hold out my right hand. I did. As he made a small cut in exactly the same place on my finger, it occurred to me just how strange this act of his was, since he is squeamish and when I have talked about my days of cutting myself as relief when I was younger, and others doing it as a self harm thing, he stated that he could not understand it at all, and was amazed that anyone would cut themselves intentionally. Whenever we saw a film (we watched lots of horror films) he would reel and could barely watch a knife piercing skin. Anyway, here we were, doing it most definitely with intention.

It didn't hurt.

Self inflicted small injuries don't. I should know.

The hurt comes more from an accident – a lack of control.

I looked at the bright red blood seeping out of my cut, and thought how healthy my blood looked. He asked me to squeeze the finger, so that more blood would come out, as he was doing. OK let's do it he was saying. I hesitated before I offered up my finger to him.

He joined mine with his, and took great joy in really getting our blood and cuts mixed up as he rubbed them well and truly together.

We were committed.

The rest didn't matter.

Chapter 34

'I desperately wanted to be with you – we are soul mates and you're my best friend.'

I got offered a job as reception manager in a local hotel, but didn't take it.

I didn't think I would get on with them and have the authority for the Management role, even though I could have – I lacked self esteem.

I was offered a number of good jobs around this time including as an Overseas Administrator abroad with a large travel company and even jobs as air stewardess for different airlines. I had to jump through a lot of proverbial hoops to get those jobs when I think back. I had to do lots of tests and role plays but in the end I turned down every one. Perhaps a self esteem issue egged me on, just to see if I could get the jobs, but the pay and actual idea of doing the job was not what I wanted and I lived miles from the major airports. I just wanted to feel capable, I guess. The statistics of initial applicants to successful applicants is very small, so I proved one thing again – I could get a job.

I was thinking about becoming a Property Manager while I had my job as a Property Management Administrator and that company paid for me to do my Property Management qualification (ARLA) which I did eventually pass.

But going to work after bankruptcy was hard; hard enough just to keep going.

I would wake up abruptly with the alarm, at 7.30 am and quickly press the snooze button. 'Just another nine minutes,' I would sigh to myself, burrowing under my duvet in search of just a little more peace. I would do this up to three times, until I made myself late.

I'd take far too long to think about the day, think about what I had to do, how boring it would be. I'd peel back the curtain slowly beside my bed and peek through the gap out the window at the weather (even though it didn't really matter what the weather was like) and then panic might hit me when I realised that I had to wash my hair and dry it or my lift was on its way. I have never been a morning person.

A cup of tea was the most important part of the morning, and a wash if I didn't have time to shower – I couldn't really leave the house without those two tasks being achieved. Mornings were a rush of stress and it was all down to me. If I got out of bed earlier, if I did my lunch the evening before, it would be better, but I was always that eternal self punisher!

If driving myself to work, I would fly up the road, to find my car wherever I managed to park it the night before. *Fucking selfish people* I would murmur towards the neighbours' houses if they parked their cars nearer to my house than me. I'd jump in the car and speed off.

Throughout the journey, everyone would get in my way for some reason. "Get the fuck out of my way!" "What the fuck are you doing – go!!!" "Oh shit, you stupid wanker!" I might even punch my steering wheel. Getting up earlier would stop those people being in my way – or the urgency anyway, but I just could not see it or could do nothing about it. The tips I'd learnt about using my senses on my stress management course went out of the window.

I could never get parked when I got there; I would drive round and round looking for a free space, but I hardly ever had time for the walk in the latter months, so I ended up in the pay and display car park near the office most days. That made me sick – to pay out of my low wages for the pleasure of going to work! But I did it anyway and still I wouldn't get out of bed earlier. It was everyone else's fault.

After running up the road into work, the lift and people were the next obstacle to making me late. Once upstairs, I would shimmy into the large open plan office, smiling and chatting, in the hope that my late entrance would go un-noticed. So that I would be seen by the powers above me as being delayed due to someone else, I might get a sandwich from the sandwich lady on the way in, as cover. I might offer everyone tea on arrival, to get on the right side. Or I might not feel like any games, and just sit down ignorantly, and get straight on with my work, hoping desperately that no-one would comment to me. I got away with it most days. If they did comment, it would annoy me profusely and I would sit there seething for half hour.

Occasionally the routine changed. If I was sleeping at Chris's, I would wake up, not alone, but to him making me tea, breakfast and a packed lunch. All smiles, he was. Sometimes I would smile, and other times, I would be miserable. The whole getting up late, panicking, and chucking on any clothes I could get my hands on would not change, although I always looked nice and didn't go out without eye shadow and lipstick, which I would do in the car.

He would drive me into work sometimes, and drop me right outside. Chris was never late for anything, but I would make us late and still be in a rush for the lift. "Yeah, bye, have a nice day." I might scowl at him. I almost hated his cheeriness and wanted to crush it. Then all day, I would at least look forward to him coming to meet me at 5.30pm. It would also pleasure me when I opened my little lunch he had prepared, to find tomatoes, fruit, crisps, gorgeous healthy sandwiches and little treats, like squares of dark chocolate.

If I got a lift from my colleague and friend Sherri, instead of driving myself, the half hour journey would be much better. We'd chat all the way there and never arrived late! That was if I was at the meeting point on time for my lift of course, which was not every time. We would have a parking space in the private office car park. Clara, who we would pick up on the way, would always organise a nice parking space as part of her job was managing the spaces and who they were allocated to – if any of the managers were off for the day, we could take their space.

We would walk down the stairs from the car park, and make tea on the way in, whilst chatting to whoever happened to be in the kitchen. "She is such a bitch, she grassed me up", "Another day, another dollar" or "You never guess what happened?" might be a few starters…

This was the first job I got during my bankruptcy period. I was there for one and half years it turned out in the end. I'd temped for six months, and then was taken on part time four days a week at my request on a permanent basis because they liked me. I stayed until I was made redundant. The job was far below my capabilities, but I didn't want anything that taxed my brain. I was getting over my bankruptcy and I trusted no-one. But that job, I at least had under control. It took only about four hours a day and I only worked a four day week, to do all the tasks in my job description, yet I had give up eight and a half hours of my time, plus travel and getting ready time, to do it – to earn my wage. To get some money in my bank, to survive, to pay my brother back what I'd borrowed for my liquidation; to buy shit and pay bills. I had to budget big time and I was under scrutiny by the insolvency service as were all bankrupts.

I had a good social life then too: more clubbing, drinking and messing about with people of all ages.

I had a grievance going on at work about part time workers getting public holiday allowances. I got HR involved too. I always found it hard to let grievances or complaints go. So, it wasn't just Chris who got the wrath of my tongue; my work and parents did too. I could be quite rude to my mum and dad sometimes, failing to listen to them or being curt when they wanted to chat. Not nice, and I am not proud of those times, but I was very angry with the world and resentment is a curse. I found it hard to deal with Chris having money when I didn't and maybe I was fuelled by jealousy too. I didn't want to rely on him and have him pay for everything, but I had no choice, which dented my pride.

So I needed to seek comfort. It was times like those I turned to memories of Agnes and sometimes I would visit her.

When I walked in through the main gates I felt at peace. As if my worries melted to memory; that time when the world was good, when I was a child. But then I'd reach the grave stone and start talking about *them*. My problems, as an adult, no longer the child now and Agnes was gone now. How long until I would visit and my mum and dad would be gone too. Who first, how would I cope? It didn't bear thinking about.

I always parked in the same place.

I always took flowers.

I always looked at the other graves; young, old and very recently deceased. I felt for every single one of them and for those they have left behind, especially the tiny babies and children's graves. It reminded me how unfair and how unpredictable life can be and how it can be taken from us in a moment.

A row of trees lined the perimeter and healthy grass grew where no graves have been dug. It was fresh up there and I found myself breathing deeply, my body relaxing as I walked.

I'd go to my Nanna's grave first. I usually talked, but didn't have too much to say; an update on Dad or some such thing or maybe just reiterate that I regretted that I was only thirteen when she died, and I wished I had been older so that I could have known her and remembered her better. I have many questions I would ask; questions that grew with each year that passed. I read the words on her head stone every time, taking in the loss. I'd fill a watering can with water from the tap just opposite, and fill my Nanna's flower pot with water, popping the flowers in one by one to form a small arrangement. Usually I took a photo.

I'd stand up from crouching, say my farewell and head right along the path, then left at the end. Auntie Agnes's grave was at the bottom. I walked slowly, never rushed.

Hello Auntie Ag I'd say. If no-one was around then I'd talk at a normal volume. If there were people nearby, then I'd speak in whispers or in my head.

I read the words on her grave stone. She was with her husband down there. I often pondered over burial and cremation. If I had a proper headstone who would visit me?

I'd talk to Auntie Agnes. I'd tell her what was going on. The girl she knew was not so happy anymore, but was trying to sort herself out. She still regretted losing all of Agnes' money.

I told her I missed her meals and her company – our chats about her life. She had been such a strong, independent woman, I wanted to learn how to be like she had been, instead of being how I was.

Sometimes I'd laugh, many times I'd cry, always I remembered.

When I left, pulling the edges of my coat tighter, I'd step back into my life... and the peace would dissolve.

Chapter 35

Going Wild

New Year resolutions for 2007

- Go to Borneo
- Gym, walk, yoga, swim
- Stop smoking
- Cut drinking
- Time 4 me!
- Keep in touch with old friends
- College courses
- Visit Laura in San Francisco
- Read books
- Stop being bored!
- Watch TV/films
- Hypnotherapy
- Australia – visit my brothers
- Tidy/throw out – do more boot sales
- Marketing website
- New job
- Restart pension
- Save money
- In 2 years – own business up and running
- Grow herbs
- Write my book and get it published

To add to everything Chris had also moved back into the family home in January. The rest of the family (his wife, the daughter who lived with her and the daughter's three children) had all moved to America and although I was relieved that Chris couldn't keep going up there to see them as he had most weeks, it meant he would want to take holidays to America see them. And it also meant he had moved an hour and half away from me, so I felt abandoned again. I visited regularly but he had left it just as *they* did – all the beds were made, messages left on the kitchen wipe board, photos up on the walls. It was disturbing, yet

I had to see Chris. I was also finally allowed to meet his mum after a six month wait, since the family weren't around now, and she *was lovely, but her health was still deteriorating.*

It was at this point the redundancy came to fruition.

Chris took me to Monkey World in Dorset, in February. I still had my old film Canon SLR and took so many photos. But what I really wanted was to see animals in the wild... and that's when Chris said he was going to Zambia later that month to renew one of his pilot's licenses. He asked me if I wanted to go with him.

Like I was going to say no?

Chris and I had a wonderful experience in Zambia. In some ways, I was nervous – of the people, eating the food. I had my own ideas before I went there. Part of the trip took us to the Victoria Falls and we stayed just by the river Zambezi, which was in the rainy season at the time. We booked a one day canoeing trip so that we could experience the Zambezi as close as possible. Our guide was a friendly man, as were most Zambians that we had contact with. We set off, with him in front leading the way. Only one other couple came, so it was great not having to wait for others. Shortly into the trip, I stopped paddling and took photos instead. Chris moaned as he had to do all the work, but I was so in awe of the surroundings, photos had to be done. The mucky looking river was so flooded you could only see the tops of plants and trees in the river or close to the edge of the riverbank. Small rapids formed as we went along, and this proved tricky in places, as we had to concentrate and paddle hard to get through them. It became apparent that this was not the normal canoeing trip this guy was used to taking tourists on, but he was experienced himself so he guided us well.

The other couple were not so up for it as us. The guy was OK, but his girlfriend was panicking a bit, so I only hoped that the trip wouldn't be stopped because she wanted to go back or something. The riverbank to the left was Zambian, and to the right was Zimbabwean, so this gave me a rush, canoeing through the middle of two African countries. Spotting a wild male elephant with huge tusks was a highlight. We stopped on a Zimbabwean island for a packed lunch and beer and set off again, and that is when the real excitement started. We were just floating along, enjoying the sounds of the birds and small mammals, watching the hippo's heads that were clearly visible on the other bank. The guide was just telling us that it was the season for births and there are lots of young hippos in the water, when he started yelling "paddle, paddle, fast, paddle!"

As I turned round to follow his line of vision, all I could see behind us was a large hippo head in the water hot on our tails and catching up fast! I dropped everything and started paddling furiously. "Chris, paddle, paddle!" He was paddling but not with any urgency. He is a calm man, and I realised that even this would not worry him. "Chris!" I shouted. "There's a hippo chasing us!" He didn't even look round. The other couple were slightly behind us so were even closer to the hippos fast approaching head. I looked straight forward and paddled furiously, water splashing everywhere, for what seemed like ages, until the guide told us we could stop. What a relief, the hippo had given up chase. The woman in the other boat threw a bit of a 'wobbly' but I was too full of the after effect buzz of adrenalin I couldn't care less – we'd done it.

But to this day, I wish Chris had looked round so he could've seen that hippo up close, seen the beauty of it as I had.

We only sunbathed for two hours the whole time we were in Zambia, and when we did we were surrounded by Zebra since the hotel was in the middle of a national park and the animals were protected and allowed to roam freely. It was without doubt the wild animals on that trip that made it feel like a home coming for me. We saw the last two white rhino in Zambia on a truck safari day in the Mosi O Tunya National Park. The last two. Just the thought of that fills me with tears. By the following June, the female was shot dead by poachers for her horn and the male shot and injured, even though the park was supposedly protected by male security guards twenty-four hours a day. In some ways, when I think of the beauty of those animals it becomes tainted by what I now know.

I guess what this trip really did for me was make me appreciate seeing real wildlife, where they should be – in the wild. Nearly being attacked by that hippo showed me the true meaning of what it is to be 'wild'. It isn't all about fun interacting with wildlife, they deserve respect. To see them all without bars and able to run free was so special, and when we came across each animal it was because that creature had crossed our path, not because we had paid to visit a zoo or sanctuary. Zoos would never be the same again. I had to question the ethics of putting animals in cages, and since we'd never put a human in a cage, except as a punishment why should it be OK for animals? They are living, breathing, thinking, emotional, caring, and have their own families, social systems and food chains.

No matter how depressed I get, seeing animals has always brought me back to life again. At home we visited sanctuaries or zoos, but to see them in the wild was best of all. Maybe what I saw in those animals in Zambia was a part of myself.

I want to be safe. I want to be confined by four walls and yet...

I want to be free like a bird...

It was in the March of 2007 after our return from Zambia, that I started working for a charity – strangely enough, one I didn't really agree with.

I was a temporary secretary for three months. When my car got broken into, outside the office, no-one there seemed to care. I got angry and left. Then I worked for a property management company and it was absolutely awful. I got picked on and I got depressed. I have never hated a job so much. So I decided to concentrate on working from home on my websites, as I felt too insecure and hopeless to even think about working for someone else.

Chris and I had been together for over two years when I finally went to see Dr Jones, the psychiatrist. It seemed that, no matter the problems, we simply could not be apart. We were tied together by some invisible cord which encapsulated some form of need and dependence, but also an overwhelming love and admiration – we were soul mates. We did nearly everything together, like go to Borneo to see the Orangutan. Finally. My dream.

We shared the intimacies of our bodies in the ways the primates I love so much, do. I've seen gorillas and chimpanzees sharing grooming sessions and Chris and I were a little like that. We spent a lot of our time indoors naked (in fact once on a naturalist beach in Spain, with men taking great interest as Chris photographed me but that was another story) When watching TV, we were flesh to flesh and I could almost climb inside his body to get closer. We found ourselves stroking and smelling each other like animals, since we found each other's natural aromas so comforting, so attractive. We loved the smell of each other. We love to smack each other's bums and kiss each other all over. The sex used to be great, but since the 'secret family' thing (he still wouldn't let me meet his family and he wouldn't push his wife to divorce him more quickly) went on and on, I withdrew sex to almost nothing – just an occasional treat. We both missed out that way.

But what we had, good and bad, was something I had never had before. He made me feel as though I was with the person I was supposed to be with. It felt right even when it felt wrong.

Like we gave each other what we needed.

But no one can have everything.

Chapter 36

Shit happens to everyone

I loved Chris but I was discontented with a lot of the things he did and my life. I was unhappy with the way I had such intense moods, basically I was unhappy inside.

And the way I was to Chris didn't help either. I wanted to make myself feel better, to understand the real me, even find who the real me was. And Chris egged me on as he always said that there was something very wrong with me. Of course he denied that *our* issues had anything to do with him, so all the pressure was on me to be the one to change.

But I wanted to change.

I wanted to feel better.

I wanted to continue with therapy to help myself.

No matter what bad things Chris was saying about me, I would let the professionals decide. I had finished with the 'open door counselling' after one year, partly because Chris was telling me that it obviously wasn't working, and started weekly hypnotherapy and Cognitive Behavioural Therapy (CBT) with Roger. He only accepted what I could afford to pay him so for me that already showed development. "Enough so it hurts a little bit, but not too much" is what he suggested, for my own good. And he offered free support by email. I was alone with my therapies though, as Chris didn't understand much of what it was all about, just so long as I was going and admitting that I had a problem, he was OK.

I loved the hypnotherapy. I would sit in a comfy leather armchair with soft cushions, and close my eyes while he talked softly, calming music in the background, creating a scene with words. Often it would start with imagining me going down some steps into a beautiful garden, very slowly and down to a waters edge. Then from there, he would talk me into various scenes to identify and visualise helpful occurrences. It was relaxing and the visions that we managed to identify when I was 'under' were very helpful to solving some issues. Hypnotherapy was utilised to explore memories and make changes to thinking. I had hypnotherapy for giving up smoking, where I watched myself in the dream he put me in, as a non-smoker and loving it, and making a new start in being happy and respecting my own self worth. We also utilised hypnotherapy for saying goodbye to Agnes, I met up with Agnes in my dreamlike state and hugged her goodbye and watched her go. It is an important lesson that one must grieve a death, or it will continue to haunt them, as it did me, always holding on, wishing the person to come back or was still there, which is not healthy.

Although the hypnotherapy was confined to our appointments, the CBT involved lots of homework – one piece of which was to work out in my own mind the steps of getting a relationship.

Well I knew about getting a relationship; but a healthy one, maybe that was something else entirely. Funny enough, I wrote down all the right things. I knew in my heart how to do it, as I did many things. I wasn't an idiot when it came to understanding people and relationships, but I did not practise what I preached – emotions always took over.

Other times we concentrated on CBT processes, which look at how our thoughts affect our behaviour. If we can change negative thoughts that cause negative behaviour, to more positive thoughts, then this should help us to behave more positively.

Sounded like a good philosophy to me; for all of us.

As a general idea, I could say I have no money (negative thought), but then I could say that I have no debts (positive thought).

I used a lot of the ideas and techniques the therapist showed me. So below I have included some of the forms he asked me to complete that show you how to look at situations as they arise, and more importantly to look at reactions to these situations. As they say *shit happens to everyone*, but it is how we deal with problems that are different. The same event can manifest in anger, upset or simple indifference. It's about perception. And I recommend you to look at your own life in this way too. It really does help you see yourself, even if what you see, you don't like that much. Here are some examples from August 2007 that showed how I took simple incidents and looked at my own reactions to them.

Activating event – Chris calling when he was on holiday with the children

Consequences – I got annoyed

Your actions – had a conversation with him, but still got annoyed

Beliefs – Why didn't he come home early from his holiday – I'm less important

Thinking error – he stayed out there because he had it booked & didn't want to let the kids down, not because I was less important.

Another one:

Activating event – 2 women rudely bumped into me in the high street

Consequences – I was angry/surprised

Your actions – I just looked & moved out of the way instead of saying something to them

Beliefs – They were both rude & unfriendly

Thinking error – They may well not have really noticed. I could have moaned about them and had an argument but I didn't, so no problem

I was invited to the wedding reception of Chris's employee, Alan. I nearly wasn't invited as it happens because Alan knew what I was like with Chris, our explosive relationship. He had borne witness to the numerous telephone calls I made to Chris at work, being horrible and shouting and slamming the phone down, but Chris assured him I would behave in public and in person, which was very true. It was shameful and I was usually left out of things Chris did with anyone else, friends or family, but never a wedding or party, where he wanted a partner to go with. I was useful for those.

16th August 2007

Activating event – I got tired of shopping for clothes and shoes for the wedding

Consequences – I was fed up & tired

Your actions – grumpy & pessimistic

Beliefs – I can't do my websites as I am doing everything for Chris and the wedding

Thinking error – It's not all for Chris, I am getting hundreds of pounds worth of dress, bag and shoes. I cheered up & so had a better shop!

From: Amanda Green

Sent: 07 August 2007 06:58

To: Roger (hypnotherapy)

Subject: punishment

Hi Roger,

Well, I got back on Saturday to find a huge bouquet of flowers, that Chris sent me while he's still on holiday with his wife's family and I was already set to send Chris a nice text. I did, but he didn't get it. After a couple of days of texting, both getting confused and upset, he finally was able to call last night and everything is fine. He has now run out of credit, so thankfully cannot keep texting me. I feel relaxed now and he is set to enjoy the rest of his time there. He is set to call me this evening and there will be no upset or punishment. We are going away this weekend when he gets back on Friday, and there will be no upset or punishment then, or any more!

It didn't go quite as well as I had hoped, but all fine now.

Will update you on Thursday!

Thanks,

Amanda

***

A good start!

Roger

I had been very excited about going to the wedding by now. It was July, sunny and it was held in a fabulous location.

I had spent hours getting ready all in all, what with manicures, make-up, shopping for the perfect dress and now I just wished I'd never been invited. And I blamed Chris.

I had just woken up the day after, with Chris beaming at me, and just by habit, I felt for the gold and diamond ring on my finger. It wasn't there. I checked the other hand – just my other ring.

"Oh no!"

"What is it?"

I couldn't speak – not straight away. I was too busy going over the events of the night before, desperately looking for a clue.

Finally, Chris lost patience. "Amanda, what is it, why don't you speak to me?"

"I've... I've lost my Auntie Agnes's ring - last night sometime." I remained cool, but was ready to explode, hate bubbling away in my brain. This was all Chris's fault. It had to be.

I remembered coming out of the toilet.

"Chris, they have Molten Brown hand cream," I'd smiled, rubbing my hands together. Like velvet they were.

Shit!

It must have slipped off without my knowledge, due to the hand moisturiser I'd plastered on my hands. I'd been pretty drunk too, since it was a social event and nerves and excitement always send me to over drinking. Both of Agnes's rings were too big for my fingers, but the lost one was the loosest. I should've had it made smaller.

Shit!

"Chris, we must go up there and find it!"

Chris was not going to argue. He knew how much that ring meant – how much the previous owner of it meant, to me. It wasn't the diamonds I was worried about losing – it was the sentimental value that they were my Auntie Agnes's diamonds. It was one of the few things I had left of hers and I admired it every day, playing with it and watching it sparkle in the light, just as Agnes's eyes used to sparkle...

From: Amanda Green

Sent: 20 August 2007 13:06

To: Roger

Subject: The Wedding

Hi Roger,

After all the worrying, the wedding was brilliant. I was really nervous going there, but Chris' mate from work and everyone were really nice and we had a great laugh. Chris as he promised me, stayed with me the whole time. We dance loads and chatted to plenty of people and it was lots of fun. On the flip side, I woke to find one of Auntie Agnes's two rings missing from my finger. I cherish them both, and was sad on Sunday at the loss. It's not the monetary value, but that it belonged to Agnes. But again, Chris looked after me and cheered me up and we had a nice day. So, all is good for now, and we are booking a mini holiday this evening, so I look forward to that.

Amanda.

Hi Amanda,

Glad you had a nice time. Make it one of many, it's worth it. Well done to you both!

Roger

Yes, from now on I vowed to make all our memories good ones. But like I said, shit happens. And not when you're expecting it either.

"My mum's died."

That's what Chris said.

He was standing there trying to catch onto his breaths.

The poor sod was usually crying over me, but this was a real tragedy.

What can you do to make these things better? I gave him a hug.

In the sadness we found solace in one another, albeit briefly. I re-evaluated my own problems, as I did when Agnes died but sometimes the patterns we carve out for ourselves are too strong and still we repeat them. Maybe for a while life stood still but even before the funeral it was back to being us; the way we always were.

And it wasn't the end of the surprises.

I'd found out that Chris's wife was actually his first cousin and that his other cousin, who had visited his mum, and who he'd never introduced me to (even though I was in the next room) was his wife's sister. So that made Chris's mum his wife's aunt – still with me? If you're confused, so was I. It had made me sick at the time I worked it all out, as Chris hadn't bothered to tell me, but when his mum died there was a real reason to fear these facts, I knew that I would not be able to support Chris at the funeral. I wouldn't even be allowed to go. The only humour in all of it was that his mum, in her delusion before she died, had told his family that I was pregnant with Chris' baby. Wishful thinking perhaps? I got the feeling she liked me. And I had liked her. And I could imagine the commotion this might have caused Chris' selfish wife, who couldn't seem to let go of him.

From: Amanda Green

Sent: 12 September 2007 18:28

To: Roger

Subject: funeral

Dear Roger,

The funeral is tomorrow and I will not be attending. Things have not been rosy and Chris did not want me to go as it would be uncomfortable with his wife and family being there as she's come over from America Unfortunately, I have found that very hard to deal with and have not been the supportive person that I wish I could say I have been - lots of upset. He did, out of desperation, yesterday, say that I could go to it so that I didn't feel out of it, but that at the end of the day, it would make him and his family/previous family feel uncomfortable, so I of course declined - the last thing I want is to cause upset just by being there and be unwelcome. He also said that if the situation were different, then he would certainly want me there. So, there you go. I wonder if this issue of keeping me out of the picture will continue in the future. He said that it won't, but I have doubts. He has advised me to think long and hard as to whether I can handle the ex-family issue amongst others and whether I really want to have a future with him. So that is what I shall do. His brother and family from America are staying at his, so I shall meet them tomorrow night, at least.

All for now, see you soon,

Amanda.

From: Amanda Green

Sent: 17 September 2007 20:39

To: Chris

Subject: a mess

Hi Chris,

I am very sorry that we have gotten into such a mess, when we were getting on so much better two weeks ago.

I had forgiven all the past issues with your family and friends, and we had both decided to move on. I understand that you have said recently that you will make a different type of effort, but the damage has been done. I understand why I didn't go to the funeral, but after discussing your wife coming to your house when I asked you not to, and you saying that everyone comes back after a funeral etc. (and please don't deny our conversations about this again) you seemed sure that you would not be stopping her from doing so. After bringing this up two times, and sending you a text to advise that I could not step foot in your house (which I had been bringing my stuff round to for the first time in any of your houses) if she came. You now refuse point blank that the conversations were had and that you didn't realise how strongly I felt. I couldn't have made it clearer Chris. I would urge that you also think about what I have put up with being the other half of a divorcing man with kids involved and that you have not made me feel secure at all.

Think about how you would feel being on the other side of your life, in my shoes – me with the ex-husband I protect and children I adore and a family I keep a secret - I am sure you would not be able to stand it. Please stop being so stubborn.

I don't want to be an outsider to your whole private life anymore and it's up to you to decide whether that would be the case. You are not an outsider of mine.

In January I will be making a decision about moving. If we stay together, and you are still not in any frame of mind to live with me then this is potentially going to split us up. I will be going to Devon/Cornwall or rural Spain (basically somewhere a lot cheaper than here).

Chris, I have these plans and they make me comfortable, but the biggest thing I could want in all the world, is to be with you forever, until one of us dies, and look after each other and be happy, like you say you do. No matter what has happened in the past and how I have been. I love you.

Amanda xxxxxxx

From: Chris

Sent: 06 December 2007 20:46

To: Amanda Green

Subject: (blank)

Dear Amanda,

Im very sorry that we have arrived at the end at last, after all our hopes for a future together, after all the lovely times we have had, after all the terrible times we have ignored because we both hoped that we might find happiness together. I have tried very hard with you, whatever you might think, you know that you are not the easiest person to get along with and I have always accepted that and tried my best to make you happy. I know that I haven't succeeded in that but please don't think badly of me. If you think that I haven't tried your wrong, Im only a human being, not a perfect person I know but for all that and despite all that has happened and all the bad and horrible things, I do love and care for you very much. I expect you will have a view about that but this e mail doesn't need a reply. I just want you to know that I will miss you very very much, that I love you, and that I wish you the very very best for the future and hope that you will find happiness soon. I don't know what Im going to do without you, I feel very down, very very low, the thought of carrying on here without you is not a very happy one, maybe I should just sell up and fuck off somewhere, anyway its not your problem. I know that you will be tormenting me in the weeks to come, it's just how you are, you can't help it I know, but whatever I say when you do please remember this mail as this is what I really think about you, and that will never change. The happiest times of my life have been with you, believe that because it's true, incredible isn't it, so much joy and so much sorrow, how cruel and unfair that we have these problems between us , life is such a cunt, fuck knows what it holds in store, hopefully not what you predict for me anyway, again, all my love to you forever and ever XXXXXXX

After these letters we actually decided we would seek relationship guidance which Roger was willing to help with. I guess neither of us really wanted to let go. But on we went, up and down, round and round.

From: Roger

Sent: 20 December 2007 11:34

To: Amanda Green

Subject: Counselling

Hi Amanda,

Sorry to hear that that things are still not going so well. I am surprised that Chris is not willing to take any of the responsibility. He clearly wasn't listening to what was being said in our session.

I think that I made it quite clear that your emotional difficulties are made worse by his actions and responses. But it is not up to me to make judgement upon choices that he has made, such as staying in his mother's house, it is up to him to make the choices that are the best for both of you because he loves you and wants the relationship to work, and that includes taking your feelings into consideration no matter how unreasonable your requests might seem to him. This is where talking and compromise come in, just dismissing you as completely irrational helps no-one. Also the idea that your emotional difficulties make everything your fault is a total misreading of the situation.

If you truly want the relationship to work you must realise that you do have to leave the past behind, it's done. If you both can concentrate on what happens from this point, discussing problems early, creating a plan and sticking with it as closely as possible, but without rigidity, you may be able to build trust. But if you concentrate on the past you will not be able to build that trust because the past will always be in the background getting in the way. Improving a relationship is about where you go from here, rather than where you've been.

Counselling is about partners making the right choices and that is not always staying together. Consider what is truly best for you.

Let me know what you think.

Kind Regards

Roger

My emailed reply to Roger:

Hi Roger,

Thank you for your reply. I think you are right about the past, so long as the future changes.

Funnily enough, Chris turned up with balloons, flowers and wine earlier, to cheer me back up and to say that, no matter what I do or say, he will not get annoyed and will remain calm so we can deal with things, so long as I make some effort too.

So, I shall give it a go.

Thanks, Amanda.

Roger said that we were like something out of a soap opera

My attempt to split up with Chris failed, as usual, and we were spending Christmas together, this time at my mum and dad's for Christmas day, which made it a little jollier than usual. It was lovely having him there sharing it with us and Mum and Dad seemed pleased. On Boxing Day we went to the Dominican Republic for an all inclusive two weeks of relaxing, quad biking, sailing, eating, drinking, playing games, getting hair braids and sex. All interspersed with the inevitable occasional argument. But I guess we were trying.

We were the classic can't live with you, can't live without you, couple

When we got home Chris hit me.

It wasn't the first time he'd reacted to my endless torment, but it was the last. We were at his flat and we'd been arguing, me doing my usual screaming, throwing things around in a non-stop fury. He pushed me on the sofa. His hands closed round my neck. I couldn't breathe. It hurt. His eyes looked murderous. He pinned me down on the sofa and I couldn't get away despite the struggle that ensued. He let go of my neck and I screamed at him. He hit me in the face, between my lip and nose. That really did shut me up. I cowered. Bastard. I cried. Bastard, I don't want to cry over you. Shit.

His face softened. "I'm sorry. I'm so sorry, Amanda." He was now a distraught and sorry Chris.

I vowed that would be the end of our relationship, but it took only hours to get over it, as I had done before, and we carried on regardless. But my endless abusive phone calls to him at work didn't stop, nor did anything else.

My hypnotherapy/CBT with Roger continued.

My CBT forms got a little more questioning - Daily Thought Record

1. Situation –

    Who were you with?

    Where were you?

    What were you doing?

2. **Negative Automatic thoughts**

    Rate believability of thoughts (0-100%)

3. **Rate Intensity of emotion**

   (0-100%)

4. **Alternative and balanced thoughts**

   Rate believability of thoughts (0-100%)

5. **How do you feel now?**

   Re-rate intensity of emotions (0-100%)

1. I went home to Mum and Dads with Chris and Dad was in the garden
2. Dad's in, will have to chat 90%
3. Anxiety – 20%
4. It'll be fine
5. Fine – even though it wasn't.

***

1. Airport on Isle of Wight with Chris
2. Chris's delaying lunch on purpose, doing what he wants by fixing the wheel on the plane 90%
3. Annoyed 99%
4. I'll get my own lunch
5. 50% it turned into a row

***

1. Going home to Mum and Dads after a few days at Chris's
2. Dad will go on at me saying 'hello stranger' or just ignore me 95% as usual
3. Anxious 90%
4. I'll handle it
5. 40% (he then was in bed anyway)

My other tips for feeling better were:

- Stop goading/testing Chris
- Stop reacting to Chris's testing of me – only reacting in an appropriate way – have anxiety, explain it and say it'll be OK – be nice.
- Rules – obsessional – stop creating rules and wanting everyone to abide by them
- No more lies and impulsively blurting out about feelings and hate – only say things I mean
- Include Chris in my plans
- Realise what matters most is good relationships with family and make it my main plan
- Recognising control early on and stopping it – be more adaptable to people and plans – stop trying to plan and control everything and everyone! Then I won't feel so let down.

Chris moved into a rented flat overlooking the sea with lovely views. I told him that *I am going to find a single man and I am going to get married myself. What a fool for waiting a year and half for sad old you.* But it wasn't just me splitting us up all the time, he said it too when he got annoyed. And he occasionally took the blame for his actions.

Things need to change to survive

Journal: February 2008

I am upset that life is constantly changing.

Everything seems to be Chris.

I made lists of what was wrong and what was right with my life just as Roger said I should. I knew I had to truly break it with Chris, and not keep going back to him. He'd never take notice of my needs if I kept threatening to leave him and then coming back for more – he could get away with changing nothing at all that way.

In fact I knew I had to change a lot of things.

The lists helped me to put things into perspective. What I didn't realise was that my whole life ran on lists by then – endless things to do, non-stop statistical analysis of absolutely everything in my life. I found them easy to make, but still didn't listen to the fact that I was feeding my OCD (Obsessive Compulsive Disorder) – which Roger had suggested I had, and in my case it was an obsession with lists and doing anything to up my stress levels, like being late and many other things. Lists could end up typed out on numerous sheets of A4 paper. Just looking at them would freak me out – how on earth could I get all that done? I couldn't, and I knew it, but it didn't stop me from spending minutes or hours a day worrying about how I couldn't achieve these things, or couldn't make the decisions I needed to, all written down, and I wasted so much time worrying I had even less chance of achieving them. My stress would lead to a few things as per – drinking copious amounts of alcohol, smoking lots of cigarettes (because yes I had started smoking again after just three months of quitting to spite Chris), a denial of food, taking my stress out on other people (Chris or whoever happened to be around at the time), twiddling endlessly with my hair which achieved nothing actually except for greasy hair and more stress, or my good and faithful old friend – masturbation. Stress still led to masturbation for me at that time, just as it did when I was nine. Not a pleasurable soft form, but a vigorous need to achieve climax after climax and some sort of relief. Sometimes it would work and others it did not.

But even with all of that, and all of the lists I couldn't see what was really happening. I knew who I wanted to be but not how to change. All I knew was I wanted to be different.

No I *needed* to be different.

And Chris was still emailing me. Sometimes I even thought he was the one who was changing.

Changing and becoming more like me.

From: Chris

Sent: 03 April 2008 21:32:49

To: Amanda Green

Subject: Amanda

Amanda I will miss you so very much, its hard to imagine life without you, when I do the prospect is a very bleak one indeed anyway I suppose that I had better get used to the idea.

The thing that hits me the most is that its all such a shame, what a wonderful future we could have had together, the things we could have done together, the places we could have gone, now its clear that whatever the future holds for both of us it will be shared with someone else or alone, and that hurts me so much I cant say.

Anyway I wish you the very very best for the future and I honestly hope that you will find peace and happiness soon.

You are a lovely girl and will always be very very special to me. I will never forget our love untill the day I die. I only hope that I will be able to get over you without fucking up the rest of my life.

Good luck with your business, although you wont need it I am sure, I just know that you are going to be very successful.

Loads & Loads of Love

Chris xxxxxx

Sometimes it's just so hard to let go

16th August 2008 – *texts to Chris*

- I am going to die and I hope u miss me u cunt

- U r not going to ignore me again

19th August 2008 – *more texts to Chris*

- u will not come round my house please. I don't want any more shit at this house.

- Ok im going out, im not having u having it out round here. Go threaten someone else.

20th August 2008 – *and more texts to Chris*

- As far as Im concerned if u want to offer and give someone something u should just do it.

The problem was, Chris was morphing into a mini me – taking on all my abusive and threatening ways and I was getting them back and learning how it felt, as he'd come round to my mum and dads when they were out and bang on the doors and swear at me through the letterbox when I ignored him. He played mind games with me, as I did him. We still couldn't cut contact though – we were a lost cause by now.

Chris made me think about his age and the probability of him dying before me, due to him being seventeen years older than me. But I knew full well that we can all die any minute, hour or day and I told him I committed in my heart to him, which to me was like committing to be married. I wanted nothing but him. No-one but him. I still don't...but I couldn't settle with him if I couldn't go to his funeral due to his secret family being there, or let him show my baby to his wife's family.

I know Chris felt desperate to help me in a way. He even helped me choose a private psychiatrist. I was very nervous as these type of doctors could have me sectioned and put away in a hospital, but they were qualified to acknowledge if someone has serious mental problems or not and diagnosing mental issues… We were at our wits end, and I felt I wanted and needed to help myself. I knew that my behaviour was out of control at times, as my screaming fits and hitting Chris or inanimate objects got worse and I felt I couldn't cope with many things by then. So, Chris said he'd pay the £250 a session and that he would come with me to support me and make sure that I said the truth about my issues so I could get the right help…

So, before I knew it, within days, we were walking up the road to Dr Jones's office…

Chapter 37

End of the line

The end of the line, as ill-defined as it is, came when I was finally given my diagnosis in August 2008 – Borderline Personality Disorder. Nine symptoms. Nine ticks. A whole heap of denial.

Although I'd apparently been suffering with Borderline Personality Disorder for a long time, I finally had a name to explain my madness. You'd think it would be simple then, wouldn't you? I had Chris, I had my family, my mum – they all knew about mental illness, but then again maybe that was the problem.

I did ask myself how much of what I told Dr Jones about growing up and the crazy life I'd led had brought me to this diagnosis. In hindsight, although it was proved that I have had far more mental illness symptoms throughout my life than I liked to admit, and have certainly had depression since I was fifteen; it seemed that it was more recent events that set me off on the one way path of destruction, namely by bankruptcy. But all that had to change. Dr Jones concentrated on my promiscuity, drug taking, eating disorders, self harm tendencies and boyfriend troubles when we were talking. I guess you could say that gave me the first glimpse of the real me.

And of course there was Chris, together for two years we'd built ourselves a cave of love. No matter the problems, we simply could not be apart. We were tied together by some invisible cord borne out of need and dependence, but also an overwhelming love and admiration – we were soul mates. We were in it together, and in spite of those three words and the journey before us there is a more immediate one – we were off to Borneo to see those Orangutans I loved so much. Seemed good and bad did run side by side.

And while I had a name for my mental illness and I knew something had to change I would put it back in the box.

But only for a while.

Because soon, like it or not, I would have look for me, the real me, the one I seemed to have lost somewhere along the way.

And my homeward journey would begin with a trip to Borneo.

Part 11

Return Journey

He who returns from a journey is not the same as he who left

– **Chinese proverb**

If I told people that I have been to twenty-four countries (twenty-one by the time I was twenty-two), had multiple holidays every year since I was fourteen, worked in Japan for nine months, toured Australia for six months and enjoyed seven months in Thailand, they might think that I'd had a blessed life.

If I told them I have worked in the hotel industry, for a sexual health department in a hospital, with prisoners in a drug cell block of a male prison, as a recruitment consultant, and many office jobs as well as having my own company and multiple websites, at age thirty-six, then they might think I'd had had an interesting life.

If I added to that a mix of mental health problems, promiscuity, drug taking, alcohol abuse, eating disorders, self harm, violence, mood swings, obsession, jealousy, loss of self worth and masturbation in public at age nine, then I'm not sure what they'd think.

The psychiatrists and doctors have their views, I have mine and you will have yours. But I believe we are all a composite of every experience we've ever had, and everyone we've ever met. This story has examined my life and how somewhere along the road I lost sight of the real me and I didn't like the person I had turned into.

But somehow, with help, I needed to find my way back.

The stigma of mental health problems had followed me like a shadow from childhood and it affects so many people, from those in the depths of depression to those experiencing the psychotic, alien, hallucinogenic schizophrenia. And as long as people keep avoiding discussion of mental health issues and avoid understanding people with disorders, this will continue to destroy lots of people every day of every year, causing many deaths along its tragic path, through suicide.

First it was about my mum, and then it was about me. I, too, had a mental disorder - what about that?

Should I look a certain way?

Should I behave a certain way?

Should I have friends?

Should I be loved?

Should I be viewed by others with a cautious eye?

Should I be in hospital?

Should I be medicated?

Add stigma to that mixture of blessed and interesting and what do you have?

You have me.

But which me? My dad told me he thought I had a split personality. Maybe I did.

Who I was? Who I became? Or maybe all of that is me?

You see behind all that confidence as a business woman, with all that travelling and all those experiences was a little girl; the same one you met in Part 1. A little girl who was born early... a little girl who was loved, that's always been loved... and a little girl with lots of worries.

Sometimes, these worries take us so far into the forest we can't see the way out. That's what happened to me. A little girl who was lost in the forest. Sometimes I was perched on the edge trying to fly away. Sometimes I was so far in I was folded into myself, looking for my colours, wondering who cared what happened to me. I could die right there in the forest. And other times I *could* see.

But to *really* see I knew I needed to find my way back into the forest and look at me. To see who I was and then walk myself back to the edge where I really could be free and happy in my own skin.

But how?

I went to see Dr Jones that day in 2008, which is how this story started, as the last option to find out what was *actually* wrong with me. And he did. He did find out. He even gave me a name for it. And yet that wasn't enough. Not really. A name meant there were other people like me. But what if Dr Jones was wrong? If I kept my eyes shut maybe it wasn't real. Look at me: Amanda G. Business woman. Interesting blessed life. That was me. Wasn't it?

But of course what you see on the outside, that's a mask. Open the cupboard and see what's inside and then you'll see the real me.

So Dr Jones gave it the name: Borderline Personality Disorder, but the whole process of working out which parts of the disorder I had and why, well that opened up a whole new can of proverbial worms. The condition didn't just appear. On the contrary, it has been with me all of my life, just as clinical depression, anxiety and obsessive compulsive disorder have. Children are not diagnosed with personality disorders as they are still building their unique personalities when young, so they often suffer in silence. And the more I researched mental disorders the more I wondered if I also fitted the 'Bipolar' diagnosis.

One of the things that fuels the stigma with mental illness is that it isn't like a physical illness with name, cause, treatment, outcome. The more I read the more I realised how mental health is like guesswork. We all have varying degrees of one form or another it's just it's not always clinical. And there seems to be a continuum with anxiety and depression feeding into all kinds of manifestations from Bipolar to schizophrenia. BPD was one such condition, a complex one at that, falling somewhere along that line.

No wonder it was so hard to work out. And so hard to find the right way to treat it.

So, had I been fooling myself that my life was grand and happy? Perhaps so! The last few years certainly had not been 'happy' as such. More like a fairground ride where the highs are happiness and excitement and the lows are depression, suicidal thoughts and intense anger, but there's no steady ground in the middle – just high or low, black or white, as I was beginning to realise.

Admittedly, I was relieved with what I didn't hear: schizophrenia, catatonic schizophrenia. All my life convincing myself I wasn't like her; my mum. Well I wasn't, it was a different disease, wasn't it?

The thing is, I *was* like her. The more I learned the more I realised I was actually like her, in so many ways.

It's just that when I think about her now I know that is not the bad thing I always thought it was. Mum was doing OK, eventually ... and so would I. I hoped.

Chapter 1

The Long road back starts in Borneo

I have adored Orangutan since I was about eight years old, which was when I first remember meeting Toga at the local Zoo. To me, he was graceful, quiet, non-aggressive and beautiful. But I'd hear people saying things.

"Isn't he ugly?"

"Oh look, it's a Gorilla."

"Look how weird he looks!"

Maybe I'd look into his eyes and remember when people ridiculed me.

And it wasn't just the kids. Adults were as bad.

I got jealous when others were there with Toga as if he was mine, and it's lucky I had the patience to wait until every visitor had gone and I was on my own with him. He was a mature male with fully grown cheek pads and I could gaze into his tiny black eyes and study him in peace. I never wanted to leave. Unacceptable enclosures for various animals stopped me going to zoos for a few years, but I guess zoos have improved now and do help conservation in small ways and they do educate and introduce the animals to children and to adults who would perhaps never see them in the wild. But I know they should be wild and free. Humans are only incarcerated for doing bad things, animals are incarcerated for just being what they are. There's a big argument there, for and against, but not for this book.

Maybe there has always been something about what I saw in those animals that tapped into my deep inner self. Hadn't I always wanted to fly away and be free?

For the past twelve years I had wanted to start campaigning for the survival of the Orangutan in Borneo and Sumatra, since they were, and still are, being wiped out by human kind, but I'd done nothing, convinced every year that I would go to see them in the wild and it would spring me into charitable action on my return. I'd been so close in Thailand too. Every year, I didn't go, and every year I heard about the rapid decline in their numbers due to poaching, the pet trade and the palm oil industry. I did feel guilty, but I also had a lot of problems of my own so I harboured guilt all of the time.

The Orangutan are so close to extinction, just a few years away, if that, particularly in Sumatra. They are regularly tortured, killed or made orphans and I wanted to help them.

As with most things in my life, plenty of obstacles blocked my path to Borneo in the Autumn of 2008, like Chris making me wait for months to book it as I wasn't being a 'good girl', countless break ups with him, and him allowing his wife to delay the divorce for what was by then two years and counting, but thankfully, they were overcome possibly because he'd let me organise the whole trip which had kept me busy and gave me purpose. So, after a lot of stressful organising and packing, I found myself at the Radisson Edwardian Hotel in Heathrow, just hours away from the flight to Borneo with Chris, my fellow explorer, boyfriend and love of my life... and that little matter of a diagnosis for BPD. But I just pushed that to the back of my mind. I could overcome. And this was the start of the journey back to me.

Or was it?

The first morning in Borneo I awoke to lovely sunshine streaming into the room and a happy head

It was a trip where we lazed on sun beds under umbrellas, swam in the beautiful seas and experienced tropical rainstorms. We saw beautiful resorts, rainforests and river lodges. We encountered Orangutan rehabilitation centres, turtle egg laying and we travelled by planes, buses, taxis and boats. I took hundreds of photos and videos; luckily I had succumbed to digital and had a nice new SLR which Chris bought me for Christmas. During one afternoon boat trip, we saw a Proboscis Monkey family playing in the trees together and another time my head was inches from a Green Viper snake. But what did I do, take its photo of course.

On an evening boat tour we saw a baby crocodile, a huge Iguana, a swamp snake, a fantastic giant butterfly and a beautiful kingfisher that I was able to stroke.

The list grew of what we saw on that trip: some amazing birds – Egret, Snake Bird (Anhinga), Hornbill, Macaques, Blued eared Kingfisher, Pied fantail, Stork billed kingfisher, plus a Flying fox, Monitor lizard and a Mangrove snake (black/yellow). But, best of all, was a female Orangutan, swinging freely in the trees with her baby clinging on. She was free – free to live wild.

But it wasn't all peaceful.

My itinerary was full on, I got a bad stomach one day and had to miss one of our boat trips, and this gave me time to ponder. To think about that diagnosis that was hanging over me and I was trying to push it away.

Doctor Jones said that I would have a fifty-five percent chance of full recovery if I took the drugs and treatment. Doctor Jones said that I had all the nine symptoms. Doctor Jones seems to have me down as some promiscuous, drug taking, manipulative nutcase. I thought and thought – it was hard to concentrate on reading my book. I read the same page over and over as my brain hit overdrive.

This holiday is just another escape from my life, a temporary fix

But trudging through the intense humidity and lush forests, alive with creatures and sounds, gave me a true sense of 'feeling alive' and stopped me thinking about my diagnosis. For a while.

But even then we fought.

It had all gone off again: the peace of the rainforest was broken. *It's his fault. Bastard!*

"I hate you, you shit, I hate you – you ruin everything! I'm getting a flight home. I can't stand you any longer!" I thumped Chris's back, repeatedly and hard.

He turned round, grabbing my arm roughly

"Amanda, calm down. You don't need to go home – we can sort this out."

He scared me.

"Get off me! Fuck you, bastard! I'm getting out of here, away from you. You never wanted to come here – you only care about them! You don't want me to be happy. Go on, hit me again. Go on, break my nose this time, why don't you!"

My heartbeat quickened, and rapidly thumped through my whole body, as I remembered the times he'd lashed out at me too.

After throwing things around the room and punching the bed, my rage soon turned to despair, as my body started shutting down.

Then the shaking started. My eyes flooded with tears and the sobbing came. I wanted to get out of that room, that country, away from him, so badly. I wanted to go home. I always wanted to go home in times of adversity. Thing is, when I got home to my parents' house, I was miserable, so I just couldn't win, but I always wanted to be somewhere I wasn't at the time.

Wherever you go your problems go with you

I felt helpless. I didn't have the strength or confidence to go anywhere by myself. A far cry from my past, when I was carefree and took risks and was bright, but this is what I had become. I needed Chris. Maybe too much. I wanted to split up with him, to show him that he couldn't ignore my true feelings, but I was too scared to be on my own, and the closeness that we had and adoration for each other was like an elastic band; it stretched, but we always came back for more.

Just moments earlier, we had woken to the sounds of the Bornean rainforest – birds singing and creatures buzzing. I had seen a wild male Orangutan before our afternoon nap, and had been so happy, clicking away with my camera, on a mission to collect as much research for my campaign as possible. What had happened?

Chris didn't understand me. He didn't realise that just because we weren't discussing things didn't mean I wasn't thinking about them; in fact they never left my mind. He didn't know I was constantly haunted by thoughts and the pain curled itself up inside of me until I was exploding with the smallest provocation. It never made sense to him, as he couldn't see what sparked my outrages; that it wasn't about what happened in that moment, but what was going on in my mind – his divorce, his lies, his issues. Him telling me he lied because he was too scared to tell me his truths. And that's how it was that day; I'd exploded in rage at something that seemed so small. I picture us lying on the bed, Chris beside me, as the sounds of the jungle swept back in through the open window. Then the guilt started and thoughts tore at my insides.

'Who had heard?'

'Would they think I was some low-life?'

''The holiday's ruined.'

'Was the psychiatrist right?'

'Oh shit, what happens now?'

'My hand hurts!'

'I don't want to take those drugs for loonies.'

'I knew he would ruin it all.'

'I should never have come.'

'His fucking wife!'

On and on, thoughts tumbling: anger, pain, upset, paranoia and fear.

But I did love him.

And at least there were still the Orangutan.

So we did what we always did, we made up. On our last expedition we came across the male Orangutan again, right above our heads and had around an hour to photograph him. It was wonderful to see this beautiful creature just feet away up in the tree, free and happy. It made me forget about everything else. *Almost.*

I have a worn, unwashed cream t-shirt in a vanity case in my old bedroom at Mum and Dad's house. I really like the t-shirt, but I can't ever wash it. I was wearing it when the most special moment in my life occurred.

It was a hot humid day in the Bornean rainforest. And there I was with a beautiful baby Orangutan in my arms, gushing at the camera as Chris took photos of me. This was not a photo shoot like the ones they did with chimpanzees in Spain, and no money or goods changed hands, but it was a moment given to me by a very kind person who might have known that it was the best gift I could ever receive.

I took my time to take in everything about her – her long fluffy red fur shooting out of her long limbs, the pinky white skin underneath, her bone structure, her coconut shaped mouth as soft as cotton wool, and her eyes – dewy, black, round eyes looking up at me. I saw the sadness in them – her memories, her lost murdered mother taken from her at such a young age whom she missed as any human baby would, the kindness of the humans who now look after her, nurture her, teach her to be a baby Orangutan. She had it all coming – Orangutan school taught by skilled and patient people, nearly seven years of it; as long as she would have had with her mother.

She was 96.4% human DNA, and it showed, yet humans killed her mother, and so there she was in my arms, just for a minute. She pulled away eventually looking for her carer; someone she could trust. I didn't like to see her in distress, so I gave her back. It was over. It might have been, but unlike many memories of mine which I try to dissociate from, this one will never leave me – this was a good memory, a happy memory, a great memory, no, this is the most special moment of my life and the t shirt I was wearing, that she touched and clung to one of my most prized possessions.

I knew Chris wanted to hold her too, but he knew it was my moment.

And I thank him for that.

Sadly, many babies just like her are orphans. All too often, their mothers have been killed by poachers, who try to catch the babies to sell as pets. Or palm oil plantation workers, who are employed to keep Orangutan from eating the palm oil crops. Some are paid commission by producing an Orangutan hand to show that they got rid of a pest. Rather unfair when the Orangutan's forest home has been cut down to make way for the plantations – where are they supposed to go to find food? I have also seen photos of Orangutan buried alive, just their head poking out of the dirt – no reason behind the torturers actions. But, it is fabulous for the few survivors who are saved and are being shown love. And, rehabilitation centres, unlike zoos, release the Orangutan back into the wild to be free for the rest of their lives, long or short. I know I would rather have a short life being free than a long life incarcerated. Since an Orangutan female only has one baby at a time, and mothers it for seven years, teaching it how to survive the rainforest, how to make forest tools, and which foods to eat, for every female killed, it makes a big difference to the population and numbers are falling rapidly across Sumatra and Borneo – the only places that these primates are found now. Together with the rapid clearing of forest to make way for palm oil plantations, the habitat and food that each Orangutan needs (a few square kilometres each to survive, food wise) is dwindling every day and so many are dying of hunger. It is why they live alone, unlike the family groups of Gorillas or Chimpanzees – it's all about food and survival – they are sociable creatures really. It was a bittersweet trip, as more heartbreaking facts came to light.

We listened to talks about the work of Orangutan rehabilitation centres and a sad video outlining some of the difficulties involved in trying to save the Orangutan and typical reasons for so many deaths each year. It showed so many orphans and images of tortured and *left for dead* adults, I lowered my head and wept silently, avoiding eye contact with Chris or anyone else.

I still don't like to cry in front of anyone

On one visit to a rehabilitation centre, a gorgeous young girl Orangutan came along and hung around near our feet. It was so exhilarating, being so close to her. She was hiding at first, underneath the visitor walkway, looking unsure. I frantically took photos and got completely over-excited about being just two feet away from her, so the time flashed by, until a Ranger came along, grabbed her hand and marched her off like a naughty child. It was such a cute sight, seeing her waddling off down the path, holding his hand, and I was really pleased to note that no-one tried to take advantage and touch her. As I had done with the baby in that special moment. But I knew it was wrong.

We also saw little Orangutan babies, watching them play in the vivid green trees of the rainforest, hanging upside down from branches by their long arms and legs, drinking from a bottle held by a human hand, and just being themselves.

During a tour in Sabah (Northern Malaysian Borneo), we were shown palm kernels taken from palm trees grown for mainly cooking oil and soap. While it brings wealth into their country, it destroys valuable rainforest. And this means the homes of Orangutan, indigenous people and wildlife. Throughout our whole journey in Sabah, no matter where we went, the landmass was covered in palm plantations.

As long as the Orangutan were around, I vowed to help them. So I was deeply affected by what I read in Jeremy Keeling's memoir (co-founder of Monkey World in Dorset) where he says on the very first page that *if you really want to save monkeys* (Orangutan are primates (Great Apes), NOT monkeys – Monkeys have tails) *then maybe you should do it with a breed that has a fighting chance* of survival.

A fighting chance of survival? Don't treat the very sick, let them die? I understand what he's saying, that some species are more viable, but I knew I could never give up like that.

But what worries me is how this message has reached thousands of readers.

Monkey World do fabulous work in rescuing primates and monkeys around the world, particularly ex-laboratory Capuchins which is great as animal testing is essentially unnecessary and a disgraceful way of treating any living creature. However, Monkey World do not rehabilitate and put the primates back in their natural home, Monkey World is essentially a zoo for the rescued primates and monkeys which I still don't agree with – they are still not free. And there are safer areas in Borneo for Orangutan to live – a whole new group were found in the last couple of years, so there are options. Another huge argument could be had about this too, but again, not in this book.

Through days, months and years of therapies and support, I longed for a diagnosis for my madness, and there I was in Borneo seeing my precious Orangutan and it was like the *best of times, the worst of times*.

Whether I truly believed I was sick, maybe, maybe not, sometimes, sometimes not, what it did do was make me think about what I would do on my return from Borneo and that was start writing again. My focus – the happy ending all good stories need, don't they?

But first I had to find myself.

Although I'd talked about my past with the psychiatrist, through my memory, I do appreciate that we do remember things incorrectly sometimes – omitting things we wish to forget, making things seem better than they were, and mistaking emotions for the opposite of what they really were. So, I decided to work through the past myself, and try to work out what was right, what was wrong, and what others in my life were going through; start as a child and work forwards…

Acknowledging I needed to unravel the past was a way of acknowledging Dr Jones had been right

But it was going to be a long journey back to find out who I really was.

And as they say; every journey starts with a single step, like stepping off the plane on my return from Borneo.

Chapter 2

Taking that next step

Once home from Borneo, in October 2008, instead of taking the psychiatrist's advice about drugs and therapy, I concentrated on a 'Save the Orangutan' campaign. I collated information and photos I had collected in Borneo. It's only when I look back now I can see how I was in denial, plunging into another venture I could obsess on. And not think about my diagnosis.

But of course, I was always thinking about my diagnosis.

I guess I just hadn't learned to take off the mask.

Keeping busy is a way not thinking

The Orangutan campaign ballooned into an almost full time affair, as I became driven by news of the rainforest destruction across Borneo and Sumatra to make way for more palm oil plantations, and the Orangutan torture. I was soon badgering supermarkets and manufacturers demanding information on where they source their palm oil; whether it was sustainable palm oil provider as most are not. I wrote to Government contacts and my local MP, and all Orangutan charities for backup. Even if people didn't love Orangutan, then many others were upset at the rate of carbon dioxide that was being released every time a tree was cut down or burned in the rainforest. I heard at the time that, in Indonesia alone, the forest was being cleared at a rate of approximately six football pitches a minute, and that is a lot of carbon dioxide.

A few months later I went in for the lottery on Saturday – just three minutes before the time was up, I found my online account details and put three lines on, one of which was a lucky dip. I got five numbers out of six! But sadly I only won only £1600. Chris and I always said that if either of us won while we were together, then we would share the proceeds, and so I did, £800 each. And one of the things I did with the winnings was to adopt two more Orangutan through my favourite charities.

I continued to raise awareness about Orangutan and used that trip to show how these animals helped me overcome depression. That's if I had overcome it, but I guess I never stood still long enough to really think about that.

I even got a double page feature in a magazine but by the time it went to press, outlining how campaigning for the plight of these primates helped me, I had gone downhill again. So there was my answer. All I was doing was finding a way to cope. But it had been there, part of me too long, shaping that alien self. I guess being involved in such a sad, seemingly hopeless campaign wasn't the best thing for depression.

At this time I also saw a lot of Chris and started doing 'restaurant reviews' for a local website I later took over, it was something else to fill my days. The attention the site got, and my ability to analyse the visitor statistics in detail through Google analytics, fed my self esteem so that was great – people were interested to read what I had found out and written about. If you looked at me then, you would think I was a strong confident woman, but it wasn't true.

My campaign helped me through. Just as I portrayed my emotions to others, covering them up, as I've purposely done when I told people about my story and my depression, I knew I had to be truthful and let those feelings go so I could really be free.

Like those Orangutan I fought to protect.

Once I finally started to write my story properly, that obsessive nature of mine took over. And write I did – with passion – for the next three and half years. I just hadn't known how hard that was going to be. Or what I was going to uncover.

Help yourself if you want to find yourself

The Psychiatrist had also advised me to take up CAT (Cognitive Analytical Therapy). Chris took me for the therapy, but at £100 per hour for sixteen weeks, I had to rely on Chris to pay for it. I couldn't let go; not really.

I had my first session on October 2008. I didn't like the format or her and she was forty miles away. Or maybe these were excuses. Whatever they were, I never went back. But I was still seeing Roger for counselling.

I also got the prescription for *Quietapine* from Dr Jones but when I read about the side effects of these anti-psychotic drugs, I decided not to take it. I did eventually – but not then. I guess it was hard to see myself medicated, the way my mum had been for years. The final admission there was something wrong?

Chris's divorce still not being finalised and us still not living together meant we were arguing as usual. I also found myself using alcohol more and more as a comfort. As I became wrought with anxiety, I spent some time in my 'office' in Dad's conservatory, thinking about songs to end our relationship that would encapsulate each other's feelings, in an effort to feel pleasant about it. But it just helped me wallow, drinking and sobbing for hours instead.

My song for Chris was *Knowing me, knowing you* by Abba. Yes, it will be empty and I have tears in my eyes. Yes, we do know each other well. Yes, there is nothing we can do about our relationship. Yes, we are through and there will be no more carefree laughter, but I have to go.

The song I chose from Chris to me was *Wild World* by Cat Stevens. Yes, he feels he has lost everything to me and I have broken his heart, but unlike me, he has kind words and wants me to be happy and if I am to leave he wants me to take good care. Yes I have a lot of nice things to wear that he has bought me over the years and I am sure that he will remember me as a child too since I act like one so often. He doesn't want to see me sad or being a bad girl either. And if I am not bad then I shouldn't be sad. Those lyrics are so true.

Then, another song by Nelly Furtado I decided epitomized the whole sorry affair – *Why do all good things come to an end?* It was my all encompassing song of the decline and end of our relationship.

"WHY do good things always come to an end? WHY does everything good come to an end? Please tell me, someone, God, anyone." I begged the sky, hoping and believing once again, that there really was a God who could help me.

I chose those three songs while looking at numerous photos of us – sat side by side or cuddling; always smiling. We look like we have everything to live for in our happy little lives and sometimes it felt like we did when I could stop thinking about the negative stuff, but it was never for long and the darkness came uninvited.

I listened to them over and over, weeping and sobbing, drinking myself into a stupor, my guts clamping up with the stabbing, excruciating sorrow of the situation. Omitting to eat, which I did regularly in times of strife, my Irritable Bowel Syndrome (IBS) came on quickly, and the pain of the spasms in my tummy fed my desire to punish myself through more hunger and pain and alcohol – a regular habit. Although connected to an unhealthy diet, IBS is aggravated by irregular eating times, failing to eat when hungry and stress – all causing air to blow out the gut as well. I knew it, but ignored it anyway.

I wrote at the time, *'When I break up with Chris, I feel lost and lonely, I want to be dead, I withdraw from people, I am unable to think about the future, wishing I could go to sleep and not wake up, and I feel sick inside my stomach, as it aches and my body aches for a cuddle, the wrenching agony as the dark cloud following me finally catches up with me and pollutes my brain, as I have no-where to run anymore. I feel like an unreal person, like I exit my body and then watch myself as if I were another person, and I want to punish that person, that bad girl, that failure...'*

It was not the first break up we had gone through, of course. Nor was it to be the last; far from it. I never was good with endings. It never got easier. There was never much time in between when we were set on staying together, committed. There was no chance for either of us to feel stability or trust towards the other, and it was no wonder that our relationship remained rocky, but the invisible elastic band of astonishing closeness to each other in the deep pits of our souls, remained in place and we always came back for more – more punishment, and more pleasure and the break ups always felt like the end of our lives as we felt we could not live without each other.

I was still sending him emails and texts going on and on at him...

Maybe we would never let go. Maybe he was keeping me sick. Maybe I would never get better?

Chapter 3

Good days, bad days

I asked my GP once whether schizophrenia was passed on from a mother to her children and he said no.

But I always knew there was a chance it could.

And this set off my paranoia.

The more I delved, the more I worried and the more I worried, the more I delved. I was trapped in a vicious cycle.

I watched a programme called *How Mad Are You?* The psychiatrists tested a group of people, some of whom had a mental disorder (Schizophrenia, Bipolar, Depression, Anorexia nervosa, Bulimia nervosa and Social Anxiety Disorder) and some who did not have a mental disorder.

The psychiatrists got many of the diagnoses wrong, labelling individuals with wrong diagnoses or suggesting something was wrong when it wasn't – upsetting for some of the 'normal' people.

The first question was the one I have perhaps asked all my life and maybe that was to convince myself was *what is normal?*

And then, *how did they get it so wrong?* There were very sick people within the group who were perceived as 'normal' and others with no mental health issues told that they were sick with serious psychiatric disorders.

And then I wondered why there were so many symptoms of so many disorders? Does 'Borderline Personality Disorder' describe them all – bring together all the symptoms?

No.

I had depression, anxiety disorder, paranoia, had had anorexia and bulimia, and I showed signs of being Bipolar, together with BPD, OCD and mood swings. I started looking up these disorders, separately, in more detail on the internet. So, I asked myself again – *what is normal?*

Is it having symptoms or not having symptoms?'

And how many symptoms do you need before you come out of the 'normal' box and are placed in the 'mentally ill' box?

I looked at my friends and family and I could find symptoms of mental issues within all of them, so were they all ill? Or more importantly are any of us really *normal?*

The big problem, as I have mentioned and keep coming back to, is this stigma that shadows sufferers of mental illness. I have already talked about how this followed me as a child and the way it manifested in the bullying. The most obvious and more widely suffered mental illness seemed to be depression. I'd studied others in my workplaces that were off work with depression, and many people believed them, but others talked about them as losers, lazy, cheats.

It's wrong to discriminate, but people do

Would you get the offer or support and friendship from others if it was you? Did I? I am afraid the answer's no.

Who wanted to befriend someone who was depressed, weak or even, as some would think, a liar, claiming to have something wrong with them when they didn't?

But there were people doing just that, and depression became an easy excuse for having time off work. I'd heard people claim depression and stress were the new *bad back*. It was rapidly becoming the *fashionable sickie*.

But what this seemed to mean was that people with 'real' depression were ignored. Some were not supported and even ousted from work events. The cause? Fear? Ignorance? Lack of compassion? Or all of the above?

As the Queen of the happy persona, no-one saw me at my worst. I stayed at home, shut myself away. I wouldn't get out of bed, the desire for being dead and being unable to cope encompassed me so I turned to drink. But no-one saw me like that, apart from Mum, Dad and Chris occasionally, but they didn't really know how *much* I was drinking or that I was hiding drink in the house. If I had taken time off work sick for my depression, told my bosses I was mentally ill, would they have really believed *Little Miss Sunshine* didn't just want a few days off? If I produced a letter from Dr Jones to prove it – what then? The words *personality disorder* would have just brought me more problems.

Maybe it was just easier to say nothing.

Depression comes and goes, sometimes lasting months, weeks or days for people. It is confusing, worrying and lonely, so it is no wonder that many people don't discuss it, preferring to face it on their own, feeling ashamed and that they should pull themselves together. Some don't make it, and commit suicide as it engulfs them too hard. Depression for me, for many years, meant running away – I would run with that black cloud following me, all around the world , but it was always there teasing me.

So, if that is how depression is seen, then what hope do people with more serious disorders and illnesses have?

What hope did I have?

With depression, often there is insecurity, which can lead to one holding in one's thoughts and emotions – trying not to get hurt. If a person with depression is unable to relate their feelings to their loved ones, or acknowledge that they have a problem then how can they expect loved ones to support them?

They cannot help themselves and no-one else can help them.

Would employers even give us a job in the first place if we told them of these problems? What if you told them that you are on anti-psychotics (as I was recommended to take) due to your psychotic episodes and hallucinations?

So, you see, how do you face up to a stigma and accept a mental illness when those around you can't? Living a lie can be the easier option for some, but covering a wound and letting it fester for years isn't the answer.

I am at the beginning of a journey that might take a lifetime

Not many people I knew realised that I suffered with depression or any other condition. One friend of mine, Sherri, stated, "There's no such thing as depression – you just have to get on with life and not be weak." Therefore, she is one of those people I did not discuss it with. On the odd occasion I saw her, I made special efforts to act happy and lively, when inside, I sometimes wished I was dead. That is how it was. If someone couldn't be compassionate, then I tried to be what they wanted me to be. That, as I discovered, was a typical symptom of BPD – changing personas to suit others. Or I just stayed in and didn't see anyone, which is a symptom of depression.

I did not feel sorry for myself. I either felt suicidal, or I got on with life. I chose to write this memoir for those facing or who have faced and conquered the same demons – to share my experiences, and maybe even help someone.

It was an admirable notion, but I didn't even know if I could win against my own demons, let alone finish a book.

But I was going to try.

Chapter 4

Too many facts!

Remember how once I walked from surgery to surgery and begged in tears for a doctor to help me a couple of years before?

And how some told me straight away that their patient list was full, others did let me see a doctor, and then said they were full.

This, I will never forget. Doctors turned me away in my home town. Doctors turned me away point blank. They did nothing, just told me, "Sorry, but we are not taking on any new patients." I felt incredibly let down by the NHS. Of course I must point out that this is just my experience and maybe other people have fared better. But it wasn't the only bout of lack of support I have received through the NHS service either.

So I could see an immediate barrier to help, finding the right doctor.

And then looking at myself; at how what I was doing, or what I had done could have contributed to my illness.

The more I researched, the more I wondered about cause and effect. And there was one big thing that had been part of my life and one that seemed to play a big role in mental illness and that was the use of recreational drugs.

When does drug use become a problem?

The drugs didn't help. They messed with an already messed up head.

Funny thing is how I took all those drugs that messed with the head but wouldn't trust medical drugs that did exactly the same, but for positive effect. Maybe that was because it was too easy to read the medication information leaflets, carefully dissecting the side effects and convincing myself that they were no good for me. Trust has always been an issue when it comes to doctors; is it any wonder when I saw my mum catatonic in hospital? Watching her helpless and being controlled and incarcerated by doctors and nurses and given frightening treatments and heavy medications. It stayed with me. If it were these days, she probably wouldn't even be in hospital. Most sufferers are out in the world, or living in assisted homes, hostels, halfway houses (read '*Henry's Demons'* by Patrick and Henry Cockburn for evidence) or one of the few psychiatric hospitals left.

Questions, questions – I had so many. I wanted answers. I wanted a solution to my life of heaven and hell. But not a pill. If only there was a pill with no side-effects that just made me well.

While I finally had that once elusive name for my condition and a possible solution, and was doing all that research, a part of me was not able to truly accept it. It was time to really look at myself. And I wasn't sure I wanted to.

Chapter 5

Save me!

I knew it would be hard uncovering things I had shut away.

It was like picking the scabs of an old wound. But hoping that what was underneath was shiny new skin.

I had not always been ill, I didn't know if I was born with it or if circumstances in my life had made it come out or even if I'd lived a different life would it have happened anyway?

But that's something I will never know. We must accept we are what we are. Warts n all. Life shapes who we become, illness or not.

This was my journey, my self-help.

But was I really strong enough?

Journal: November 2008

I'm lying in Chris's bed. My brain matter saturated with paranoia – what if the police come? What if I get into trouble? What if my dad finds out? I have just had a screaming match with Chris at his flat – screaming, swearing, hitting him, throwing things about. Then calm.

I lay on the sofa deflated and numb. He goes to sleep in bed.

After a couple of hours of torture and worry, I realise the police are not coming and I just cannot stand the thought of Chris being asleep – in a peaceful place away from this chaos. No, I have to wake him, my mission now to keep him awake all night! If I can't sleep, why should he – punish him, punish him.

So, I start again, jibing about his fucking wife, his unfinished divorce, about how he panders to her, and not me, how everyone is better than me, his secret friends who I'm not allowed to see with him, his secret life altogether, how I am not good enough for the precious people in his life, the children who he cares so much for even though they are not his, how he takes no notice of what I want and just does everything to suit himself – a monotonous and endless stream of verbal diarrhoea in my usual fit of anger.

He pauses. "Oh no, the neighbours have turned their light on – now I'm going to get kicked out – oh no, why do I deserve this? Are you happy now? You want me out you bitch, you fucking mental bitch" he shouts. He has that look in his eye – like he would like me dead.

That's when my mood changed, and I suddenly felt scared to death and was quiet. I didn't like it when Chris got angry, but it was occurring more and more. And one day those police might come to take me away.

I need to leave him. But I can't.

Chapter 6

Writing is my new therapy

November 2008

There I was, running down the college corridors, a month after my return from Borneo, flustered by both the nerves of meeting new people, the fact that I was late, as I was for everything, and the temper of the argument I was in the middle of with Chris. Finally, I found the correct room. I took a deep breath, plastered my signature smile on my face and checked my posture before entering through the classroom door, to greet my new teacher and fellow students. (There were only six of us.)

That bit was fine, and I quickly took a seat, hellos and apologies out of the way, then came the bit I dreaded; the formal introductions.

"Welcome to the 'writing your life' class. First of all, let's get to grips with who you are and why you are here, so that we can all make the most of the four sessions over the next four weeks. Please state your name, why you are in the class and anything you would particularly like to focus on – who would like to go first?"

Since I have spent my life attention seeking, it may seem a little strange that I still had issues when all eyes and ears were focussed on me, but I've always been the same – as she spoke I started shaking, my temperature rose, my breath became irregular, yet I knew I wanted to get it over and done with so I quickly volunteered.

"My name is Amanda," I said, "and I want to write my life to help me understand my depression. I started to write my childhood two years ago, in 2006, and managed twenty three thousand words, but I got to an upsetting scene and couldn't write anymore. I have collected memorabilia and communications as well as writing diaries and journals since I was fourteen years old, and now I would like to make some sense of my life through them."

The other women listened intently, keeping eye contact with me as I spoke a little shakily, and they smiled as I finished. Then it was their turn to speak, one by one.

What I had said wasn't quite true, but was as true as I was willing to be at that point – I could hardly tell them I was a raving loony at times, had been diagnosed with an illness that turned me into a remarkable impersonation of the bunny boiler in the film, *Fatal Attraction*, and that I had been plagued with difficulties for more years than I could remember. I still wasn't even sure if I believed all that anyway. In my heart, I was good. I wanted nothing but to be good to others and be happy, but that thing inside of me would take over. It wasn't my fault.

I realised I was drifting off with my thoughts again instead of concentrating. I found it hard to focus in those days. One woman was writing to get over her tormented childhood, two women who wanted to gain some writing skills as a personal hobby, and finally a woman who wanted to document her interesting childhood growing up in a caravan while their house was being built and the way outsiders perceived them as a family at that time.

We did a writing exercise, to describe our childhood home, read out what we'd written and finished up with a homework assignment. I love homework so I was most happy about this. The two and half hour session complete, I left the room feeling uplifted, optimistic and excited – I could do this, I told myself, which was quite a contrast to the person who had walked into the room. They liked my essay describing my childhood home and said that it sounded like there were family issues in my portrayal of how it looked and felt.

So, that was really how that three and half year journey of writing started. I did warn Chris that I may well feel and act worse in the meantime, rather than better, since I'd be uncovering ALL my past – every detail – and I knew that there would be some surprises and horrors in my drawers that would most likely hurt me when I got them out – particularly negatives I might learn about myself. He didn't say a lot, only that he wanted me to get better, but I repeated myself to get the notion across, and promised him that there would be no miracles. Nothing would happen really fast, but that in the long term, I felt that it would be the best thing to do – to close the lid on the *Pandora Box* of my past that had been opened so many times by previous therapists once and for all.

I would then move on in my life in a positive way, living in the present, instead of the past. I truly felt it was a risk I was willing to take, for the purposes of my long term future.

The mission was to feel better and decide if all the problems in my life were my fault, whether I really did have Borderline Personality Disorder and to see if I could overcome my severe depression and my relationship with Chris could stand the test of time. The ability to cope with normal occurrences was my goal.

Two weeks later, and the people at my writing class seemed to like what I transcribed from memory, even though it is serious subject matter. I wrote my memory as a little six year old girl, in the car with my dad going home after a visit to my mum in the mental hospital. They thought it poignant, that it posed questions and made them want to read more and the tutor agreed, particularly praising my piece describing my family home as well. I felt shivers of satisfaction through my body as they spoke about me so encouragingly. I liked the class – it got me out of the house, I concentrated on my writing and I liked meeting and mixing with people again. I felt like part of society once more. I had not been out to work for a long time by then as I had been working from home on my websites, and had hardly any friends left, so my social life consisted of just Chris and my mum and dad. I felt a bit embarrassed writing about myself. I mean, who was I? No celebrity. Who wanted to read about me? I wasn't special. But, everyone in the class was writing their memoirs and they all had a story to tell. Who doesn't? We have all lived and learnt so much, we all have stories inside our minds. All the while, I *beavered* away at home, delving, researching and writing my life and I began to feel confident in my writing skills.

Journal: November 2008

I have just won a Nintendo Wii for writing the star letter to 'WOW!' magazine about John Sargeant leaving 'Strictly Come Dancing' – I was on his side and wanted him to win. I also got letters and tips in other magazines about the X Factor. I realise that this writing lark might get me somewhere good. My websites are all about marketing, therefore, all about writing things that will make people want to read my stuff and do business with me. So, here I am, starting my book, after years of thought, partly for self therapy and partly to get published. I do hope that my story will help others in my situation, but I will just have to see what happens in the next couple of years. My 'Writing your life' college course is two weeks into its four week existence, and I am happy with it and learning lots.

I stopped writing my diaries when I was twenty-four as I felt I had 'had my life' and nothing was worth writing about afterwards. It was a mistake, as, not only did writing help me to finish the day – I mean 'get the day out of me' and helped me to get on with the next day fresh - I also knew there was something I could give to others out of it. Maybe it would be just an understanding of 'different' (less 'normal') people or maybe something to read that would inspire, should I come to a happy ending.

Chapter 7

Christmas is a time for reflection

December 2008

It was a sad day.

I had split up with Chris, *again*. Was feeling low, had a cough and David with his overpowering and difficult personality had been giving me grief; about everything. He had been over from Oz for more than three weeks and I had seen him only four times. I guess it could have been more if I had felt better and happier, it could have been more if he hadn't been difficult about me calling him half an hour late on Saturday and deciding that it was then too late to arrange to go out that day. It could have been more for many reasons. Still, that night I had said farewell for another year, two years, maybe more.

I had fun with his son though – my gorgeous nephew who was round-faced with pink cheeks that made me want to stroke them softly. He was such a lovely boy; well tempered, kept himself amused, was not needy, and had the most amazing smile, as well as being a very handsome lad! His name, Alfie, suited him, and in just the small amount of time he was with us in the UK, he grew up so much. He turned up with just a couple of words, mixed with plenty of chatter in his own toddler language, and he left with quite a few new words, like 'dark' (meaning the sky is dark, as he loved looking out the window at the sky), and 'hat' (said as he put just about anything on his head) and quite a few others. I love being called 'Auntie Amanda' (or in his words, 'Manda') too but I often feel that the title is too high for me – am I a good auntie? Do I do enough? Am I really an auntie to him when I've rarely seen him since he was born and lives in Australia? Well, I AM his auntie by blood, so I guess that is enough, even though a mother by blood who abandons her child, should not, in my eyes, be called a mother – not a proper mother anyway.

So, I spent four evenings at home with Mum, Dad, David, Linda and Alfie. I got on with Linda. Actually I wondered if there was anyone in this world who would not get on with her? She was a 'glass is half-full' woman – very easy going and would not hurt a fly. She has taken all the verbal abuse and flack from my brother for the last sixteen years, and at one time I wondered if I respected that? Shouldn't she have stuck up for herself more? Shouldn't she leave him? In fact, the last time I visited them in late 2001/early 2002, I think she was considering it, according to my brother. But, she stuck with him, and got her son as a reward, even if she worked and David was the stay at home father figure. Still it would appear (upon the short visits from them anyway) that they were on a more even keel – as even as my brother would allow it anyway. For example, he still couldn't hold his tongue when Linda realised that she forgot to give Alfie some food, and had to tell her what a bad mother she was – her reply was 'yes, I am a negligent mother.' That says it all. And if David has fallen out with any family members, then she doesn't bother contacting them either – happy, it seems, to be ignorant.

I phoned Chris. I had one last suggestion; that I move in with him for three months, temporarily, to see if we really could make it work – *either we try living together or don't bother anymore.* I suppose I knew we weren't really right for one another but the heart likes to rule and I was bloody miserable without him. He wasn't particularly supportive of my suggestion and then he said he'd visited my therapist/hypnotherapist Roger, who agreed it was an abusive relationship from *my* side, that we needed relationship counselling to make it work, that Chris needed to decide if it was a relationship worth saving. Then he declared he was going to visit his ex-family in America the following week. I was angry for two reasons. Firstly, that he had been to see Roger on his own, MY therapist, and that Roger had crossed the confidentiality line in talking to him about me (therefore I did not want to see Roger anymore) and secondly, that the first thing Chris thought about was going to see the children.

I told him to 'fuck off if that was his priority' and hung up the call in my usual fashion.

So, as I emailed my therapist angrily to tell him how unhappy I was about him discussing me when he saw Chris and that I would not be having any more appointments with him, I also wondered what Roger thought of Chris telling him about our fight just over a week before and whether Chris would have told it in his favour or the truth if, of course, he even told him at all?

And some fight that was; which typifies why, when I look back now, we really shouldn't have been together. But like so many things I couldn't see it at the time.

I'd woken, bleary eyed and hung over that day and remembered what I had done when I saw Chris's black eye.

The next day I was having my hair cut at the hairdresser Chris and I both went to. Carl the manager, loved to talk while he cut and snipped away proficiently at my blonde shoulder length hair.

I always choose a stylist who is sociable, as I don't like to sit in silence while they are in such close contact with me.

Carl was always telling me how much Chris loved me and that he cared for me and I got the hint that he talked to me about Chris and to Chris about me, but *at least he's interested* I would think.

I had been there about fifteen minutes when Chris walked in, all smiles. He'd often turn up at the hairdresser's, catching up with me while I was out and about and away from the addiction of my laptop and websites. He knew I liked to go out after having my hair done as I felt it a waste to have it styled just to sit at home.

I greeted him politely, tinged with annoyance that he was showing his face.

"Oh Chris, what's happened to your eye, been fighting again?" Carl teased.

"Erm, I fell over," said Chris; unconvincingly.

The conversation became a little tense and Chris left, arranging to come back in half hour when I would be finished so we could go get some dinner together.

But Carl was not satisfied, and after a minute or two posed the question to me about Chris's eye.

"Did he really fall over?" he asked, scrunching styling mouse through my hair.

"No, he didn't. I did it." Carl stopped, looking me in the eye of my reflection in the mirror opposite.

"Oh."

"We had an argument, I got out of control," I continued "He's hit me before too."

Due to my true dislike of lies, I had to tell him the truth, but on that particular occasion I found myself saying too much. I found a new hairdresser after that day.

Is honesty the best policy? I do ask myself sometimes. I was to find out in the future that it isn't always in my case...

I was so tired of that relationship that I decided when I said enough is enough I really ought to mean it. Moving in wasn't such a good idea, was it? I should move on and find happiness.

Happiness, eh? Will I ever know it? Will I ever get it? That's what I used to drive myself crazy thinking.

I'd look at my parents...

After everything, after many years of taking sides for both of them, I realise that my dad has just put up with, in some ways, the most horrific of marriages, rearing four children, and still remains to be able to carry on. Unfortunately, most of his 'protection' has been with his wife. My eldest brother, Peter, says that you should protect your wife, as she is the person that you will be with for the rest of your life, not your children, but who is he to talk? At the end of the day, as far as I am concerned, you should make an egg fertile, knowingly, with the complete feeling of making a child. There should not be a 'shag' or 'fuck' or caring but un-protected 'lovemaking' going on, risking unwanted pregnancies, but it happens Dad didn't know better – he was told by certain doctors that having children would benefit Mum and her disease, without a thought for the children that would be born and discover the down sides of that decision and advice. I have thought about this many times in my life, and I do not blame him for the decision to have four children given the confusion he must have been living in, and his dedication to wanting to give my mum some happiness, yet I still find it amazing and dismay that myself and my brothers were all born in some ways. We all have a stubbornness and strong personalities, but we are now much older, and have all found our own paths, except me, and I hope I can find a happy one.

Luckily, I learned to think differently about our family in the future.

17th December 2008 – Texts to Chris

> *– no I didn't I said to give it 3 months living together on Monday + u were only interested in seeing the kids. Little did I know u had a trip planned 4 the next day. Im just an idiot.*
>
> - *yeah lets upset Amanda a bit more shall we*
> - *no wonder u told me LA was shit and put me off going. Wel bye then, il take ur advice. Im glad for u that work don't NEED u this week. Have a nice holiday.*
> - *I will not sit here waiting for u again. I made that very clear every time you go on holiday to see them wherever they are. U have fun and im gonna too. Iv got a good plan to cheer myself up. Now I neva want to hear from u again after this. I mean it.*
> - *I am going to be mature and say goodbye nicely x*

Despite everything, particularly Chris going on holiday to see his family and booking it without telling me, we booked a last minute trip to Florida to leave just after Christmas. See, in spite of all this it was like we couldn't let go.

But the thing was, in all that aggression and anger towards him, trying to punish him, I was really only punishing myself. I was the one getting the most upset, the most obsessed, spending my time bullying him when I should be getting on with other things. When I should've been concentrating on my therapy; on getting better.

But there I was, off again on that trip.

When we're somewhere else we can pretend everything's OK

I would not have chosen America, but Chris said I would like it, as it would be exciting. He was right. We had a ball. I sat by the villa's private pool in Orlando for a couple of days, writing. We went to most of the theme parks and Sea World was awesome! We hired a car, and headed up to Mount Dora for a few days, taking in the Blue Spring National park, as the huge, yet graceful Manatees came into in the shallow waters there for the winter. We headed south and stayed in Miami and Key West, did jet-skiing, wildlife watching and exploring.

And we hardly argued at all. There wasn't time to argue.

We got back to the UK welcomed by white covered lands – the snow was like a perfect white blanket; serene, quiet, pure, untouched – it covered everything, like a concealer. And so peaceful. It was like a clean slate, yet spoiled by footprints. Wouldn't it have been nice if we could've come back home and kept that. But in the end nothing is perfect. And even those snowy landscapes can seem bleak at times.

I ordered lots of films and books that dealt with the subject of BPD and Schizophrenia, and scanned websites for more information on BPD. I felt worse than ever. I didn't want to go to hospital or prison. I was scared.

Will I ever get better?

Chapter 8

The glue that holds us together can tear us apart

Chris always said 'why can't I make you happy?'

But how could he when I didn't know how to make myself happy?

And how could I love him when I didn't love myself?

Every so often I'd get a strong urge to bite him – his ear, hand, arm, anywhere. I felt like tearing chunks out of him, like a vampire. I am not sure if this was related to hunger or stress or desire.

It's funny the things we choose to remember. How we are selective with our memories. Do we remember things the way they were really were or the way we wanted them to be? Truth hurts.

My unstable relationship with Chris, the on and off, *loves me, loves me not* of it was only getting worse. When I started this 'self therapy' idea, I did warn him of its possible adverse side effects, and how my responses to my home truths could well backfire onto him. I was prepared for the pain it might cause me to unearth realities about myself that were undesirable and I was right. I was right for once.

It was good to look for truth, to see how I got to be where I was. In some ways it was a journey into the unknown – because I had little idea of what I would find out about myself, I could not measure the truths or the affects they would have on me, correctly. I had already upset myself enough over the last six months, with my childhood truths and I was going to shock myself with more truths nearly every day for the next year, maybe more. Could I handle it? Would I give up, like I did with everything eventually? Would Chris and I still be together at the end of it?

Questions, questions questions.

But what were the answers?

Would I ever love myself? Forgive myself? For what? Did I love Chris enough that if I had to I would let him go?

It was that invisible elastic again, or glue. Maybe we all are bound to those around us by glue, and to our pasts, and sometimes we need to dissolve it.

Write what you know

I started writing fictional short stories, to help me practice my writing skills, and 'Marie' was my first attempt, about a woman with mental health issues. Or perhaps I was really using my writing to look for the answers about myself, to start picking at that glue.

They say you need to pull all the pieces apart and stand back to see how they fit together. Deconstruction.

But what if then they can't be put back together?

29th January 2009 – Text to Chris – *Amanda and Chris forever xxxxxxx*

29th January 2009 – From Chris - *And ever and ever xxxxxxx*

From: Amanda Green

Sent: 24 February 2009 16:29

To: Chris

Subject: over

We are born alone and die alone, and that is probably the best way for it to be. We're over.

Reply from Chris to Amanda: *If you want some company to commit suicide let me know.*

Strong glue?

I went to see Auntie Agnes's grave and cried for the first time in a long time.

I was thinking about how selflessly she looked after us and how we could turn up any time and she would welcome us. She would cook us dinner and never wanted any help and how liked she was – always receiving flowers – putting them pride of place in the lounge. She got shit from my mother but never let that put her off as she cared for us and saved all her money to give to us. She always wrote to me when I was abroad and missed me when I was away. I visited her but I think she should have got more support when she lost her husband, Albert, and when she got ill. She was ninety-nine when she died and I only twenty-five. We talked a lot. But it was never enough.

She could've helped me find myself again. And I think she would've told me my obsession with Chris was only holding me back.

But she was gone, wasn't she?

A letter was published in another women's magazine, earning me £25 and a writing magazine gave me a critique on 'Marie' which I paid for. They said I had a promising start, but I'd tried to fit too much into a short story.

I guess I've always had too much to say.

Chris and I went to Dudley and did the 'zoo day' (one of my Christmas presents from him) in the snow. It comprised a whole day feeding and meeting animals – from feeding steak straight into a tiger's mouth, feeding milk from a bottle to an Orangutan, flying an owl and feeding lemurs from my shoulder and feeding penguin's fish straight into their mouths to tickling a Tapir; much more than we were due to do on a typical zoo-keeper day, maybe because we were adults. It was fabulous, apart from the Orangutan enclosure, which was in a terrible state, but after two years of emailing them, I was pleased to hear that they had finally secured the budget to build a new one and the female had given birth to a healthy baby.

We stayed in a hotel that had a swing in the bedroom. It was a proper swing, so after a few beers, we had lots of fun swinging so our feet touched the ceiling, videoing ourselves and trying not to fall off.

For Valentine's, Chris flew me to Ostend and made me heart shaped toast for breakfast. He always cooked breakfast anyway, but that was really sweet. (He also did all the cooking, or took me out for meals, and all the tidying and cleaning up, while I did as I liked; writing or talking about my story in all its developmental stages.)

I started watching films more and more that portrayed mental health issues and Chris watched some of them with me. I guess fact and fiction are not so different. I guess I really needed to understand myself.

- **The Saint Of Fort Washington** (Schizophrenia)
- **Angel Baby** (Schizophrenia)
- **A Beautiful Mind** Schizophrenia)
- **Benny And Joon** (Schizophrenia)
- **Girl Interrupted** (Borderline Personality disorder)
- **Prozac Nation** (Depression, but she seemed Borderline to me)
- **Betty Blue** (French film about a young woman with horrendous mood swings and rage and her relationship with her boyfriend)

In some ways these were helpful, but in others, they terrified me; hospitalisations, medications, out of control behaviour. They were ringing bells, memories and thoughts in my head that were spinning me downhill.

I could recognize myself in too many of the characters

I knew I was like them even if I didn't always say it out loud. When I look back I said it enough times, ticked boxes, agreed with the books but I wanted to pretend it wasn't me.

I had reached the end of the line, brushed myself off and started on this journey into myself, but was that enough?

I was writing and researching every day but was I really changing?

A knock at the door – it was Dad. He was back from his skiing holiday, which had been ruined. I'd been worried about him.

After letting him in, he walked in the lounge and I sensed something was wrong, and it wasn't just the bandage round his shoulder and arm. He seemed a little unsteady on his feet.

He said "Hello, I'm back" but his mouth didn't seem to be moving in its usual way.

We greeted him, cheerily, Chris, Mum and I, as Chris had come to our house, and we all sat at the dining table, Dad facing me.

"I had a bit of trouble at Gatwick as you know," he started… but when he spoke I could see clearly that one side of his mouth was drooping, slightly paralyzed, and he was slurring.

I looked at Chris, for acknowledgement of my dad's delirium. He smiled at me. I smiled back. Then I frowned. I saw that my dad's hands were shaking. I needed to get him to continue talking.

He told us that he felt very tired, and when his plane landed at Gatwick, he retrieved his case from the carousel, but he got lost in the airport. He couldn't work out the signs and what they meant, so he kept stopping to ask people the way to the drop off point where his pick up would be waiting. But, every time he walked away with the directions in his head, he had forgotten them. All this information came out slowly and slurred and I began to feel tense with dread. My dad was not a forgetful man.

Mum made us some tea and he spilled it on the table, unable to hold it straight.

"And what about your shoulder, what's going on with that?" I asked.

He had already told us a few days before, when he called us from his hotel in Andorra, that he was steadily skiing with big turns on pristine snow in the sunshine, when he was hit so hard from behind by an out of control snowboarder, he was thrown down the piste landing on his shoulder. The girl who'd collided with him apologised and left he remembers in a daze, and the next thing he knew he was being carried down the piste on a stretcher, by two guys from the emergency services, like I had been when I was a child.

After X-rays it was found that he'd dislocated his shoulder, but the shock of the injury had made him feel very drained and sick and he'd spent nearly all the rest of his holiday bored in his room. At seventy-seven years old, it was a surprise that he had gone on this holiday, but before he left he said to me various times that he didn't feel good about going and didn't really feel like it. I don't always trust my instincts either, and I had wanted to go with him, as I felt something wrong about it too, but I just couldn't afford it. Once he phoned about his accident, I had wanted to go out to be with him, but I couldn't, so I'd had to wait for him to arrive home.

So, back home in the lounge, he continued to tell us snippets about the accident and how he felt, urged by me with question after question, but his answers were fragmented and he seemed to forget what he was saying mid sentence and talked gobbledegook in between.

I had a quick chat with Chris outside to ensure it was not my imagination or over-reaction that clouded my perception of the scene, as sometimes I suffered with delusions, but he agreed that my dad was certainly not himself. He was shaking so much too and was so unsteady on his feet I thought he had the symptoms of someone who'd had a stroke which was on my mind as they had been advertising the symptoms on the TV every day at the time. So, within a few minutes of Dad's arrival home, I phoned the emergency doctor, wasting a quarter of an hour with him. I explained my concerns of a stroke, but he said that he wouldn't come out. I started shouting at him that if anything happened it would be on his head. He said that if I was that worried I should call an ambulance, so I did. I wanted to cry, as I couldn't bear to lose my dad, or for him to be ill, but I forced myself to keep it in so as not to upset my mum who was already fretting and clueless as to what to do.

The paramedics came impressively quickly. Dad was bewildered. I hadn't told him they were coming, but he thought they were there about his shoulder. They didn't find him in any danger, but took him to the hospital, so Chris and I went in his car to meet him there, leaving Mum at home for ease, after reassuring her everything would be OK.

We waited a little while in A&E until Dad was transferred to a temporary bed to be checked by a doctor. Dad was complaining that he was tired and wished he could've just stayed at home. *This bed's uncomfortable. How long are they going to take? I want to go home.* Huffing and puffing, sighing, moaning. I felt so sorry for him as the bed looked like a wood board, and he'd been travelling all day, but he had to be checked over.

The doctor asked him which year the Second World War was. He asked his name and his age. Dad answered correctly. They had various machines attached to Dad, and had been coming and going checking the traces.

The doctor came over to me and said that he couldn't find anything wrong, apart from a temperature and that my dad was OK. I protested: he *is not OK*. I told the doctor that he didn't know what my dad was usually like, but he is a very young seventy-seven year old who has all his faculties. I explained that he was not talking, acting or moving as he usually would. The doctor looked a little puzzled but said that he would take my comments into account.

In the meantime, Chris and I were getting very tired too, as we had been there a couple of hours, hanging out near my dad's bed in the temporary A&E ward, which was far from comfortable. It was around midnight. I felt bad in case I was wasting the hospital's time, but I knew there was something wrong.

The doctor ran more tests then decided to put my dad in a ward and keep him in a few days. They found he had a very bad chest infection and had to be looked after. We accompanied Dad to the 24-hour watch ward where Dad would stay for the night to be surveyed in case he got worse. Poor Dad was left on a bed that didn't look much more comfortable than the first. He was far from happy to have to stay and being a 24-hour ward, it was busy and noisy. I wished I could give him a pair of my earplugs.

The following day Dad was transferred to a normal ward which he shared with five other men, where he was put on an antibiotic drip and he stayed for three days. His shoulder was also X-rayed and held tight with fresh bandages.

Note from Mum – *Dear Amanda, thanks for calling in late, I slept til quarter to three, then off and on till 6am. Please let me know which ward dad is in, is it Woodgrove General. I hope he is feeling a little better. Thank you for what you did for dad love Mum xxxx*

Chris, Mum and I visited him. Mum also went to see him on her own on the bus. Dad had his lunch at one point, and it smelt revolting, turning my stomach, and I thought how horrible it would be to be ill enough to be in hospital and that got me thinking about all the poor, sick people in the surrounding wards and around the world.

When Dad finally arrived home, my brothers called him to see how he was. I heard him say, "Oh it's all Amanda's fault, she put me in there, worrying over nothing." Of course this upset me because Dad had been told he'd had pneumonia after all, but Dad did say to me quietly, "Ah, you care about your Daddy!" I just smiled. What he said was true of course, but I couldn't admit it. We don't communicate such nice things to each other.

I guess what I really realised when Dad was ill was one day we will all be gone.

It was when Chris and I fought around that time I realised that what annoyed me most about Chris was what annoyed me most about Dad.

Maybe it was normal behaviour, but the fact that my dad was willing to section Mum so easily when ill, yet cuss me when I put him in hospital when he had pneumonia, showed how he hated being in hospital and out of control, yet he was always able to offer that hospitalisation and drugs to my mum for years on end.

My black and white thinking was ruining everything, distorting. One minute I was able to see my own problems, accept something *was* wrong – and the next convincing myself there was nothing wrong. One minute someone was nice, the next I hated them. This is one of the reasons doctors find it hard to treat a borderline personality – a person can be out of control, possessive and delusional some days and appear perfectly *normal* functioning, likeable human beings on others.

Through my research, my prognosis seemed terrible, there was no cure. And I appeared to have all nine symptoms of BPD plus Obsessive Compulsive Disorder, anxiety/stress, deep depressions, a lack of self esteem and an underactive thyroid (this is linked to depression and moods) as well as other health issues such as IBS, haemorrhoids and back problems. It all seemed virtually hopeless. But they say ONE THING that helps a person is if they have ever known love and support and I had and I had never forgotten it which I guess is why I held onto what I had with Auntie Agnes.

And my mum and dad.

Mum always loved me, it's just she had her own demons to face and that was harder for her than I could ever imagine; or frighteningly now as I look back, I probably can imagine. In fact I can probably imagine better than anyone.

Now that's some realisation.

I finally found it in me to leave the house and go to my favourite place.

I slammed the front door as I left Mum and Dad's house where I still lived and headed off through the gate.

The air was filled with noise, what with the buses, the industrial estate, cars zooming past down the hill, and women who insist on driving their children to school in 4 by 4's. *Don't they think about the carbon emissions? In this day and age, they should do – it's all over the TV for goodness sake.*

I started with a decent pace, passing my old infant/junior school on my left and I could not wait to get up the hill and have a minutes respite from the concrete jungle. It didn't last long, as the whole town is concrete, except the woods at the top of the hill. I was not so fit, so I had to scramble up the hill. I could have chosen to go right and take the long hill up and round the block, but I took the short, steep hill instead, to get the slog over with.

Hurrying past the rows of semis, a noisy Subaru flew past. *It is so dangerous, driving like that near a school and those silly road bumps they put in a couple of years ago, don't stop the 'boy racers'.* To drown out the noise I turned my iPod on, inserting the speakers in my ears and shuffled through to my number one track *I don't feel like dancing* by the Scissor Sisters. *At least I've got some good music – just not anything else in my life is good right now!*

It took me back, to the summer of 2006, a good year; a good year for music. It was that summer I met Chris and we shared these favourites, dancing round his flat to them as we got drunk, smoked cigarettes and he cooked dinner; good times. We were naïve about each other then. Scissor Sisters, Justin Timberlake, Nelly Furtado and Shakira… I still love listening to them years later.

Trudging up the hill, past the trees, slightly out of breath at the top, I kept up the pace, as I stepped to the beats pumping into my ears through my earphones. I saw a postman, and wondered if that might be 'the job for me', as he can roam around posting, smiling and being a good face of the postal service, but then I think that *not every day is going to be like today and I can't smile every day, or can I? I probably can to others actually. Doing that job would be fine in the warm sun, like this, but not in the cold dark mornings of winter – I'd never get out of bed!*

Onto the busy main road I felt a bit sick, as I inhaled even more exhaust fumes. I began thinking about putting rights to the world and sorting out this global warming thing. *Oh, those poor Orangutan!* I drifted into thoughts of this for a few minutes as I trod the path – arms and legs thrashing back and forth, army fashion. I was on a mission and those thoughts drove me to pick up my pace more and more. *I am angry with the world – but what is new there?*

Stop thinking about it, try to enjoy it! I tried to clear my mind and stay focussed on the present, just as my therapist's told me to. *Use my senses. Smell – well, it stinks of petrol* fumes! Sight – I can see concrete, a Ford Focus, white vans, a young woman pushing a child in a pushchair, with her knickers showing over the top of her skirt, with a crop top... nice. Taste – I can't taste anything. Sound – I can hear cars, vans... that's about it really, lots of traffic noise! Touch – I can feel my feet pounding the concrete and my back hurts, but what's new there... Oh yes, I can feel the warm sun on my face. I stopped to concentrate on that heat, and I felt a little better. I stood for about a minute and indulged myself. *OK, I am ready to move on. There's something positive!*

After another two miles of busy road, I got to my destination, down the lane and to my late Auntie Ag's old bungalow. The lane was much quieter, and a relief. I felt comfort, as I sat on the bench outside, looking at her ex-home, and remembered those good times that happened inside it and in that garden – the meals, the gardening, picking the veggies, the love... And as I sat there, the warmth of that sun was so calming...

I have known real love.

My mum, my dad, my brothers, my auntie. I know that now.

Chris.

They say there is a fine line between love and hate don't they.

But knowing that I have known and do know love is the single biggest power I have.

Borderline Personality Disorder is also known as 'emotionally unstable personality disorder.'

If you have love and support, you have everything you need.

But you have to learn to love yourself first.

And that means seeing yourself – your real self – and then accepting yourself.

Chapter 9

Barriers

Writing my book was still making me feel worse than ever. It was supposed to be my therapy.

I couldn't believe what I was reading about me was true. I thought it was so much better than it really was; that I was more innocent. What was wrong with me? I knew going through reflecting on it would be bad, but not as bad as it became.

I suppose I didn't see it all happening, how using my journals was opening wounds, picking slowly at the glue and while I knew I was ill and I had a name for it I was still in and out of denial, even then. I was learning all there was about the illness and still wondering if they got it right; if that was really me? I exhausted myself, and I see that in my writings here, the way I changed from moment to moment. A yo-yo of acceptance and denial. No wonder I was so exhausted. It's exhausting just to read it. Maybe that will help to paint a more accurate picture of what it was really like. For me. For those around me. And let's face it, it wasn't just BPD as I kept reminding myself.

I was writing my story and wondering who she was; the child, the young girl, the woman I read about. My alien self? And all this time I was throwing myself into building my new projects, my websites, my writing. And capturing my whole journey in writing.

I guess as one part of a person unravels, another is formed. Like I was holding my life together as best I could while the other end fell apart. But it was too late to stop now. This was my journey back to me. The closing of *Pandora's Box*.

Another magazine asked to use my photos of the Bornean Proboscis Monkeys. Of course I said yes. I even had some published in a photography book. Chris took me on 'photography' day trips in the car.

So it seemed my photography publishing was taking off, but I needed a goal, to keep it all together. What I needed was to get some writing published outside of my own websites. I don't know if it occurred to me then how much of what I was doing and what I was learning about me might be something someone else wanted to hear, or if the story of this stranger I was rediscovering, might actually be something that other people would relate to. I suppose then it was about me, perhaps I wanted to find out that I wasn't ill, that I didn't have BPD. Me? Not me. I wasn't like any of those people in the books or the films I watched. No. Not me. Not Amanda G.

But I was getting to be a good writer through all of this and maybe that was my future? The websites, the photographs, animals... maybe I would be so busy recreating this new Amanda G I didn't need to think about the old one?

I guess it would be a while before I could see what I was really learning.

But learning I was.

Although Chris and I watched lots of films, around this time, when we were not out eating or holidaying, or working, we were also watching *Benidorm* and *Gavin and Stacey* and they helped us to keep laughing, through the arguments and horrors.

My mental health campaign was also building, as I started to get involved in supporting mental health charities and organisations. It was all there... my past, my future, I had so much to offer... it's just a pity I didn't always see it for myself.

A pity that, with all of this, I was hiding it from the people around me, as if I was different.

I am still alone with my diagnosis

One in four of us will experience some form of mental health issue in our lives. Actually I think, with today's fast paced, stressful environment and economy, there are probably even more than that, but many people live with mental health issues without even knowing it. They think it's just a side-effect of their busy emotional lives. And maybe some just don't want to admit to it; the way I didn't want to be like my mum. And when I think of what she had to go though, all those terrible treatments, it was no wonder. It's different now, but those images of people in sanatoriums, having shock therapy and never being the same again: that lives on and haunts us still. We don't want to be like that. Who would?

But there is nothing to be ashamed of with mental health issues – they should be treated just the same as any physical illness: a diagnosis, a treatment, a prognosis. It is no less the fault of the sufferer than a bout of influenza. But it's always difficult when the condition comes in so many guises, many that look to the untrained eye as just being human and emotional, and OK maybe out of control sometimes. I guess this is the crux of what I had to struggle with. Was it an illness or was that just me? My personality? Was I a bad person or was I ill? But then the condition BPD even insinuated it was a disorder of my personality. And it was, it is, just that and it's time we all stood still and tried to understand that.

But this inability to accept the illness, and when you do, for other people to accept it, can really hinder recovery. It is very hard to talk about with others as they may either not understand the problem or not want to understand the problem, least of all talk about it. This can make life for a sufferer a very lonely place and I experienced a whole spectrum of reactions when I first decided to talk about it after all those years of silence.

Having depression or mental illness doesn't mean you're mad or antisocial – on the contrary, many sufferers are kind-hearted and docile. The media doesn't help either. For example, they have been known to suggest a person with Schizophrenia is violent and a menace to society, which is utter rubbish. In fact, sufferers are more likely to harm themselves than others and are usually not violent at all. Mental health illnesses portrayed in film and news are most often sensationalised, and sadly this impacts on belief and augments the stigma. Yes, I was violent at times, but usually because I was drunk as well and I am not typical.

Education is what's needed to help more people understand what it really feels like to suffer with depression and other mental health disorders. It is real. We are not making it up. Look at my journey, I didn't want it, I don't want it. I denied I even had it. So do you really think I'd want to tell people I had it, if I didn't?

The stigma is real. The more I tried to 'come out' and talk to people about my problems, the more alienated I felt. People would change the subject, telling me to *get a grip*, (would they say that to a cancer sufferer?) And these were from people that were supposed to care about me. It was a very difficult barrier to overcome: I wanted to share my experiences, tell them how lonely and desolate I felt, how much I wanted to be dead really – I wanted to let people know so that they could help me, but how? What *was* the right platform for it?

When I sought help professionally, the obstacle became the way I looked – because I 'look alright' I can't be too bad. Yes, I do look alright – my skin does not portray the years of angst, turmoil, drugs and alcohol abuse - but if I was not *alright* I would stay indoors, as I often did, unable to get out for days. No-one would see me when I was not alright. But this is no reason to ignore someone's pleas for help.

People 'discriminate' against others with mental health problems and therefore are in effect confirming that the 'stigma' is true and correct, yet it clearly is not.
Something really needs to be done to ensure that this attitude changes for the benefit of all.

I would like to suggest that we take another stance on our thoughts on mental health, and realise that those who suffer from one also need care and charity from others, and some understanding for who they are. They are just like you, apart from some of the things they think or feel, but they are not bad people or mad people.

And those with a problem need to speak out and tell others, so that they can be supported, and not hide away and worry about what others will think or how they will react – there is a lot of support out there, it's just a case of finding the 'right' type for you. Of course that's all very easy to say but when your illness itself makes you scared and insecure - how do you ask for help? Or even recognise you need it when, as you have read, my mind was a yoyo of highs and lows. Saying you'll get help, you'll change, you accept you have an illness is one thing but what if the illness makes you deny it doesn't exist and you're fine the next day?

<u>What can **you** do to help?</u>

Whether you suffer from a mental illness, know someone who does or just want to dispel the stigma and understand…

- Learn about the issues/symptoms of some illnesses – watch a film portraying mental illness, read a book – a memoir written by a sufferer or an informative book (you have already taken that step), look on websites or in libraries.
- You could watch films which are based on mental health issues, such as *A Beautiful Mind* or *Bennie and Joon*. They can be very therapeutic and educational, although please note that some are not totally correct in their portrayal of all symptoms and are sensationalised. A very useful website I have found is http://cinematherapy.com/filmindex/mentalillness (as viewed in March 2012) On this website you can click on the mental illness you wish to see a film based upon, and they come up with a list where you can find out more about the movie descriptions. Don't just be shocked by the behaviours you see, try to empathise.
- Help others you know with a mental health problem – friends or family – be more understanding and supportive. This can be difficult at times, as the symptoms of some illnesses can affect you directly too, or can be difficult to understand, but be patient – it will be worth it in the end!
- Bring it up in conversation with others – you never know, you might just be giving someone a chance to open up to you who has issues – but getting people talking can help iron out myths and educate.
- Visit one of the charity websites and find out other ways you can help – MIND, Time to Change or Rethink in the UK.
- If you have a mental health issue, talk to others – your doctor, a therapist, a friend, your family or one of the charities– don't stay silent – get help! And don't give up!

The famous have power

So many celebrities now are 'coming out' and talking about their experiences with mental health conditions, which is a great way to bring it to the public. It can help raise awareness, although I do find it hard to accept so many celebrities talking of suffering with depression and Bipolar, like they are acceptable, but not owning up to having Schizophrenia or Borderline Personality Disorder. Statistics will tell you that there ARE celebrities with these illnesses, yet who are they and why don't they talk about it – come out? Because of the stigma of those two illnesses in particular, that is why. Mentally ill people can be extremely creative and successful, so I wonder who is hiding their diagnoses. I plan to campaign somehow to try to get some celebrities to talk. To help dispel all stigma.

Knowledge is also power

I talked to my brother about how much people knew about Mum's illness and how it seemed they ignored her. He said Mum never mixed well with people of a similar age to herself, and has tended to gravitate towards older people; those who accepted her for who she was. The fact that Mum didn't talk to other Mums could be either she didn't want to or she didn't see what was happening. Maybe she thought if you don't talk about it it's not real? But that makes me like her.

David said something else too. He said you couldn't always trust Mum's version of events. Maybe she remembered things differently. And that made me think about me, reading my journals, wondering who my alien self was... so as I keep saying and will say again - were we really so different? Mum and me?

I remember how some of the kids at school got to know that Mum had been an inpatient in Hinton Hall and how that made me feel, what they used to say. This is why I feel the stigma is unfair for people with mental health issues and I am supporting http://www.time-to-change.org.uk through my website. They are dedicated to changing peoples' views on others with mental illness, trying to beat the stigma and educating people into understanding and accepting those who are suffering.

Aren't we all a little bit mad?

The UK BBC TV soap *EastEnders* did a lot to bring awareness about mental health issues and the character Stacey and her mum's Bipolar share similarities with my own struggle. As I also watched Stacey I realised how similar I was: desperate, needing attention, drugs, drink, depressed, excitable, confused, having affairs, needing sex and men, unable to cope at times, all leading to paranoia and anxiety which led to psychosis and loneliness... similarities to me, except.... she killed someone... which is not a portrayal of Bipolar, as, I will repeat, a percentage of people with mental health problems want to harm or kill themselves, but not others. However, it did remind me of a day I felt like stabbing Chris. Not that I would've done it, but the thought was there to shut him up from telling me I was mad, and that was scary. I always thought I was Bipolar like the fictional Stacey and her mum in the show and I did even discuss it with my psychiatrist later on. Stacey's mum's Bipolar blighted Stacey's childhood, where she had to look after her mum and herself instead of the other way round. Watching would make me cringe, cry and laugh at different times, and I would feel uncomfortable in a way sitting next to my mum who's an avid *EastEnders* fan, watching something so similar to us being played out on the screen and not being able to talk about it with her. Stacey became my favourite character because I could relate to her and I think her illness was portrayed quite well.

TV shows like this and, in fact, with the way media is even more a part of our modern living with social networking, we really have no excuse not to be more informed. And TV shows I believe have a responsibility to portray mental illness in a way that is accurate and informative and shows like *EastEnders* with considerable ratings will and should go a long way to help dispel this stigma.

Chapter 10

We are all obsessed

Obsession has always been part of my life: from the incessant diary entries to writing my story. I have used that obsession in a positive way in detailing every event of my life, as presented here, but obsession can also be debilitating. Living with OCD is not easy and OCD is common as a co-disorder, in BPD sufferers.

Some useful terms

- **Obsession** – this is a constant fear or worry about something in the mind which can become overwhelming. This might be a fear that our actions may lead to harming another person
- **Anxiety** – thinking about this obsession over and over can bring anxiety and panic
- **Compulsion** – to reduce the anxiety and panic, one might stop going out to avoid causing any harm. This is a compulsive action carried out to try to relieve ones worries.
- **Temporary relief** – this compulsive behaviour may help at the time to relieve the anxiety and panic, but the obsession will come back and one has to continue the compulsive behaviour in order to relieve oneself again. It is a vicious cycle which cannot seem to be broken.

We can all have worries or suspicions but many people can think about them logically and dissolve them with explanation or positive action. Those people can get on with their lives and put their worries to the side. But for others with OCD the thoughts, obsessions do not stop and what's more others may form a perpetual cycle of rituals and routines, the only way to stay safe.

Fear of leaving the oven on, setting the house on fire, harming others through your actions, cleanliness issues, or a need for perfection are a few traits.

Often a sufferer will know that the compulsive behaviours are not logical, therefore they are not psychotic, but they can't stop. For me, when I finally moved into a flat of my own again, an example would be to think I hadn't locked the door when I left the house. I would have to go back to the house, no matter what time of day or night, to check that it was locked, even though I knew it was. Or, I would think that a glass near a window would set the house alight because the sun would shine through it and cause fire. I knew that these things were not viable, yet I absolutely *had* to go back home to check, no matter where I was. Every time I did, the door was locked and there was no fire, but it didn't stop me from going through the same process again and again. I'd even have to get Chris out of bed at 2am to drive me home to check. He wouldn't argue either, as he knew there was no point – he couldn't talk sense into me.

No one really knows what causes OCD; it can run in families. An increased blood flow in the brain has been found in people affected with OCD which returned to normal after successful treatment and recovery.

The neurotransmitter chemical, Serotonin, which transmits information from one brain cell to another has been increased with certain anti-depressant medications, and has helped recovery from OCD symptoms.

Stress can make OCD symptoms worse and adverse life events can bring OCD on in those with a tendency for OCD.

If loved ones reassure an OCD sufferer that they did turn the oven off or did lock the door, for example, this can lead to the sufferer not getting the outside help they need to recover.

Diagnosis

It's not easy telling your doctor about symptoms that might sound ridiculous, but you must. It's essential to discuss it with a doctor to find the right treatment. This is also important with family or friends. I did both of those things. There is nothing to be ashamed of and this illness can become very destructive and hopeless if not treated and can be very long term.

OCD severity – how much do your symptoms affect your ability to function on a day to day basis

- If obsessive thinking and compulsive behaviour occupy less than one hour of your day = mild, if they occupy one to three hours of your day = moderate and if they occupy more than three hours of your day = severe.

Treatment

Cognitive Behavioural therapy (CBT) and Serotonin reuptake inhibitors (SSRI's) anti-depressants are best known to treat OCD – the intensity of treatments will depend on how severe the symptoms are. If necessary, anti-psychotics may also be prescribed as well as the above.

CBT works as 'Exposure and response prevention' which is basically working on a variety of situations and examples that cause the anxiety, obsession and compulsion. One has to experience the situation that causes their obsession/compulsion but NOT to carry out the compulsion. So, for me, it would be to NOT go home and check that the door is locked. Stay out and try to forget about it, challenge it and when I get home, to find that it was locked and it was OK not to go back earlier will gradually help my brain to stop the obsession forming. It essentially dissolves the belief, therefore the obsession. One has to prioritise each obsession and work on each one until they are diminished.

Depression can co-occur with OCD (and BPD as well) and if the depression becomes severe the sufferer may sometimes have suicidal feelings. It is VERY important to get help, support and treatment.

Like many other aspects of BPD and indeed any mental illness, it's about a continuum, with what might be seen as normal at one end, how to normally deal with the situation, and then at the other spinning out of control, that's when it becomes clinical and when it needs addressing. And why we often deny, *we all have these oddities, it's OK, I can control it...* but can you? Do you know when it's no longer *normal?*

We all have obsessions

My eldest brother was obsessed with religion and his wife's desires.

My middle brother was obsessed with how his wife behaved. She rarely did or said anything right, according to him.

My youngest brother was once obsessed with body pumping and steroids, driving fast and fighting.

Mum was obsessed in other ways; hers had a name, like mine.

Dad was obsessed with... what? Making sure Mum was OK, making sure we were OK. But is that obsession or is that love?

Like all the other symptoms of BPD on their own, or to a lesser degree we can all perhaps recognise ourselves in those behaviours. But it's when you put them together and when you see just how far I would take them.

I used to count.

I used to count everything – steps as I walked along, and pavement squares. That started when I was little and was trying to keep up with my dad's steps. He'd hold my hand walking along in town. We'd be alone, don't know why. But the counting the steps continued for years even without my dad there. Counting other things too; words in my head, words I would say over and over in my head.

I didn't notice the compulsions because I blocked them out

I was a perfectionist. I needed everything done in a certain way and if it wasn't perfect I'd reject it, like the garage leaking in the flat, meant I had to sell the flat. I was afraid of fire. I would salute magpies and not walk on three drains in a row having to do things three times for luck, like taking three lots of toilet paper, or touching things three times…odd things obsessions, as you don't really realise you have them until they are pointed out or you catch yourself doing them one day.

It was only during my therapies I began to realise the full extent of them. As I made my list of 'Amanda's mental symptoms' these things were all added over time and I realised just how many of them I had. The more I wrote my book, wrote about my illness, wrote about my symptoms, the more it became apparent just how OCD I was. No wonder I felt mentally and physically worn out! It became clear that having constant conversations with myself, going over and over thoughts and worries, having all those routines and habits were wearing enough by themselves, and that's without any of the other symptoms of BPD or depression. But, some of these things were tackled last since they were not the priority on my list of symptoms. When I realised how destructive my daily task lists had been I stopped doing them. But I had many more to eradicate and that was to be sorted out later on. I didn't want to continue with my internal conversations, my hair playing, my nervousness, but I decided that anger, rapid mood swings and my fear of abandonment were much more important and should be dealt with first.

Control, but no cure

I still do some of these things. I play with my hair, twiddle it endlessly annoying everyone I know. And there are the obsessive dreams; recurring ones about being chased and *they* are catching up, or I am paralysed but awake and hearing what's going on around me, but I can't wake up. We will all relate, in one way or the other to these I'm sure.

Some obsessions come and go, some sit deeper in our brains. So deep it seems we can't shake them off, often stress and depression act as triggers. Some obsessions are more like 'habits'. All the same, it is wearing to have them and repeatedly worry about them or practise them. But it was a part of recognising me, and it is a part of me – still.

Like all facets of my illness it's about control. I control them; they don't control me

I was slowly discovering who I was and why. And I was slowly moving forwards.

A couple more wildlife magazines printed my photos from Borneo and I could see I was getting addicted to being published. Another obsession? Or maybe it just fed my self esteem.

Thankfully my book was going well, but it will come as no surprise that I was obsessed with it. There was much to plough through – emails, texts, letters, photos, boxes of mementos – it was never ending and hard work. It was hard because I had to get everything in order of date, tonnes of it, all those bits of paper, then read them, then type them ALL up, sort all the photos into order, printed and digital, sort all the emails out and paste them in, write up hundreds and hundreds of SMS texts, read all the letters again, typing up whole diaries, sometimes with one day equalling a whole page; years and years of them, taking months and months to plough through, then sorting out what I wanted in my story, or what was useful to my self therapy, then cutting, and cutting and adding and adding, and narrating and cutting... a huge job that took so long because I wouldn't let one note go, EVERYTHING had to be logged on the computer in my book word documents – hundreds and hundreds of documents, postcards, little notes, a whole life written up, then trying to find a way to turn those hundreds of thousands of words into a story that people could read cohesively– then writing scenes, going back in time and writing hundreds of pieces about different times and events and people, going back and remembering; feeling, tasting, smelling, visualising and listening – triggering all my senses from the past, trying to relive them in the present so I could write them down.

It made me more ill; getting lost in the past, but with sheer determination to beat my demons – I was not going to give up. I knew it was going to hurt, but nothing prepared me for the pain. When I think of it now I am pretty amazed I got through it on my own. And I was on my own by this time. No Roger, no counsellor. I had no-one around to talk to who could understand – I mean *really* understand. And I mean it when I say I do not recommend looking back as the best way to cope. It doesn't work for everyone.

Look at what I had to go through.

My brother Ian told me so many times to stop writing my book because he could see that I was feeling worse even from the other side of the world – he didn't know how bad I was, but he still cared. I knew he was right but there were two things I couldn't let go – I had to get myself better and I couldn't give up on the biggest commitment I have ever made – I had to finish my book, and by doing so I would prove so much to myself about my inner strength and dedication – I was not going to fail this one, I had failed too many times and this was my chance to prove myself and help myself.

I was researching my disorders, reading mental health memoirs, reading books that told me I had no hope of cure. And I was taking this out on Chris, who despite everything was still around. And he still went from telling me I am a *crazy fucking bitch* to being wonderful.

BUT, I also got lost in my writing. It wasn't all bad. Slowly, sometimes one step forward and another two back but slowly, slowly I was getting better and so was my writing. I was achieving and I was keeping very busy.

I'd started another four week writing course at the college and I was loving it: *creative writing*. I would read my work out and get feedback, whilst learning new skills. We concentrated on writing short stories, and how to get them published. This led me to writing a few more short stories; another route to self-expression.

I decided to write letters to everyone important in my life: friends, family even therapists. I would write a separate letter every day and I told them everything I wanted to say.

But these are things I could never say directly to them. Perhaps some time in the future I'll repeat the exercise to see if I feel better about them. Since I felt so negatively about most people, I thought it would be a good way to analyse whether I have beaten my negativity.

I wrote, be it the letters or my book every day. I turned off the internet (unless needed for research), emails, and anything else that might distract me. I taught myself not to try to do many things all at the same time, to concentrate on one at a time. I won. I taught myself to stop writing massive lists and work on goals that I could achieve. It helped my daily stress levels no end. I was changing things little by little – destructive habits and behaviours. I needed to change, I knew that. I needed to cope better with life and to stop running.

    I needed to look at it differently.   And I was.

Chapter 11

Don't just look: see

I will not take drugs. That was a pledge I made with myself.

I will not drink. But that one I knew I would break.

I would not use tranquilisers: How could I find myself if I was absent?

Sometimes, I wanted to go into hospital, to see what it was like and felt that it might have given me the break that I needed, but I was too scared.

As far as I could see, it is about what you do tell the doctors, and also what you don't tell them that moulded their decisions. Had Chris not been there, at my appointments, I would have probably been smiling all the time and making light of the situation and my problems as usual. Maybe one of the symptoms of BPD was acting.

Where was my OSCAR then?

I would ask myself so many questions. Was it them? Was it Chris? My ex-boyfriends, friends, family who have the problems or was it me? It was a rhetorical question even if I didn't want to admit it.

None of us are perfect. If it was time for me to finally open my eyes and see what was really there... then they needed to do the same.

Because it was never all me.

And I guess understanding that was part of my journey back to myself.

It depended how I felt on the day as to how I progressed. I could feel really down, excited, or suicidal. I would think everyone cared or no one did. Sometimes I wanted to die sometimes I wanted to live. But this changed daily or hourly. I even wondered what it would be like to swap my life with someone else. I have a feeling even what seems on the outside to be the most perfect lives will have scars and cracks. We are all broken.

Who has the perfect life?

My journey of self- discovery really started that day Dr Jones said to me... start at the beginning. Only this time I had my eyes wide open and instead of just looking... this time I *really* saw.

June 2009

A secret hell – that was my life.

No-one understood me.

Thank God for my websites. Without them, I would have to go to work. But I was done with all of that.

Journal: 25th June

Mum and I are similar in many ways. We go for ice cream, coffee and a walk down the seafront after and bump into one of Mum's friends who has had cancer and she is with her disabled son who stares at me and my body.

Chris has disappeared. He kept calling me because of this morning, and crying and wanting to know if I was finishing it with him or not.

I just watched a programme on celebrities pretending to be homeless so they could mix with people that were really homeless, and they all dealt with it differently. Heroin, alcohol, prostitution – one of them said that he wished he could hang (and he would do it himself) all the murderers/rippers and put the money for pensioners and homeless – our money is being wasted on prisoners he said. I felt sad and ashamed in a way that I mostly ignore people begging on the streets. I decided not to anymore. 129 k people are in the homeless hostels and that was their next 3 night stay.

The next morning I confronted Chris.

"Where did you go last night?"

"I was out."

"Where?"

"A couple of places."

"Where?"

"The Bull and The Cornfield."

"Who with?"

"No-one. I bumped into a couple of people…"

"Well, now I am going to get you for ruining my evening and turning your phone off, you piece of shit – I will make you suffer today."

Silence, so I put the phone down.

How was any of that helping me?

David wanted a couple of examples of why I suddenly accepted that I did have BPD, when I finally told him about it on the phone. But had I accepted it? If I had, I would say it was gradual, no single defining moment; no point in time when I could say this is it, or that I could hinge my book around. Enlightenment, if that's what it was, was slow, some days I accepted it, some days I didn't.

I told David of the abandonment – if Chris wanted to do anything without me I phoned, texted, threatened, and hit and abused him. I think David was surprised. I also talked of my drinking every night and sometimes during the day. And that's when he said something I wasn't expecting. He said what if he was borderline too? I don't know if he meant it or was joking but I shrugged it off, but I suppose it was possible. He said the drinking part sounded fun though. Then I told him how sometimes I wanted to die.

And I told him I could get so depressed it engulfed me, like a tidal wave and I couldn't see a way out.

And I told him nothing about BPD was fun.

He laughed and suggested anyone would be depressed still living with their parents.

I supposed he wanted to understand.

But he wasn't like me. He wasn't. Really.

Over the years I have managed to talk to my brothers about what they thought of me as I was growing up, as the adult I became.

They told me I took too many holidays. But still never seemed happy with life. I was moody at times, always playing with my hair. Seemed unable to stick with boyfriends or jobs, or settle down. I guess what I really wanted to know was if they ever thought I was like Mum. What I hadn't realised was what they were most afraid of was if *they* were like her. Just as David had said he could well have BPD. Maybe he *was* serious then? I felt sad that he was still in Australia as we couldn't talk about it all properly.

Peter said that growing up with Mum as she was had a very negative effect on him, at times, but he never really said any more than that. My other brothers said more, and they told me they did see problems in my behaviour but they had no idea of the intensity of them or what really happened in my life. They still don't know much. Only my book will really show them what it was like for me. The odd thing is I am sharing all this with people I will never meet, and my brothers are right there and I can't really say it.

Chapter 12

Discovery

I was like a sponge. I loved to watch documentaries about people, animals, nature, illnesses crime, anything.

I also loved to watch all kinds of films; horror, thriller, romance, real life experiences, comedies.

Journal:

I am watching a documentary about a hospital accident emergency department in London. Video cameras run round the clock for a 24 hour period capturing the doctors, nurses and staff efforts and the patient experiences, stories and illnesses or accidents. There are drunk people falling over and hurting themselves, there is someone shot in the head, there is someone who's been stabbed in the stomach. There is also a young boy who has been thrown off his bike into a wall, hit by a car. All sorts. This programme is a real life look into the world of the emergency services. The boy's head is being supported by moulded blocks so that he cannot move it. His body is lifeless. He is very sick the doctors keep saying. He needs every effort by the staff to keep him alive so that he can be operated on and fixed. Traumatic. Rush, rush, trauma; they are all so professional and I admire their ability to keep calm and how they know exactly what to do. I respect them for taking that kind of job and for studying for all those years to help others. It is humbling.

I lie on my sofa, my stomach tensed, tears dripping from my eyes down my face, I begin to sob. Poor boy, he must survive, he is too young to die.

Later I lie on my bed and I think my life is over. My life isn't worth living. I am a bad person. No-one would miss me if I died. Everything is doomed. How can I die? Can I do it? I cannot cope. I must do something about this. How can I be so unhappy when my life is not so bad? What is wrong with me? Oh shit! Think of people worse off than me... I think of all the people in poverty around the world and how lucky I am to have a western world life, medical services and a roof over my head. I think how people are struggling everywhere, and in every way – disease, famine and corrupted governments. Suffering everywhere. I visualise the scenes. So sad. Devastating. So many people unable to help themselves. Babies born to die, Mothers unable to feed them, clean them. Awful. I know all this vividly because it makes me cry whenever I read about it or see it on the TV. I always donate some money for Red nose day, or other major charitable events. I have to do my bit. I cannot sit and watch it and do nothing. I cannot directly help them all so a donation is the least I can do. Then I think back to the Orangutan, and I remember that I am trying to help them with my awareness campaign on my websites, and the adoption schemes I go in for. Then my thoughts turn dark again, as I imagine the little Orangutan babies running scared as their mother is shot and killed by poachers as they cling on. It must be so scary for the vulnerable little primates, suddenly orphaned. I start sobbing again. This world is shit. Life is shit. Why are there so many bad things going on in the world? I hate this world, humans are bad...

I try to think of those suffering more than me again, so that I can appreciate my place in life, but it just makes me sob uncontrollably in despair. Maybe my ability to have empathy comes from this ability to really put myself into people's situations and scenes, I can taste, feel, see what they do. Destructive for me in a way. Mum and Dad are going to die before me. I cannot cope with that loss. I want to go first, so I don't have to. I can imagine my reaction. It doesn't bear thinking about. I cannot be left behind. And my brothers, will they die? Poor Ian with his epilepsy and going deaf. Why him? He doesn't deserve it. And David keeps getting health scares. And Peter is stressed and underweight. And I am so unhappy. I've been happy, why can't I be now? What is wrong with me? What did I do to deserve this? I should be happy, I can't understand it. Fuck it! No, I cannot think about this anymore. I feel sick. I am a bad person and I don't deserve to be here. What do I do for anyone? Nothing! I pour another glass of wine. I am going to get drunk. That will make me feel different, even if not better. Feeling different, drunk, fuzzy in the head is better than feeling like I do now. I have a plan. I am going to do some work on my websites and get very drunk indeed.

12 Things About Me

Jolly

Angry

Sad

Lonely

Persistent

Selfish

Hard

Loving

Cuddly

Pessimistic

Controlling

Childish

Chris

Selfish

Controlling

Caring

Thoughtful

Hard

Tidy

Responsible

Relaxed

Adventurous

Positive

Dad

Responsible

Caring

Strength

Worker

Routine

Positive

Wastes money

Gullible

Giving

Normal people – do not live like this

My life was full of contradictions. One minute I could fool everyone and myself that I was fine, and the next remember that I was far from fine. I could convince myself that I wanted one thing, and then when I got it, or nearly had it, I didn't want it. Control was what I wanted. I wanted everything my way. I wanted it when I wanted it. I wanted people to behave how I wanted them to. But no-one wants to be controlled – not really.

I think realising this was a big turning point.

I don't want to waste my life and die

Many doctors do not believe you can recover from BPD. Particularly, as they say, when combined with other anxiety based mental problems – in my case, depression, panic attacks and obsessive compulsive tendencies.

I was soaking up all this knowledge and writing all these lists and ideas and what I was and how I got there. I was talking to my brothers. I was doing all of that and yet really, deep down I *still* saw myself as a lost cause,

But I was wrong.

Chapter 13

Mission Statement: 'To feel better and be happier in life'

I wrote a mission statement at this time, my way forward and I was going to stick to it: I was going to face my demons and I was going to do it by finishing this book. What I knew was finishing it, completing something, was part of my journey, and by sharing my journey I might just help others.

And perhaps I wouldn't feel as if I was taking that journey alone.

Writing my story from beginning to present would finally 'get it all out of my system' and into some understandable order, so I could move on with my new life. I knew if I were to look NOT at the disorders, but at symptoms, one by one, prioritising their importance, then I could tackle them. If I was to look at BPD, OCD and depression and accept them all, then I would have given myself a life sentence of hell.

You cannot fly until you have learned to walk

And I told myself: *If my plan changes, that will happen and I will not change this book, as it is a journey that you are on with me. If I change round what happens, it will be even more disjointed than it already is, and so here it is... Maybe I won't even ever publish it – be too scared, too daunted by the outcome...*

Chapter 14

Good and bad

These diary extracts show though how my moods could change like the weather. A mission statement was one thing, but what about the bad days?

Journal: 8th August 2009

It's ten past four on Saturday afternoon. I'm at Chris's I'm listening to the sounds from outside. Out the back, I can hear children playing. I go to look out the front of the flat, on the seafront. I can see sun, blue skies, clouds, beach, sea, people swimming, sunbathing, chilling out, and walking along. They look summery in their little dresses, shorts and t-shirts and it is very warm out. I feel fucking awful. I feel like dying, I feel like giving up.

16th August 2009 – *I want to die. I want the arguments with Chris to stop. I want to stop living in this tiny room at my parents.*

All at the same time I was conversing with David as he, Linda and Alfie were coming back to live in the UK, but even that didn't cheer me up.

Paranoia can stem from the simplest things

Looking at the blackboard menu, the words 'mackerel, ' home-made soup', 'grilled plaice', 'belly of pork' glowed in white chalk, as my mouth filled with saliva.

"MMMMM, let's eat here tonight, shall we?" suggested Chris, embracing me with a kiss.

I looked around me at the lunchtime diners. "Don't do that in here!" I told him knowingly, pushing him away gently.

Smirking, we turned to seek the table we desired and gave our booking details to the barman. We visited Arundel castle for the afternoon and bathed and dolled up we headed down to the pub for our long awaited dinner. Settled in our requested table, it took about ten minutes to choose the wine from the fabulous listing. All set, and food ordered, we relaxed and took in our surroundings.

"Ahhh, we aren't sitting together tonight – I can't touch you up," said Chris turning his bottom lip over so that I could see the inside of his mouth. *Bless him!*

"No, we aren't, but it makes a change as we always sit side by side. Most people sit opposite each other anyway and I can see you better like this..."

"...Cor, that guy's fish looks fabulous," I said energetically, as a nearby diner was served his meal.

Arching his neck round Chris caught view of the man's plate and took a long look.

"Alright!" I said abruptly. "No need to stare."

Chris brought his head back to our table and said "Yum!"

We talked about the group of people behind Chris – why they were there, what they looked like, whether they were enjoying themselves. We ate loads, drank loads, giggled when the waitress accidently threw the man with the nice fish dish's coffee all over him, we discussed what to do the next day and how we were going to watch X Factor later on the ITV website as we had missed it by dining out (we would usually watch it in the room and go for a late Indian if we are staying away, such was our dedication to the programme). We also talked about lots of other things like my family, comparisons to other restaurants, our favourite wines and general stuff with plenty of laughs here and there. I have always said how sad it is to see couples out for dinner saying nothing – how could you have nothing to say? We always had something to say.

The whole restaurant was busy apart from two tables for two. One was by the restaurant entrance and had lots of space around it, and the other was right behind me. A couple came in and chose the latter table and I braced myself to deal with this. I had hoped no-one would sit there.

The man sat on the opposite side, and the woman sat right behind my chair. As she tried to settle herself in, she kept knocking my chair, and I decided it was on purpose.

"What's wrong?" Chris asked me. "You look vacant," and I realised that I had stopped laughing and smiling and chatting.

"Oh nothing," I replied, and forced a smile. "Carry on, what were you saying?" and I leant back in my chair and flicked my hair.

The woman behind me now had her chair right up against mine and I could feel every small movement she made. This was not comfortable, but she was not going to win. I flicked my hair several times more.

I wanted to go to the toilet for around an hour before we eventually left the restaurant, but I couldn't move - I wanted to stay put. I did it too; what an achievement! Thought me.

I cannot really remember what Chris and I spoke about after the couple behind me came in and sat down, but we did have a dessert and more wine and I remember Chris saying that he "Can't work out why your mood has changed…" and he didn't seem to be enjoying himself anymore. Later that evening, we argued and went to bed not cuddling. I never liked it when we didn't cuddle.

Another time Chris and I went to a Cantonese restaurant, argued with the rude manager and later I convinced myself they were Chinese mafia – and they were going to 'get' us… And every time I heard a siren, I felt a pang of fear, thinking it was police coming for me, even if I hadn't done anything wrong.

Why do I always feel like I'm being watched?

Journal: August 2009

Public places, dancing in a nightclub, standing talking or eating a meal. So many times I cannot enjoy myself as I am so aware of what I am doing out of my body, like watching myself and convinced that I am being watched. Perhaps this is why I prefer to see one friend at a time – there's less pressure. It also might be a perfectly good reason why I always get drunk so much or took drugs in the past, as they made me uninhibited.

Writing in my diary, as a child, was my way to let out my thoughts, and if something disturbed me, I could write it down and forget about it – it would be gone, dealt with. It was an escape and a saviour; a hobby, yet a secret. Everything was internalised and dealt with by me. I'd write them in my room, in bed usually, writing fast and furious with my biro pen into a variety of diaries. I kept them under the bed, in carrier bags and later on, locked them into a hard cased suitcase in Mum and Dad's loft, so they've certainly been protected. Ten years after the first one was written, I made a 'pact' with my best friend at the time, Jane, to burn them should I die. My life has always been one big secret.

Moods swing like pendulums...

I live at home with my parents. It doesn't feel like home – nowhere does. I live in a tiny bedroom, where everything is in a mess, it has some damp and you get those wood lice coming in and crawling on my single bed. I hate it, It's noisy because it's near an Industrial Estate. So much traffic: buses and lorries and it never stops. I wish I hadn't moved back. I wish I could live happily ever after with Chris.

I want a home of my own. I want a cat. I want my own space

I told Chris I want to kill myself again today, just like yesterday. These phases of depression and suicidal thoughts did not last long; minutes or hours

I remembered the statistics... 2% of the population have BPD.

10% of BPD sufferers commit suicide.

And what's more, BPD sufferers also make up 20% of all psychiatric hospitalisations.

I am always on the edge. Life is the border.

Chris found out that I could get a referral from my doctor to a 'Community Mental Health Team' who would give me an assessment by another psychiatrist and treatment.

Apparently, there was to be a new thing in place that would mean that you do not need a referral from your GP to get mental health help and it is called Improved Access to Psychiatric Treatment (IAPT). This was after my doctor (GP) said I wouldn't get help as I wouldn't be high on the list due to looking alright and I wasn't a drug addict.

On 20th August 2009, a year after my initial diagnosis, I got a referral to the Community Mental Health Team. Chris insisted I needed more help; that what I was doing wasn't enough, that I wasn't moving forwards. That I wasn't getting better, I was getting worse. It was OK to write lists and missions statements about what I was supposed to do. It was another to do it. I had been advertising Mind, Time to Change and Rethink on my website, since April, as a place to go for help for everyone else yet I hadn't asked them for help myself.

14th September

Went to the appointment with the Psychiatric Nurse at Clinton.

An hour's interview went fairly well. I took my list of symptoms. I was a little nervous as it was a mental health NHS place, but I was a bit late so I only waited one or two minutes. We went into a small room with four low seats and talked, while he took notes. I talked a lot and told everything I could. He asked if I was 'jealous/thought about suicide and how my concentration was/promiscuity/the rape/the drug taking/how I sleep/how I eat and how much I drink now and I told him I was very angry and changeable and about Dr Jones and Borderline. He also asked about the help my mum gets and I said none now but she had been in and out of hospital for twenty years. I said I was scared at how similar my behaviour is to hers and that I am scared of taking medical drugs and hospitalisation. He asked only a few questions and advised that it was not a diagnostic session but an assessment. They have various routes to go down afterwards, such as CBT, counselling, psychology or a psychiatrist, depending on what the patient needs. He said that he couldn't make a choice right at that moment, as it has to be discussed next Monday at their meeting, where psychiatric nurses, psychologists, psychiatrists and counsellors all get together to discuss their weekly business and current patients. They would make a joint decision on my case and although he said that he doesn't predict anything to a patient, as it could be seen as a false promise, he did say that he expected it was best for me to see a Psychiatrist in order to discuss the many problems I have in more detail.

We said goodbye and he will call me next Monday or Tuesday to let me know what they think. I told him that I find it easy to cover things up with my persona but that I came there because I am 'desperate'

28th September

Dad and I decided it best that I write my book anonymously. He doesn't know all that it's about, but I guess he gets the gist, since I told him it was a memoir about me.

14th October

Went to see a new psychiatrist, Dr Singh. I got there on time, I could hardly believe it! He seemed OK, but he kept looking at the clock above my head. We only had 45 minutes, so I guess he had to hurry up. He already had my notes and so asked me how I am right now. I told him that I am quite good today – not happy, but not angry or sad or depressed. I am looking forward to doing some work on my websites and going to college tonight on my creative writing course. I told him that this was a good day and that my bad days were quite different.

"*I feel like I am two different people – one that is happy and fun and wants to go out, and eat well, drink good wine, and chat a lot. The other one who is miserable and wants to die or is angry and violent*"

"*Are you like this with everyone?*"

"*No - my boyfriend mostly. I love him one minute and hate him the next.*"

"*I see.*" *Dr Singh was quickly scribbling notes and I realised that there must be quite a few 'stories of Amanda Green' around, since I have told the same stuff to so many different therapists and doctors. I wished, once again, that they could swap notes and save me the trouble. He asked me to tell him when I first decided that I have a mental health problem. I said it was a year ago that I accepted it, but knew there were problems long before that.*

I take out my anger on Chris because he's there

He wanted to know about all my previous therapies. He asked about the diagnosis of 'borderline' and what had been recommended. I told him 'Quietapine' anti-psychotics and 'CAT' therapy. He asked if I took any medication for depression or the Quietapine, and I told him that I started with some anti-depressants a few years ago, but I didn't get on with them and I was too scared of drugs to continue with them or try the Quietapine. I told him of my mother and her treatments and her hospitalisations and my experience at the hospitals as a child, and I cried when I told him. I said that I was scared as I had seen her suffering her problems and treatment which is very true.

Then we got onto some other stuff; my sleeping pattern?

The stress in my belly and beating in my ears keep me awake

Do I take recreational drugs now?

"No. I stopped ten years ago and have only had them a couple of times since"

"How much do you drink?"

"I have half a bottle of wine every day, up to a bottle of wine on a bad day" (although I can drink two bottles on a bad day actually, but I didn't tell him that).

"Do you think that is OK?"

"No, I think it is too much"

He asked me to go through my life, which I did in chronological order, but very rushed, as he continued to glance at the clock and hurried me up at times...

"Sorry but can you talk faster, as we only have a short space of time..."

So, I rushed through it. At least he is not £250 per hour. Lucky I have been concentrating on my life, as I wouldn't have even got to 10 years old in that time. But all that happened was that I told him what I had done in my life, brought out the dieting, self harming, drugs and running away abroad, and not much else. He asked me about my work and I told him enthusiastically about my websites.

"Well, I don't think you need any drugs. You are scared of taking them anyway and you don't need them. You are not bi-polar or schizophrenic, as your state of mind does not stay bad for very long. Bipolar's have the mood swings but they stay good or bad for longer. You do not. You get stressed with what is going on around you. You are obviously smart, and are getting on with life generally. I think you could benefit from some CBT to help you. You may have a personality disorder and stress, but it can be helped with therapy."

So, that was that.

I felt numb. I questioned him on this simple outcome, but didn't really ask much more and I didn't get much of a reply and he didn't really think I had a problem, although he said he would see me in a couple of months to check on me. I shook his hand and left.

As I went to my car, I realised what he had done. He'd released me from a 'mental illness'. He'd told me I don't have one. So, I am OK. I will have to write this in my book. Should I now change my book? Although rather than my book, I felt relieved and self assured about 'not having a mental illness'. So Chris can get fucked telling me I am ill all the time. I am OK.

But I knew that wasn't true.

Chapter 15

What I was and who I am

So there I was: ridiculous, crazy, unhappy, excitable but hiding behind the mask of a strong confident woman.

Reading my diaries and all the other stuff offered me a good understanding, but it was hard. *Really hard.* But I had to do it, because that's when I saw me... and what I was, and how I acted around Chris. I saw the child and I saw where that behaviour started.

But to get to the real roots I knew I needed to dig even deeper.

What was a positive, though, was that late August had brought my brother, David, home for a one year trial of living in the UK. Linda went almost straight into work and David remained the stay at home dad. They moved into a flat just half hour drive from me so I saw them quite a bit – during the day and for dinner. Alfie loved it and we soon became close. He would get very excited when his auntie Amanda came round and it gave me purpose once again.

October 2009

I wondered if I would ever make it to the end of my book.

What if I died first?

What if I killed myself?

Then, I'd think about that. I'd examine it. I'd pull it apart. I'd live it in my mind – the whole scenario of death as I could, as I was able to imagine it. Then I realised that wouldn't happen to me; I was not in that 10%. No matter how many times I willed it, longed for it – the quiet peace of not living, not worrying and all that stuff – I realised that I was too strong to give up. I also lived the emotions that it would put my family under, at my funeral, realising I killed myself.

I would use the symptoms, the obsessions, the passion, the all-consuming need to show the world who I really was. I would turn it on its head and make it work – for me.

So there I was, the real me: trying to help save the Orangutan, lifting the mental health stigma, sharing my views, stories, photos and experiences with others, and most of all, most *of all* I was sharing the experiences of living with a mental health disorder, first hand, with those in this world who needed to hear it. I knew the purpose, what I was supposed to do with my book – writing it to help myself and others - and I was. I was doing it only I couldn't always see it.

Do you see now?

I wanted so much for my experience of the madness I knew to benefit others; that the idea of it being to no avail, would make my life seem almost worthless. That is why I knew I would finish it; I would get to the end of telling my story and that in doing so I would find myself. Maybe there isn't such a thing as *happy ever after*…but it's a great way to focus the ending of a story.

And my life.

You can have a cold and call it flu, or you can have a cold and get on with it.

You can control your mind: positive or negative.

You can say I can't do it. Or you can say you can.

You will.

You did it.

How well do you know yourself?

It's selfish to die.

That's what my family, my old friends, my boyfriends might have said about me.

You're self-obsessed, Amanda, they might say if they wrote a letter about me as I did about them.

Maybe.

But I could use that; to help other people understand. It was an illness but it was also about being human.

Mixed in with the horrors of the problems in my head, were fun times, laughs, adventures, serious discussions, friendly gestures and motivational actions just like normal peoples happiness – condensed into short spasms. This leads to intense highs a third of the time, massive lows just under a third of the time, and the rest of the time a *relative normality*

So there it is: a snapshot of me – the real me. That is who I am and how I live.

Take me as I am

I did some research about who might publish my memoir.

I took a mental health test online to prove I was normal. It didn't.

I will help myself

27th October 2009 *We had a blazing row in the morning and I hit Chris loads of times because he wouldn't shut up. He dumped me again, told me to fuck off and took me home in silence. Then he went to see his mate so I texted him abuse. Horrible day in some respects, but I took the day off and went out with Mum for lunch and then tea outside at Clinton castle (Salvation Army café). It was a nice day out and sunny. Then went home and Dad cooked roast chicken and I got drunk. Didn't do work, but watched TV.*

29th October 2009 *Spoke to Chris and we are going out for an Indian*

30th November 2009 – *Woke at 7, no more sleep – too stressed about Chris. Debbie* (my school friend) *came to see me, we had lunch out and chatted about her pregnancy, being a mum, making the decision to be a mum (as I am nearly out of my mind on making this decision whether I would like children or not at times and whether I was worthy and capable) and it got me thinking. I was quite wired through lack of sleep and too much drink lately, and it went by in a flash and she was going again. Every second is gone just like that. As I write this word, as you read this word, those seconds have now gone, and we cannot get them back.*

I showed dad one of my published pieces in a magazine. He didn't read it or look at it properly – he just glanced, as usual and asked, "Are you getting paid for it"

I found that very aggravating as I am trying to get published and known and it will not happen in five minutes, sometimes I get paid sometimes not, but to him if I'm not paid it's not a job and it's not worth anything. Of course it's not just him, many writers, artists and others will come across this negativity. But life is not all about money

I worried all the time that I kept feeling worse because I was dragging up the past – instead of healing, I was re-living.

Journal: 29th January 2010

I am in a complete state, screaming abuse, hitting things and wanting to break and throw everything in sight – I hurt myself again, punching the arm of my chair as I sit here in total disruption and anger. Another screaming match today with Chris – I am used to it now – him pulling on my weak points and me pulling on his. All he had to do was get divorced in the two years that I committed to him. It's been more than three years now! Ok, I was a bit abusive from the very beginning, and he has been at times, but he stayed with me, just like most of my boyfriends have wanted to stay with me, but my gosh this one has upset me – is this what love does to you? I realise this is the only person I have loved properly as a boyfriend, so I don't think I like love – it is too hurtful, too difficult, too everything! It just adds to the rollercoaster I have been on and off for years. I want to get off and stay off for good – I am sick of riding and feeling sick, claustrophobic and trapped – extraordinarily happy one minute and wanting to kill myself the next.

I WILL get better and BE NORMAL again.

But my self therapy, it got harder. I sought solace in the memoirs I continued to read about other peoples' journeys, both identifying with how they coped, feeling less alone and also encouraged that in the muddle of false starts and a tumultuous relationship there was a place of control and I could get better. And not only that my journey, like those I was reading about, might make others feel less alone as well.

If I could get to the end.

Sometimes I had the TV on for company while I wrote, some trash, some decent programmes...

Jeremy Kyle said today that too many people blame the past for their current behaviours

But are we not all shaped by our pasts? And isn't that knowledge, that appreciation of how we got here a way to unlock it and get better? What I learnt when I worked in the prison was that many of those who had committed crimes had been brought up by parents who did drugs, didn't work, stole, had little money. I know this is not always the case but it is a common one and everyone has to take responsibility for themselves as an adult. Patterns are often formed when we're young. Children are moulded by their caregivers, usually their parents, and they learn their ethics from those people. Too often it is a vicious circle – bad parenting, bad child, becomes bad parent, has a bad child. I know this is a simplification, but life and people are not simple. And for me, while I was no criminal I was shaped by my past. While I can blame some of that on living with a mentally ill mother, I also knew what I was doing.

No one made me sleep with all those men or take drugs. We do have to take control of ourselves and there is an argument for everything.

In the end all actions have consequences.

It was always easier to write the bad bits

Shouting, screaming, pacing, accusing, texts, phone calls to Chris – mobile and work. I could've stopped it, but I didn't. I remember my hypnotherapist telling me that I have to change.

It was the day before the Easter break, and Chris was busy at his work.

Journal: 1st April 2010

He took 4 ½ hours cooking his bloody lamb casserole last night, and by the time we had it, several glasses of wine and nicotine fuelled smoke from cigarettes had passed my lips, basically numbing my taste buds with a film over my tongue and upsetting my stomach in the process, so I felt immediate indigestion on trying to eat his pride and joy feast. He knows full well that if I don't eat when I am hungry my stomach will bloat with air as my IBS takes hold and then I will be uncomfortable and in pain all the rest of the night and will need hot water bottles, paracetamol and I will be moody. It happens every time, so why doesn't one of us learn? Also, today I felt a little trapped in his flat. I'm staying round there again for a bit. I feel trapped as I often have done, and something holds me back, doesn't allow me to get out and do something nice, even when the sun is shining. The sun hasn't shone much for two weeks, and this winter of 09/10 has been so dull, cold, long, rainy and snowy, that I, like many others I know and don't know, have had enough of it. It has zapped me in its own right. It has nothing to do with BPD, bipolar, mental health or anything else – it is natural.

I can't help but feel upset by the lack of support given by Chris at times. He reads my life story stuff and understands more and more my problems, yet he seems to throw it back in my face when we argue and uses it against me, knowing how to get at me and upset me the most. He sympathises at times, but usually when I don't want sympathy.

I want empathy not sympathy

He feeds me, but at times that he wants to eat, not considering me and my stomach or wellbeing on many occasions. He says *"If you are nice to me, I will be good to you"* but what does that do? I have problems and cannot always be good. I told him *"I can get myself better, but I cannot work miracles"* so many times I lose count, and I am getting better, but I cannot be good all of the time. It is a disease that I need to control at all times. It hasn't gone away, it's controlled by me and it needs constant diligence and effort to control, as the habits are so deeply rooted. I have done so well, and I will continue to. I learnt that it is not about what others do, it is about how you react, and that is what I am still working on. But Chris finds it hard to empathise; to really think how I am feeling, a depression, a panic attack, a bout of paranoia – it is so strange to him that even with careful description sometimes he just cannot get it. He just sees ludicrous behaviour and says that no-one else would do it, least of all him. He only sees it from his own point of view. But he's not me, I am unique as we all are, that is the point!

I feel resentful that Chris wanted me to take those pills – those atypical antipsychotic tranquilizers. I don't want that shit in my body; taking over my brain. I didn't want to change my brain matter, and turn into someone else who may need drugs forever to keep calm. I'd just be numbed, sedated, but not fixed. Only I can do that from the inside. Drugs cannot change habits or behaviours. I also hate the way he compares me to my mother. I hate it. Why keep doing it? Whilst I am repairing my lost soul for once, why do that? He is not all bad, and in many ways he is a great support, but diplomatic he is not as he blurts out stuff that he doesn't mean but that hurts me, and he knows it. I do it too, but I am the sick one right? And I now admit it to myself and him.

March 2010

Mother's Day was an effort.

It was my idea and a late one at that, but I mulled it over with Chris, who remained open to anything, and gave my mum the offer of a meal out at the carvery or he would cook at his flat. She chose the latter, as it would make a change for her. We picked her up, albeit about an hour late and I think she felt a bit let down as she had been waiting in her coat before the scheduled pick up time; eager I guess. Anyhow, I did call her to let her know and we took her back to the flat where I, on my mission to uncover all the past, went through some old photos of Auntie Agnes and Nanna, not remembering at the time that she had never really liked them. Lunch was a quick affair, where she got us to serve her from the bowls of food one small plate of chicken, chips and salad, and that is all she ate. Mum doesn't eat a varied menu – chips, roasts, meat, salad, carrots, fruit, cakes, sweets and crisps just about sums it up. We had Pouilly Fuisse which we all liked. A very good wine. Too good for the occasion? Nah. She started falling asleep on the sofa. I let her. Chris and I smoked cigarettes on the balcony, and I crashed on the other sofa, not making as much effort as usual admittedly. Mum then got up, and stated that she was going home, by bus (we had joked earlier about her getting a bus home, but you can never joke with Mother) so we managed to sort it out to take her home with some effort. I was very relieved to leave her there and escape back to Chris's... It is what I'd call a negative Mother's Day. I would usually take her out on my own, or with Dad, we'd have a nice meal, I would give her a lovely card, have a bouquet delivered to her house to make her feel special, and take real notice of her; not the usual half listening and being too busy malarkey (that I did all the time with mum and dad and then felt guilty about afterwards), but really concentrate on her as it was her day. It's just that this one was different. Was that because Mum was different? Or me? I think the latter.

We go out together regularly

Mum shows me off when we are out 'this is my daughter' and she loves it when people say that I look like her. She likes feeling younger than she is and hanging out with me, going in pubs, for walks, out shopping. Sometimes when she has a lie-in she says what a waste of time it was, wasting the day being asleep and other times she says that 'oh at least it made the day go quicker.' She likes Chris as well, and we surprised Mum and Dad on their holiday in Spain, knocking at their hotel door. Chris flew us all to the Isle of Wight for their 50th Wedding Anniversary, and we gave Mum a good start to her coach holiday in Devon, turning up at her hotel before her coach got there and staying for dinner, one night and the next day. She loves all that.

Is it time to go to Oz again?

Journal: April 2010

So, here I am in prêt a manger – just stuffed myself on a tuna baguette and tomato soup and now onto the cappuccino. I got a free muffin too, but I can't eat that. It is busy in here. I got a table by myself and am sitting here happily typing. Well, not happy, but typing anyway. I have often thought about this – sitting in coffee shops writing. I am a writer and I write in coffee shops. That is cool! Perhaps I should do this more often. It is inspiring because of all the noise and people I think. Music is playing but the hum of conversation is overpowering it, so if you tried to concentrate, you wouldn't know which to listen to. A tramp outside was being clocked by police earlier. Whilst here supping on my hot tasty soup, he was out there barely able to get up from the concrete floor. What sort of an existence is that? I am lucky. Am I? Maybe he is happier than me – maybe not. Where does he go to the toilet? What does he eat and drink? How does he get his money? What a state to get into, but it is rife here in London.

Two girls on the train earlier were chatting about her nephew perhaps – Harry his name – born 6llbs 4 oz. He is gorgeous apparently and his mother breastfeeds him. The conversation was sweet and they seemed happy girls. I think how I was like them once. I sat there wallowing in my misery of how shit I am, and how shit Chris is whilst listening to the jolly banter. It was nice to listen to, but I was a little jealous of them and the woman with the baby they were talking about.

So, off to the passport office soon to get my new ten-year passport renewal. I've had to make a big trip for this because it is such a last minute decision. It is exciting really. I wonder *whether to go to see Billy Elliot over the road this afternoon as I have a four hour wait before I can pick it up. Should I treat myself – will I feel lonely in there? Will people stare at me on my own? What else am I going to do anyway though? I might just go and ask about it and how much it is if I can drum up the confidence. I don't have to go in even if I do enquire. You never know – watch this space!*

I have a good window seat here. There are people sitting outside, as it's quite warm and dry at the moment – at last after that shitty long cold winter! To my left, people are sitting and I can see right across to two streets. Lights, red buses, people rushing, all colours, all creeds. Busy busy busy. In front of me stands the Victoria Palace theatre with the big Billy Elliot sign. There's a Garfunkels and loads of other restaurants and shops. Busy Victoria!

I've been sat here ages now, and I just don't care – I would stay longer but I have to go soon for my first appointment. I hope it all goes ok. I'm sure it will. Shall I go to Oz then? That is the question. Or do I stay here, get a job and move out with the money I now have, care of Chris? (he gave it to me to go to Australia with) I must evaluate this and not jump in without thinking, like I always do. I can't spend too much more money without thinking or it will be a waste.

This self therapy isn't working as fast as I would like it to. Should I get more therapy – what to do? Perhaps I will evaluate whilst away from everyone and everything and see how I feel in one month's time. I can then restart my book, and hopefully I can look at it in a different way. Right now, I would write it and make myself look really bad, as everyone is telling me how shit I am throughout the years – they can't all be wrong can they? What if they are right? What if I am really bad and there is no hope to get better? What if I am trapped in this hideous mood swing forever?

Dad spoke to me about Australia. I don't know why, but we'd often have a chat about me, my boyfriends and my life, since I was a teenager. He tried to advise me each time, despite the fact that I often didn't act on his ideas. He took a little time out one evening and I explained the mess I was in. He said that he realised that I had issues with all my boyfriends and always have done. He agreed that it would be nice for me to see my family and to get away from my problems, namely Chris.

David was not so encouraging. I told him once the trip was already booked – he said I shouldn't be spending money on holidays, but trying to sort myself out – but he did think it was for the best to get away from Chris (he didn't know Chris was paying for me to go despite our recent split which I told everyone about). I think all my brothers had mixed feelings about the trip, same as Dad. I guess they all saw the repeating patterns in me – get a job, leave a job, get a boyfriend, have problems, take responsibility, then run away. But Ian had suggested it during our last phone call. I told him I felt like dying. He thought I should try to make a new life in Oz.

But maybe this would make me see a life without Chris? And that is what happened. I *could* do things without him.

I was away for five weeks in all and was reading an American book on BPD during the trip; *The Borderline Personality Disorder Survival Guide* as well as parts of *Borderline Personality Disorder for Dummies*.

We look for answers in all kinds of places

My mind was so full of questions. I was supposed to enjoy Australia for a few weeks, cycling, walking, spending time at the beach on my own. But instead I couldn't stop worrying about what I would do when I got home and what my future would hold. It was hard to stay in the 'present' and I should have used my mindfulness techniques, but I forgot. I did go out with Elsa for bike rides and days out to see an aquarium and zoo, and at the weekend we all went out to theme parks, on train rides and much more, but otherwise I stayed in and wrote some of my book or read my BPD book, hanging out with Michelle and the children she looked after as her job was day care at their home. But the questions about my future kept on coming, from me, in my head and from my brother. Did I want children was one of them.

But I had no answers.

Then Michelle told me about a psychic she'd been to see who did tarot readings and looked at your health. So I went, armed with photos of Chris and all my questions.

She found my spasms in my gut (IBS) and the tension in my shoulders. She said she could see me ferreting in and out of a suitcase constantly – yes, going from Mum and Dad's to Chris's every few days, as I had done for the past three years. She said that I was quite a fun person and *go go go*, no sitting around, bouncing from here to there. I could be creative if I allowed the time to focus – I flit about. I like to be in charge, in control, that everything is how it should be, my tendency is to be organised but also disorganised as time is a big issue to me, and I don't have time – everything's got to be 'now.'

She told me I needed to use my heart to work out my relationship for the big changes she predicted were ahead of me. She said I'd gone as low as I'm going to go and that I would be brighter and have new perspectives from then on. But I had to change my thoughts because the constant questioning was draining. I was to empower myself to deal with the change and the loss of a relationship.

She also talked about my parents.

How much they loved me, and how I could release my pain and my fears to the angels and ask them to take care of that. She said my parents did the best they could in the circumstances and they loved me the only way they knew how, so if I can forgive them, I would not carry it around anymore.

Cancel, clear, delete – clear the mind of negative thoughts, as we can put out negative ideas and it can attract them too – don't allow them to come into my space.

I came out of that appointment calm yet shocked at how much of what was said was true and how positive the whole thing had been. It helped me to feel good about the future and gave me extra strength and conviction that everything was going to be alright.

It was so lovely to see everyone on that trip. I had missed them so much. And I had missed five years of my niece growing up who I'd been so close to. She loved having her auntie there and I loved being an auntie. And I felt so responsible taking her out on my own, given my recent behaviour issues. Ian and Michelle couldn't believe we could spend so long just hanging out at places and chatting. And apart from the odd worry about driving their car, albeit my very good driving record, the only paranoia I had was when we went to an adventure park. We were shown macadamia nut trees, and the guide broke some open and gave one to Elsa which she ate. I then was convinced that he had HIV and he may have a cut hand and gave my niece HIV. It bugged me for days as I panicked thinking it would be entirely my fault if she got HIV and died.

Chapter 16

You gain control, and then you lose it...

I started on Chris at his work and his home and terrorised him for three days by telephone. I had only been back from Australia a week.

Then Mum sent me overboard with comments about not being able to put the washing out and she couldn't use the spin dryer, because I was in the conservatory on my computer next to it. It wasn't true. Of course I would let her do as she pleased in her own home. I flipped. It didn't take a whole lot.

"Don't you fucking lie, you can do as you like. You're just trying to cause trouble," I screamed at her just a few inches from her face. I'd been away from it all for five weeks. I was sick of placating and just couldn't keep doing it; always having to ignore and accept her bad moods, doing things to please her, pandering to her, cheering her up, Dad telling me to do it, walking on eggshells, letting her get her own way all the time, protecting her from issues, listening to her being nasty to my dad and making him unhappy... on and on. I was exhausted with it all.

I spoke to Chris about it on the phone and he invited me to his for the night, despite my being horrible to him. Next day, I went back to Mum and Dad's to pack as Chris and I had booked to go to York for a few days. Dad was in. I tried to avoid him.

He said hello quietly and slammed the door to the bathroom, while I packed my case in my bedroom. Then we argued without even looking at each other – him in his bedroom, me in mine.

"Oh, by the way, I understand you had a go at Mum yesterday?" he called out.

"What? Oh yes, kind of…"

"She said you were right in her face, being really nasty and I'm not having it."

"She started it, and I am not putting up with her shit anymore."

"I don't care, you'll have to pack it in, do you understand? I get it in the neck and I am not having it."

"It's disgusting! You get it *in the neck* without doing anything anyway!"

"Well, if you don't like it, then move out."

"Yeah, I bloody well will."

"Good."

He went downstairs.

I shouted: "Since I pay you forty pounds a week, when I'm hardly ever here or on holiday, I expect a little more respect, not all this fucking shit!"

"MMMMMM, you can keep your swearing for Chris, he seems to like it and comes back for more."

"Just as well I've got someone eh, there's no-one in this house on my side."

"Well, you always have Chris to fall back on."

"Yeah."

I flew down the stairs to tell him that what I had done to Mum the day before was the same as I had experienced many times as an innocent child when she was horrible to me and to him, and it was because of the two of them that I was like I was. He was nowhere to be seen. Chris turned up while I was looking for Dad, through the bloody back gate, which Dad doesn't like and I had asked Chris many times not to do, but I didn't say anything. I told him what had happened and he got my stuff in the car and we headed off to York for a few days in his plane, where, despite arguments and issues during the trip, we had fun and made time to chat about my situation at home.

Chris said calmly that I could move in with him, if that would help. I took him up on his offer, and didn't go back home, although I only took a few things with me and left most of my belongings there. Despite spending half my life staying at Chris's home for so long, that time I vowed would be different.

I had been paying Dad £40 a week towards bills and food, and I continued to, just as he continued to take it from the kitchen table where I would leave it on a weekly basis. But having been away for a few months, what with Australia and living at Chris's, I didn't think I should keep paying £40 per week just to keep my stuff in his house. So, many months after I moved in with Chris, I left Dad a note on the kitchen table stating that I should now pay only £20 and couldn't afford to keep paying £40. Storage at a storage centre would be cheaper. Dad soon sent me an email in reply:

From: Dad

Sent: 25 October 2010 21:45:34

To: Amanda

Subject: storage

Amanda,

I received your small note via Mum. It would appear that after two requests to come round for an informal chat (about your situation) you cannot be bothered, although you have had plenty of time. Well Well.

Reference this so called storage. This is not on. Let me remind you that when you came back to us last time it was initially for about six months to a year till you sorted yourself out. How long has it actually been, quite a few years now.

I have actually lost track. As you said in one of your very short notes you have been away for the best part of six months and I will accept £20 per week as you are pleading poverty.

Under the circumstances I feel it would be best all round that you move your belongings to a suitable depository and I suggest 6 months to do this. This will bring it up to end of April 2011 which I think is very fair.

By the way what happened about the job you were going to get mentioned just before Xmas last year?

Love

Dad

x x

I decided I didn't like my dad anymore. I continued to live at Chris's and that was fine with me. I was better for a while after that.

Then I had another argument with Chris.

Things were changing, between us. Somehow I felt less scared of being on my own. I realised that, no matter what he or my dad said, I was getting better. And I was doing it by myself. Other people couldn't see it so well, since most of my torture was happening in my mind and they didn't know the half of that anyway. But I could see it, feel it; very clearly. It seemed that Dad and Chris were the two people that held me back though, and I would be much better without them. Maybe that was extreme, but who the 'fuck' were they to tell me what and who I was and what was wrong with me?

I came to see myself in a way I hadn't before. As if I was able to see my real personality, my true self. Bubbly, kind hearted, reliable, putting myself in other people's shoes, capable of learning and a good friend and lover.

I wrote down my more negative personality traits and how I might work on those aspects of me. Like messed up relationships, jealousy, inability to deal with emotions, out of control reactions, impulsive behaviour, self-destruction, depression, suicidal thoughts...

I decided that by working on these undesirable traits, and eradicating them from myself, I would be left with a pretty nice person, who I could be proud of with a happy future. This extensive list has the traits I attributed to my different conditions – the BPD, the OCD, the depression. This was, and still does serve as my guide, and my check list. This is listed in the

Further Reading section of the end of this book. What it enabled me to do was one by one, pick off the traits, learn to change ... until I found me.

And amongst everything else I found my happy memories.

I would video take offs and landings when Chris flew us places in his plane, so we'd have memories of his flying – you never know when you won't be able to fly anymore.

"Oh wow, this is fabulous," I cooed into the headphone microphone, as I scrambled for my camera.

Only Chris could hear me, as we were in his aeroplane – a four seat Cessna 172 and we were 'coming into land' at La Rochelle, France, Chris calm as ever at the controls. He had cleared his path to land with the control tower through the radio system, and as long as he wasn't talking to important people involved in our trip through the sky, he and I could exchange conversation though our headsets.

"Lovely," he replied, smiling and squeezing my leg. The view was marvellous; azure blue skies, occasional puffy white clouds and dark blue sea. The visibility was so good everything at ground level had vivid detail. A bridge stretched out in front of us, across the water, which led to a narrow strip of land to our right – an Island called the Il de Re – and the mainland of France spread out to our left, and the city of La Rochelle. Being a coastal airport, the landing route took us into a left turn, so I could take one of my best aerial videos of the entire landing. I loved to video landings, each one caught on film forever. Chris liked me doing it. He was always busy when landing, getting the levels and direction right, talking to air traffic control and sorting out where to park once we hit the ground. When he got time, he watched them on the laptop once I downloaded them. I told him he can keep them forever and if the time comes he cannot pilot his plane any longer, he will always have lots of mementos.

Although not every trip was a happy landing.

I went on a writing course/retreat and my mind was full of questions, anticipation and fear of being left alone without Chris. Chris flew me there is his Cessna, it was down in Devon, which would make the trip more interesting and not as long, so as to help my aching back from the immobility of a long car ride. I kept myself busy photographing any and all villages and towns along the route, and when the clouds became too thick to see below us, in front of us or indeed anything outside our car interior sized cockpit going through the air at 100 mph I'd bury myself into reading something or staring at the controls in panic. It was true, I was a nervous passenger and I worked hard on stopping my panic attacks. Sometimes all I could think of was opening the door and jumping out, moments of terror fuelled by adrenalin. I'd fly through the air at speed towards the ground, and then nothing.

I'd be gone forever. Why did I think that way?

Except on that trip to Devon, it almost happened.

It took a while to find the tiny farm air strip near the village I would stay in, but once we spotted it we were soon coming in to land. I was doing my usual scanning of the inside of the cockpit with the video camera, Chris at the controls, and the green country views outside. It looked beautiful, with small hills, lots of farmland and plenty of green space – so different from home. Holding the camera up high coming in to land, I realised the strip of land was running out and we were not even on the ground yet. But we were so low, all I could see was the row of high trees coming up fast in line with us. Shit! I dropped the camera, I couldn't look, *we are going to die*. I couldn't speak or move with my head bowed and eyes closed, ready for impact.

Quick incline. The engine working hard.

Going up again.

Oh Oh Oh.

We hadn't hit anything. I held the camera in the air to log our crash in case the camera survived the impact.

But no impact, we climbed.

I looked up feebly.

Yes we were up, I could see the sky ahead, we were up, up, up. I could breathe again. We didn't crash. We are up, but Chris was turning left to have another go.

"Can't we land somewhere else, Chris?" I asked softly with a hint of begging.

"No, no, we can land here, it's no problem…"

Oh God.

It's a shame I'd panicked and dropped the camera. Watching the video you see the trees ahead, then the floor of the plane and then us skimming the tops of the trees by just about two feet as we go over them. You can see the urgency that was needed in that split second decision to miss our landing and ascend. But Chris was as cool and calm as any pilot should be and the odd bad weather scare or small issue never phased him.

My pilot, my hero.

You are part of me, Chris. You help me breathe

But what I never said then, or when I was flying, and felt free... was maybe that what I really needed was something I could never say.

Maybe I needed him to set me free.

Chapter 17

Whatever it takes

It was August 2010 when I finally decided to try anti-psychotic drugs, like the doctor had advised two years previously ... a small dose of Quetiapine. I was still living at Chris's flat, so I felt that he could keep an eye on me for side effects or problems.

Quetiapine – began 50mg August 2010

When I first started taking it I felt suicidal. And I was always tired. I took it at night, but always woke up with a foggy head. I would sleep an average of ten hours a day, but could have slept more. I'd have very vivid dreams.

During the day I wanted to sleep. I was depressed – sleeping stopped me thinking. I suffered dizziness sometimes. I doubled my dose as advised to 100mg which would lead me up to 200mg, but it was too much to bear and within three days I was feeling so suicidal and so hopeless I reduced the dose back to 50mg. I had read that these were possible side-effects.

On the whole, the drugs did help my paranoia and anxiety. I was able to eat in restaurants without thinking everyone was looking at me and talking about me. I felt more able to tackle my depression. Slight weight gain (1/2 stone) but when I doubled my dose, I lost a few pounds as I stopped wanting to eat.

Other side effects...

Nightmares

Some insomnia but mainly too much sleep

Pain in legs/stiffness and tingling

Sleepiness and lethargy

Blocked nose

Foggy head

Still paranoid about little things

Feeling weak

Add to this the symptoms of my illness:

<u>Emotion dysregulation</u>

Unstable emotions and mood swings – happy, angry, sad – changed rapidly on an emotional rollercoaster

- Easily stressed
- Unable to take criticism
- Take offence to things people say or do.

Intense or out of control anger –

- Hurt myself
- Hurt Chris

- Throw things
- Shouting/screaming
- Angry with myself and punished and blame others
- Cannot stand traffic, noise and other annoyances – become out of control at very small things

Interpersonal dysregulation

A regular pattern of unstable and intense personal relationships

- Lost friends – my choice
- Happy to hate
- Rollercoaster
- Good/bad, black/white, love/hate – nothing in between – no grey
- Conflict
- Fights (physical/emotional abuse)

Overwhelming fear of abandonment

Annoyed and sad and lonely when abandoned

Behavioural dysregulation

Impulsivity that can lead to self harm

- Spend money
- Drive fast
- Alcohol - lots

- Smoking

Suicidal or self-harm thoughts or actions

- Suicidal threats and behaviour
- Self harmed in the past, but hit objects with my hand now and drink, smoke and stay in to punish myself or don't eat properly.

Self and identity dysregulation

Variable self image

- Personas, pleaser, fit in
- Doing different websites/interests – forever changing them
- I was always changing jobs even when I was good at them
- Different vocabulary and behaviours with others depending on who they are
- No clear future, but getting better
- Lack of confidence
- Cut my hair off to change who I am
- Change my clothes often (style) to suit how I feel
- Loss of self – don't trust myself and my thoughts at times and often change what I think – no balanced view
- Always moving around – don't 'belong' anywhere.

Feeling empty inside like there is no hope

- Empty/void/feel unreal sometimes (not myself)

- Feel worthless and blank

Cognitive dysregulation

On reaching high stress levels, paranoid thoughts or dissociative symptoms can occur

When stressed or upset I:

- Can be paranoid about what others think
- Paranoid what others might do to harm me
- Suspicious and negative consume me so that I believe the stories and thoughts in my head to be true
- Worried that people are looking at me and judging me
- Feel as if nothing is real under stress, bordering on mild psychosis

September 2010

1st September 2010 – *I realise today that Chris cannot cope with me anymore. He gets annoyed and is paranoid that I will flip at the slightest thing. It's clear that in allowing Chris to lie to me about so many things for four years and get away with it, has done nothing but encourage him to continue doing it as he'll get away with it. It's too late now and he will never change. As I know you just have to want to change.*

Australia proved I can live without Chris

My writing course showed I could go places on my own

So maybe I could live on my own too? But where?

I wrote down: Clinton or Spain? I could stay or I could run away again.

I am not perfect.

>Guilt has often driven me to be good to my mum.

>I have very few photos of her.

>Writing my life healed me. I could feel it working. As if it was slowly releasing me from my past, my interrupted therapies, my moods, and let me concentrate on today and tomorrow and what I had then. I had something to give.

I'll always keep 10% of my heart to myself, just to be sure.

Journal: 23rd September 2010

I think I am going mad. I hate, and yes I mean it this time, hate Chris.

I'm going to get away.

A woman called Sofia contacted me about a local event for 'Mental Health Day'. After a few emails were exchanged, it transpired that she was in the same psychiatric hospital as my mum and she started to divulge all the scary horrors of the treatments at Hinton Hall; treatments I realised my mum may have suffered when I was a child, most before I was even born.

The more I learned the more depressed I became. Sofia would send me old pictures of ECT machines they'd use. She named the j-peg 'brutal'. I think of how frightened my mum was of that treatment. Sofia told me about the hours forced into ice cold baths. What if they bathed my mum like that too? I stopped emailing her, it was too painful.

I'd also reached the point in my book where I had gone through all the past and was pulling my four-year relationship with Chris apart, text by text, email by email, as if I was picking the flesh from something that had once been so perfect. I was seeing what we really had, it was perfect in places, but we were hurting each other, over and over and although he tried to understand, it was too hard. But I knew. I knew we would have to find a way to find an ending, so we could still be part of each other's life, but only keep the good bits. Maybe not as lovers. Not anymore.

In the end I told him I was heading for a breakdown. That some days I still wanted to die.

I am a nice person, really I am

Journal: 25th September 2012

I don't want for things to go wrong. I don't want bad things to happen to me or others. I don't. I want a happy life, but the more time goes on, I am becoming more scared than ever, and cannot see a way out – I cannot see happy anywhere. I cannot see anything nice. I think I want to die now. How can I be responsible? Will I ever have a family? No, that's one I bet I can answer. Fuck this illness, I hate it, fuck how I can't be normal and have a family and friends like everyone else.

Bipolar – split personality – Obsessive compulsive disorder (OCD) – Post traumatic stress disorder (PTSD)? – Psychosis – Neurosis – Borderline Personality Disorder (BPD) – depression = me?

My life was tumbling again.

Lists.

Photos to wildlife magazine

TAX return

Cancel BT and internet

How could I afford rent on my own?

I could go to coffee shops or out in the car if I needed to get out.

Dad used to do the food shopping

My book – I just needed to have the printed chapters and use red pen and the laptop to edit and make a more finished piece. I could go through and turn it into a story, then go back and edit or do it in one go. Perhaps I should do it twice. First go would take five weeks, then another six weeks to finish. (Of course in reality it was going to take a lot longer than that. I couldn't see it at the time).

Mum did all my washing before.

I could probably get some work in Clinton.

My money would not last much longer.

It's all spinning too fast?

Does any of it make sense?

One week to sort it out, one week before... what? I explode?

I was so tired, tired, tired.

The words are flowing out, no more lies

I wrote. I edited. I emailed agents. I went on retreats. I was so immersed in my writing I was blind, I was living another life, seeing the real me in the pages. But was I getting better? Was I just thinking I was?

Or perhaps I was realising who I really was in a mad cyclone that became my life.

I was coming to the end. An ending of my book.

It was helped along by watching *The Notebook,* in which two lovers split up and they found each other later. She got Alzheimer's years later and her husband only got to spend a few fleeting moments now and then with her when she really knew who he was. It is desperately sad but they used a love letter in it and it deals with the issues with such remarkable honesty.

I realised that the end was right then, when I read my journals up to date. What a journey it has been and finally I could now leave it all behind.

It was a slow process, where I knew the information a long time ago, but I just couldn't put it into practise until I had completely worn myself out. I was there, exposed, the cyclone had ripped apart my life, torn up the roots and the pages of my life were scattered like the pages of my book on the earth. Me, me, in the pages, in the rubble, but even in all that mess, I could finally see who I was. I had to deconstruct to reconstruct.

I know now in my heart, that everything will be alright.

But I am not 'fixed' I never expected to be.

My problem was that I had tried so many things throughout my life, some were bound to go wrong, but many didn't, like many of the risks I took in Thailand and Japan; the drugs. I read *The Buddha and the Borderline* and I thought how understanding the protagonist's boyfriend was, who validated her while she claimed her family and others did not. *Get a job, get some therapy, it'll all be alright,* but it won't and they have no idea how to empathise and believe in that person.

My brothers, Dad, Mum all said, "No you're not ill, you just need to…" what? Get better? But they didn't know the pain, maybe Mum did but she refused to accept that I was like her. I tried a few times, broaching the subject carefully, but all she said was, "No, not you, you're alright, Amanda, don't tell other people all that will you…"

I guess she wanted me to be alright – not cursed with a scary illness like her.

Perhaps she chose not to see the medication I took. You'd think it would help, we'd be able to support one another, but that's not how it was for us.

Dad knew about the medication too but I don't think he could quite figure it, all those years of helping Mum with her medication, but it was like it wasn't the same for me; it wasn't quite real. I never told Peter. I told David eventually as I've written here, but when I got back from my trip to Australia he turned it against me, telling me to sort myself out, that I relied on Chris too much for money; that all those holidays ought to make me feel better. He told me not to hide behind an illness. Since he was training to be a counsellor I expected more. I also told my friend, Sherri, who I still saw occasionally. She just brushed it off, saying that I was fine, and she changed the subject if I brought it up, even when I told her I was on anti-psychotics. So although I was able to tell people, I always held something back; I used to think I didn't want them to know how 'mental' I really was.

Darkness and white anger made every little thing that happened to me a trial. But, even realising that, knowing what was me and what was my illness somehow made me feel better; able to work on it. I was more in control than I thought I was. My eyes were open at last.

But then I had to ask myself, was I allowing these symptoms to occur?

The more people didn't understand me the more they continued to invalidate me

Chris did this. When I got angry he made it worse. He apportioned blame. Saying I was at fault, it was my problem, instead of trying to understand it. And, of course, I blamed him. He didn't ever even buy a book or attempt to read one of mine, to learn about BPD. Instead, he'd repeat something that Dr Jones said to him– '*it's very, very hard to live with a Borderline…*'

But that didn't mean it was impossible.

It was so hard seeking validation. 'You are ill', 'You are not ill', 'You are wrong', 'You shouldn't feel like that', 'You shouldn't behave like that', 'Most people wouldn't do that', 'You are out of control', 'Just get a job', 'Just sort yourself out and stop hiding behind an illness', 'Just be normal, like everyone else'. Endless reams of comments as if suddenly the world had an opinion and yet they knew nothing about it.

What I needed to hear was: 'I understand why you feel that way', 'I understand why you do those things', 'I know things are difficult for you right now, and I want to help', 'What can I do to help'…

Invalidating environment – what is it?

An invalidating environment is one where the people around you don't help you to deal with your emotions, whether they mean to or not. They may say you are wrong for feeling your emotions or punish/ignore you when you get emotional. I have had a lot of that from ex-boyfriends.

Someone may use words or actions that upset you repeatedly, yet indirectly.

Simply growing up in a family where everyone seems different from you can be invalidating, even if no one is telling you there is something wrong with you, you may think there is – like you are the black sheep or outsider. I know about this as well because I was surrounded by older men and a mentally ill mother.

Abuse can be prevalent too – emotional and physical. My mum had severe mental illness when I was young, and could be very loving one minute but destructive to me the next. I was sexually abused at fifteen years by an older man and was bullied by one of my brothers from a very young age.

When growing up I always felt different to everyone else. I still do.

In summary, invalidation can be:

- People ignoring you when you are emotional

- Getting angry with you when you are emotional

- Dismissing you when you are emotional

- Rejecting you when you get really emotional

The combination of emotion vulnerability and environmental invalidation is what leads to Borderline Personality Disorder (BPD).

Many people are emotionally vulnerable but never develop BPD if they are not in an invalidating environment.

Similarly many people have stressful invalidating or abusive childhoods never develop BPD, because they are not so emotional.

But neither factor is to blame. Being emotional can be great as it can make a person charismatic, interesting, passionate about life and feel others' pain deeply and are often empathetic and sympathetic. People who are less emotional may not know exactly what to do with a very emotional person, especially an emotional child. It is back and forth with an invalidating environment and an emotional child/person.

The caregivers therefore are sometimes unable to deal with it and say 'get on with it' as they don't know what to do even if they do care.

So if you are told not to feel something, then you may feel it worse, get defensive or feel out of control, becoming even more emotional than you were before. Then the caregivers may feel even less able to deal with it and feel out of control themselves, upset or angry.

One amplifies the other. When this happens repeatedly, emotionally vulnerable people may find it even harder to manage their emotions and may become afraid of their emotions and find them intolerable. This can lead to the spiral of wanting to self harm or worse.

One should feel validated with ones feelings, not to be told they are wrong in how they feel. It isn't about emotions being wrong; it is about trying to understand what those feelings are and why a person might be feeling that way. Empathy is very important, and without it, invalidation occurs.

In short, if we grow up as a child without having our emotions validated by our caregivers, how are we supposed to know what an emotion is and how to deal with it? If we got sad when a friend moved away when we were six years old, and our caregiver said 'Oh come on stop crying, you will make new friends' it doesn't teach us anything about that emotion we were feeling (in this case, sadness at the absence of our friend). So, next time we feel sad, we might dismiss it, hide it from our caregivers or turn it into a different emotion outwardly. We may feel weak for being sad since our caregiver didn't help us to understand it before, they made us feel like it was wrong to feel sad, or silly. If we were told off for being sad, and were punished say, then maybe we would learn that when sadness comes on we should be hurt because the emotion is bad. So we might punish ourselves for the sadness – what a terrible scenario!

There are so many ways a person can invalidate, sometimes it might be on purpose, other times the person didn't mean to, but it all results in the same – invalidation of a child's emotions leading to a misunderstanding of what their emotions mean and how to deal with them. But, often the invalidation isn't just in the childhood as many people invalidate others as adults as well, which just continues the momentum of misunderstanding ones emotions.

I have had therapies where the therapist was 'on my side' and validated my feelings, but they didn't understand how ill I was – maybe because they couldn't see it and maybe because I didn't show them how mucked up I felt inside.

But I could also see how I allowed ex-boyfriends and friends to invalidate me when older, telling me that I was over emotional, that they couldn't understand why I felt the way or reacted the way I did, or just ignored me when I was emotional instead of trying to understand me. When I realised the whole scenario of invalidation and how it has affected me in a negative way, I could understand that I needed to get into a relationship where my partner understood me and helped me to be well and to dismiss the invalidating relationships which were destructive to me.

Maybe that's why I felt like I was taking the journey alone.

Well, not entirely.

In October 2010 my referral came through for my new CBT therapist, Psychologist Dr Lamb and she was to commit to helping me for five weeks on a weekly basis. She worked with me on my core beliefs, so that we could find the root of my issues in my subconscious. It is apparently the core beliefs that set off emotional triggers when things happen, such as jealousy or aggravation so that's where you start.

And so I slowly emerged out of the darkness. Not quite alone.

Chapter 18

Healthy body, healthy soul

During 2010 I utilised various techniques and eventually the outside help from Dr Singh and Dr Lamb, to find my way. Since re-looking at the *om namah shivago* meditation chant and the whole ethics of Thai massage, and reading the *Buddha and the Borderline* and *Eat, Pray, Love* memoirs, I came to the conclusion that meditative practises were good for my mind and body, and I was going to delve into the calming effects of meditation. I was already using one meditation technique again, 'Mindfullness' where I concentrate on my five senses one by one to bring me back to the present moment and relieve worries, so that was a good start. Eating strong flavours like aniseed twist sweets or salt and vinegar crisps would also help me to feel 'in the present'. I thought of things that would stimulate the senses. Taste: yummy food. Touch; my soft teddy bears to hug when sleeping. Sounds; favourite music, good memories. Sight; reading nice emails or letters from people that make me feel good, look at happy holiday or family photos. Smell; perfume – I remembered visiting one of my mum's friends who had cancer and she said how lovely mine was, so I decided it was time to wear perfume more, don't keep it, use it. I bought treacle sponge and custard to remind me of my late Great Auntie Agnes who I loved. I watched films or listened to music that hold happy memories for me. I had my teddy bears and ornaments and things people have bought me out on show, out of their boxes now so I could see them and remind myself that people love me. And I liked to listen to 'downtown' by Petula Clarke as it reminded me of my mum when we happily played records when I was little. Yoga focussed the mind and the body. So I restarted that. Dancing and music have been something I had managed to get lost in all my life since I was about eight, and I hadn't realised how absent music was from my life. I hadn't been out to a nightclub for a couple of years, nor listened to music at home much. I was going to look at dance lessons at the school in Clinton.

Someone to talk to

Nov 2010 to May 2011

CBT

Outcomes:

I was no longer getting depressed.

I was no longer feeling quite so tired in the mornings from the medications.

I was feeling more positive.

I was no longer feeling paranoid.

I was ready to be on my own.

Cognitive Behavioural Therapy is a structured psychological treatment. It aims to tackle everyday difficulties through problem-solving techniques, also to replace negative thinking patterns with positive ones. Although CBT is usually focussed on the present, it can be modified for BPD taking into account previous experiences which may have influenced a person's fundamental beliefs.

Dialectical behaviour therapy was derived from CBT, but changed to help people who really struggle with self-harming behaviours. CBT was good for me though.

I only had five or six of the BPD symptoms after the therapy. If I gave up I smoking and my impulsive drinking it would be four or five and, if four, I wouldn't be classed as a BPD anymore. If I could stop getting angry, it would be three.

Maybe it's not as simple as that, but it was a way to see a resolution; one thing at a time and I had a way back. *Finally.*

Journal: January 2011

Check

- *I am still getting depressed, but only for minutes and I can snap out of it quickly*
- *I still get paranoid, but not in the extremes that I was which also relates to the lower level of psychosis*
- *I seem more able to take my pills – not as tired in the mornings*
- *I feel more optimistic about the future most of the time (that I can make it)*

Maybe the pills were working?

Since New Year, I'd had two more sessions with Dr Lamb as she continued to increase the number of sessions I could be offered. She said that after a shaky start with me being late and going off on holiday, she realised that I WAS committed to seeing her every week, so she was willing to give me ongoing support. At first, we discussed the abuse and violence with Chris and she was worried that he was hurting me badly or would in the future, but I defended him (as always). She was worried that he might, one day, 'put me in hospital' from hitting me. I said that he hit me when I was being too aggressive one day, but not enough to really hurt me, i.e. to end up in hospital. Dr Lamb said it didn't matter what I was doing or how much I provoked him, it was his actions, not mine, and he didn't have to retaliate and hurt me back. I remember when my dad hit my mum that day when I was young. He had been frustrated and couldn't take any more. Seeing it from the outside, even as a child, I could see it clearer.

In that first session, we also discussed the 'family mosaic' service and she said that she would help me to apply for housing with them in session if I would like to, so that I could move out of Chris's place since our constant arguments were damaging us both and he couldn't cope with me anymore. We discussed possible benefits I might receive – although it would have to go through my psychiatrist and council housing, which are both different to the family mosaic system. I said I wanted to be away from Chris as soon as possible. I could see what was happening, I'd been able to see for some time, but sometimes things are easier said than done.

Because there was always a dichotomy between the professional person I was on my websites I questioned whether the family mosaic would look me up and say 'no way, she doesn't need any money or help' but then Dr Lamb made me realise how Chris had paid for it all and that on my own, I have nothing.

Dr Lamb then broached the subject of my 'luxurious lifestyle'. She asked me to think about life without all these luxuries – Chris supporting my businesses and future professional plans, the holidays I would miss, eating out... She said I should weigh it up.

I did. At home I wrote out my conclusions to take to her the following week.

That first week, I was very unhappy, since Chris and I had such a horrible Christmas and New Year. The second week, I felt much better, so Dr Lamb focussed on getting out of me 'why' I felt so much better and happier despite the adversities. My business going well: which meant I was getting 'good attention' and that had cheered me up and made me forget about the shit. We said we would need to get to the root of my issues, and we found the root of this one was the need to have attention/compliments/appreciation from others. It probably stemmed from my dad, who didn't come to parents' evenings at school, and who didn't know how hard I was working and what great marks I was getting. I have strived all my life to be appreciated by Dad. That became clearer. I told Dr Lamb that, how writing my book had showed that.

So we had one core belief that we could work on: fear of failure

We looked at the circle of CBT – a thought sets off an emotion which sparks a reaction (action) and that action sets off a thought, which sets off an emotion, hence a repeating cycle.

So, she wrote down an example –

Thought –

- I am being excluded from Chris's life
- I am not worthy of meeting them (Chris's step grandchildren and family and friends)

Emotion –

- Angry
- Depressed

Action –

- Argue

Then, we discussed how much worse these issues with Chris and his family made me feel. She told me:

Feeling ill makes me angry/depressed, and makes me argue with Chris

We cannot change our emotions, only our thoughts and actions

But how?

I had to think myself worthy, of Chris's love, acceptance by his ex wife, his stepchildren. And change my actions to something more positive. I said that I had unearthed my exercise/yoga videos and could do one of them. I also could do some more of my positive working ideas, such as promoting my aerial photos to local newspapers etc.

Dr Lamb said that was on the right track.

What did I do?

Journal: 21st January 2011

I realise that Chris has had the Patient information leaflet for the Quetiapine (seroquel XL) for months, since I started using them, and he has never asked me about taking them – all he knows is that they make me sleepy in the morning and help me to sleep all night, but he has never asked me what they have done for me, if they have, how they may have helped or not helped my feelings, or any other questions. He has had no questions at all in all this time.

It is time to wake up. I have known some of this, but have hung on for different reasons, but I cannot punish myself with his actions or my reactions anymore. I must meet people who are going to be good for me and my esteem. And who care about me.

Alcoholism can have adverse effects on mental health, causing psychiatric disorders to develop and an increased risk of suicide.

I was looking up information about *Dad's Army* actor, John le Mesuerer, who died of cirrhosis, and I started to realise I was an alcoholic.

Journal: 22nd January 2011

I did meditation today to tell myself 'I am going to feel better, I am going to give up drinking and smoking'. I repeated it many times, for many minutes, and yet as soon as there were problems with Chris, I got to drinking wine and smoking. I had told myself I wouldn't but just did it anyway.

Chris would not take responsibility for his own actions; only that they are reactions to something I started. I could not make him listen. Did he even care?

Chris threatened to 'section' me

But all this did was make me worse.

It was the lowest Chris and I have ever gone at a time when I needed help the most. The final confirmation that enough was enough. But why was it still so hard?

I was given five more appointments for CBT – making seventeen in total – my favourite number. Maybe that was a good place to finish my book, on the 4th March, on my last appointment with Dr Lamb and contemplating how far I have got, together with her conclusion.

Or was it?

Chapter 19

Endings are new beginnings

February 2011

Days and weeks were a mixture of anger, love, tenderness and sadness. Was I winning? I was still living with Chris. But it was as fraught with ups and downs as always. And his ex-wife. She wasn't in our lives, only in my head but wasn't that the same? She could still hurt me if I didn't address it. They'd all moved back from America and lived just an hour and half drive away, so Chris was back to his 'visits' and I couldn't stand it.

Thought pattern

> Situation – Chris went to visit his family and he didn't invite me or he didn't try to arrange something for me to do for that day so that I was amused.

> Thoughts - I am excluded. I am not good enough to be part of his life

| Body/physical sensations — stomach problems/ spasms/IBS | Thoughts – you make me ill/you don't care | Moods and emotions – anger, depression |

| Behaviours – what I did/didn't do – I have an argument with Chris |

And it goes round again

Circle of thoughts – event, thoughts, feelings, behaviours, events, thoughts, feelings, behaviours...

I'm a hamster turning on a wheel... but where am I going?

I have to move out

Dr Lamb was pleased when I said I was moving out as she said that it was the only way to prove to myself that I could make it on my own, look after myself, keep myself company and be fine without Chris. We worked out my main core beliefs that get in the way of my happiness and life.

My Core beliefs

Self:

I am not able to cope on my own

I need others to feel OK

I am a failure/not good enough/worthless

I have no self esteem

Others:

People are judgemental

People are not supportive/lack understanding

Men should not be trusted/will use me

So, taking the assumptions about *myself*, I made these assumptions and rules:

- I need other peoples' attention to feel good about myself
- Other people must show me attention at all times
- If I don't get other peoples' attention/approval then this means that I have failed/am not good enough
- It is horrible/awful when I don't get other peoples' attention/approval
- I can't cope on my own, I need other people to support me
- If I make mistakes then this means that I have failed.

Thinking 'I can't cope on my own'

- Caused anxiety = confirming to myself that I was right, I *can't* cope on my own
- I stayed in the relationship and rely on Chris, for practical and emotional issues = confirming to myself that I can't cope on my own
- I would stay in negative situations

Thinking 'I am unworthy'

- Made me become needy
- Caused even lower self esteem
- Led to thoughts of being a failure
- Made me resort to self destructive behaviour as punishment

These thoughts lead to:

- Low self esteem
- Neediness and feeling abandoned
- Lack of trust

- Choosing the wrong men – saying no to nice ones and choosing the bad ones and going back for more

Going through this, I realised that this is what Roger had been trying to teach me, through his CBT sessions with me, but I just hadn't been ready at the time to understand what he was saying, or take responsibility for myself. It was all becoming very clear now though.

Through CBT I learnt to challenge those thoughts, for example:

'I can't cope on my own – I need people to be happy'

We logged various thoughts, behaviours and outcomes throughout the therapy and we looked back to find evidence that I CAN cope on my own.

Gradually, logging all this evidence that I was getting better convinced me that I WAS getting better, and the continuing proof that I was overcoming, one core belief, one action, one thought, at a time.

So I did move out.

I moved out on the 14th February 2011– Valentine's Day. Chris helped me to pay for it – he gave me a lump sum as long as I 'move out of the flat within a week'. I had been scouring the internet for some time looking for somewhere suitable and I found the perfect thing – a one bedroom flat with all bills and broadband inclusive, in the form of an aparthotel. It's the sort of place utilised by people splitting up, people waiting for work to be done on their houses, or for those who are working in the local college. But perfect for me – I knew what my monthly payments were with no surprise bills and no responsibilities of paying bills. I could also walk into town for shopping and food. But, it was just the other side of Clinton to Chris. Chris had come with me to view the flats and decide which one I would take.

I moved in. But still I wasn't letting go because I still met Chris for dinner, since it was Valentine's Day. But it was a beginning; a beginning of an ending.

I logged some of my thoughts:

Event – woke up to realise how much I have got to do to pack up and leave and set up my new home

Thoughts and images – me getting stressed, it's all because of Chris and his thoughts about his family

Moods/emotions – anger and stress started and low mood – fed up

Behaviours/what I did or didn't do – got really annoyed, blaming Chris, feeling hateful and telling him we'd never stay friends now that he has chosen his feelings for his wife over feelings for me and has made me leave his flat.

Body/physical sensations – angry, uptight, stressed and tense

Thoughts/images – He doesn't care (because he is ignoring what I am saying), he cares only about his wife, family and himself, I hate him

By the 17th February just three days later, I was so stressed Dr Lamb noticed I wasn't myself. I felt strange and dissociated. Stress was doing it to me. Worry about being alone in my flat – being abandoned. Could I cope? I got to my appointment because I couldn't miss it but I couldn't remember driving there. I felt empty. It was like my head was in a TV or something, and I was looking out, but not really present in the world that I was looking out onto. I was going through the motions with my body and mouth, and I could see what was happening in my surroundings, but at the same time I wasn't noticing, I couldn't really *see*. It was mild psychosis due to stress and depression, and it wasn't the first time I had experienced it, but it was the first time I had been out of the house and experienced it. Luckily Dr Lamb encouraged me to talk and coaxed me back into the real world.

She discussed how I must get out and not stay in the flat on my own, hibernating and drinking which I was so prone to doing. She did a pros and cons for it:

Stay at home

- Even if I stay at home all day I will have more chances to worry about things and drink
- If I know I have to go out then I work harder, and I am more productive
- Staying at home makes me feel low, think about the past (doing my book) and I end up drinking

Go out

- I will be pleased and proud for myself for achieving things
- If I am pleased and proud for myself then I will feel less depressed
- I will not drink and this will help me feel less depressed
- I will break my self destructive patterns and I will weaken my self destructive beliefs
- In the past when I didn't listen to my self destructive part I did something constructive and I felt good about it

GOAL: going to yoga once in the next week

I also checked my symptoms list every week to track which symptom to work on next and to tick off any that had been overcome. Every tick gave me a sense of relief, progression and hope. I worked mainly on my adverse symptoms of depression and OCD first to take some pressure off myself as they were worsening and compounding my very strong BPD symptoms.

Journal: March 2011

Dr Lumb– what we have achieved so far *– finding my core beliefs, overcoming the loneliness, finding more motivation to go out after I moved, overcoming being late and understanding why, time management, writing down the circle of how an event triggers a belief, which triggers a reaction and how I should have dealt with it, so that I can learn how to stop bad reactions and outcomes occurring. Taking responsibility for myself without being scared. Core beliefs are that I am a failure, I have no self esteem, that men are horrible and I have to affirm this by my actions which will make people not like me, make me have* unstable relationships, and drink so that I self harm and don't look after myself. And if a depressive episode came on, I could recognise it and not give into it – stop and take action before I spiralled. It became clear that I was overcoming depression and that was a big step; a whole load of symptoms I didn't have and the control I was gaining gave me less symptoms to work on, and gradually I would kick them all in the butt.

A Women's Magazine asked me to tell my story, and so I said yes, of course, with no worries about rejection, although she said that my story was so big, it would be like a snap shot focussing on my depression, since that is an illness people can relate to and know more about and by then, since I felt depression was something I could manage, it felt like a positive action.

Appointments: I kept a diary of times I had to attend an appointment whether with Dr Lamb, the dentist, doctors, hairdressers, and reasons why I was or was not late. I used blank hour by hour diaries, which Dr Lamb supplied so I could plan my hours/days/weeks better. My mission was to stay busy but also find time to relax – keep a few gaps. Thing was, I kept doing so many other things in trying to go out and do nice things, it stressed me out that I wasn't working enough on my book and websites, so I logged my work hours on the diaries too.

I like having my own space and am getting used to the idea of it

Dad said I could move back anytime. He said they are always glad to see me and I was always welcome to live there again.

I just thought he wanted my money. Some things are less easily changed.

I was still writing my book, printing it out and editing it over and over, but I focussed on the end product. I knew it would be worth it.

Letter from psychiatrist to GP – 21st March 2011

Progress update – I saw Amanda Green in the outpatient clinic today. She attended the clinic on her own and reported that her medication is helping her. However, she said that she is taking only half the prescribed dose because it makes her feel unwell.

She reported that she is seeing the psychologist Dr Lamb and her input has helped her a lot in her mental state. She said that she sleeps well and her appetite is good.

She reported that she has just moved in to her own flat after splitting with her partner and that sometimes she has bad days when she feels very depressed. However she is generally more anxious than depressed. She described her anxiety as a form of intrusive thoughts or OCD. She reported that she is worrying unnecessarily whether she had locked the door or left it open and continued going back to check it which made her late for an appointment. She reported worrying also that if she leaves a glass on the window and the sun shines on it that the glass may catch fire or burst into flames.

Mental State Examination

She is a young Caucasian lady who attended the clinic with good personal hygiene and established a good rapport and good eye contact. Her speech was normal in all aspects and her mood objectively was euthymic however she described her mood as generally anxious and sometimes depressed. She denied having any suicidal ideations, plans or thoughts. There are no psychotic symptoms reported or observed during the assessment.

Plan

1. *To continue taking her current medication which is Quetiapine M/R 100mg nocte.*
2. *To start taking Citalopram 20mg od*
3. *To attend the next outpatient clinic in three months time.*

I remember how I'd left his office, got my new prescription pills from the chemist, gone to Mum and Dad's, and how I felt angry about being given anti-depressants when I thought I was better.

Everything has side-effects

We all need ways to cope

When I told Dr Lamb, "I've been given anti-depressants, I'm not better!" this is what she said: "You are generalising. You have made lots of progress and changes for the better. You cannot say that you are not better. The doctor probably gave them to you for the short term to help you cope with your current situation." Of course, what I didn't realise was that anti-depressants are very helpful for the anxiety side of depression and extremely helpful for anxiety driven OCD traits. I still thought depression was just being sad and suicidal and feeling useless.

We sought evidence of me *getting worse*, but it was clear **I was getting better**. I was. What I didn't want was to be doing my photo shoot for my story on getting over depression on Monday and thinking the whole time I was lying and a fake that I was better when I wasn't, but **I WAS better.** It took up quite a lot of the appointment, but Dr Lamb went over many concepts that we have worked out from the past, as I was in overdrive, talking and worrying about getting angry with Dad and David and Chris and she said to do a pros and cons list for getting angry with them, to see if I am right to get annoyed and whether it is worth it.

I told her I still had black and white thinking. So she did a thoughts form with me and there was no reason to feel depressed about the pills. I was not suicidal, I was getting out, I had finished my book more or less. She said that I did not have schizophrenia and I did not have psychotic depression either which is where a patient goes into catatonic states and often needs ECT to get them out of it. I wasn't my mum. I WAS ME. AND I WAS GETTING BETTER AT BEING ME. I decided to stop looking at online forums and symptoms as I was slotting myself into all sorts of diagnoses, but was wrong. One must NEVER self diagnose a mental disorder; it must always be done by a professional in the field.

This helped me:

Situation – who were you with? What were you doing? When was it? Where were you?

1. **Moods – describe each mood in one word. Rate the intensity of each mood (0-100%)**

2. Automatic thoughts – what was going through my mind just before I started to feel this way? What does this say about me? What does this mean about me? My life? My future? What am I afraid might happen? What is the worst thing that could happen if this is true? What does this mean about how others think/feel about me? What images or memories do I have in this situation?

3. Evidence that supports the HOT thought – circle the hot thought in the previous column for which you are looking for evidence. Write factual evidence to support this conclusion. (try to avoid mind reading and interpretation of facts)

4. Evidence that does not support the HOT thought. Ask yourself questions to help discover evidence which does not support your HOT thought

5. Alternative/balanced thoughts – ask yourself questions to generate alternative or balanced thoughts. Write an alternative or balanced thought. Rate how much you believe in each alternative or balanced thought (0-100%)

6. Rate mood now – copy the feelings form the second column. Re-rate the intensity of each feeling from 0 – 100% as well as any new records.

And to tackle obsessions, I was advised by Dr Lamb to challenge them. DON'T go back and check the hairdryer or oven. DON'T give in to the paranoia. Then when I realised that the house hasn't set alight or something bad hasn't happened, then my brain will realise after time and give the obsession up, naturally. But, to keep going back to check is like telling my brain that I am right to have the obsession of fire, the compulsion to go back and the automatic fears will continue. I had to write down the 'HOT' thought (the obsession/belief) and write what evidence I had to support it and I couldn't find any. There was no way the oven could turn on by itself. There was no way a glass could catch fire...

Dr Lamb also gave me a handout on depression so that I could understand it more fully. From it, I worked out what was relevant to me:

There are many forms of depression, which can have a negative effect on moods and emotions, thinking patterns and how a person views life as a whole, physical fitness and energy levels, the ability to concentrate and/or sleep and interest in sex. At the lower end of the scale, it could describe a period of being in low spirits, which could impact the quality of things that people do, but wouldn't affect the day to day activities that they carry out. At the other end of the scale, depression can affect a sufferer in a much more adverse way – stopping the normal functioning in life and sometimes the loss of life if the person gives up on life completely.

Depression can manifest as:

• Depressed mood, which incorporates feeling low, sad, guilty or numb

• Increased anxiety and worry about things that may not have caused anxiety in the past

• Low self esteem

• Crying and sadness

• Persistent negative thoughts about yourself and life around you. This can be distracting and the lack of concentration it causes can affect their memory, which in turn makes them feel frustrated.

- Increased anger and feeling irritable, perhaps with an increased intolerance of others

- Confusion and inability to decide and be clear about goals

- Decreased enjoyment of activities or lack of interest in activities that were once enjoyed

- A reduced sex drive

- The inability to enjoy or take part in activities and confusion about life can lead to self criticism where they can believe that they are worthless, inadequate, bad, useless and disliked

- A sense of hopelessness can prevail in severe cases where there is a strong belief that there is no hope of being happy gain and no point in carrying on. They get into the rut of not feeling any desire to help themselves and this can lead to consideration or carrying out of their suicide. (suicidal thoughts and actions is also a symptom of borderline personality disorder)

- Psychosis (loss of reality, delusions, hallucinations, feeling of running on automatic) can occur if the stress and anxiety gets too much. (This is also a symptom of borderline personality disorder.)

Physical symptoms:

- A loss of energy is common, with the person feeling tired very often

- Eating patterns can be affected, with the person either eating much more or less than usual

- IBS and constipation can occur, as the stress levels affect the gut and bowel.

- General fitness is reduced, and aches and pains are very common

- The menstrual cycle can be affected

- Lack of sleep – either difficulty getting to sleep or waking up very early – this will also affect the persons energy levels and can turn into insomnia

- Loss of interest in sex

Social symptoms:

- All these negative symptoms can affect a person's abilities and concentration at work
- Withdrawing from social activities and friends, due to irritability, lack of motivation and inability to concentrate.
- Not taking part in previous past times
- Difficulties in relationships with family, friends and work colleagues

What can affect the chances of getting depression?

- Possibly an underactive thyroid – those with an underactive thyroid have slower metabolic rates than others, which can cause lethargy, weight gain and depression
- Some recreational drugs can influence the chances of depression
- Physical illness, low fitness levels and poor diet can all promote depression
- Losing a parent when young
- Those who have a very low self esteem
- Single mothers who do not have much support
- Those with a repetitive cycle of negative life experiences (divorce, moving house or job, loss of earnings etc)
- Unemployment – when for a long period
- Those who live in Cities
- Abusive or neglectful childhoods
- Those who do not have a supportive network

- Unresolved mourning of the death or loss of someone close

- Major life changes such as changing jobs, divorce etc

- Loss of job or status

Depression forms a vicious circle – depression can lead to feeling more depressed that you are depressed and negative thoughts about oneself and the world can get out of control and the depressive symptoms can get more severe as time goes on, if the cycle is not stopped. Whatever caused the depression in the first place can get lost, as the depression reeks havoc on ones life.

Thought processes that can occur:

Black and white thinking – Everything is black or white, with no grey areas – good or bad with no in between or mix. If you fail an exam, you may think 'I'm useless' which is not true, you just failed one exam. Someone does something you don't like and you think 'He's a horrible person' when there is no proof of this.

Generalising – When something is wrong, one might think that EVERYTHING is wrong, when it is not the truth. A negative thought is carried over into many other areas and positive things can be thought of as negatives. Looking on the dark side of everything and jumping to conclusions.

Living by rules – Making unrealistic rules and expectations about our lives and how we should be can lead to disappointment, guilt and a feeling of failure.

Catastrophising – When an event occurs, we might see if for far more than it is – how bad or how awful. In this case, the prediction of failure or real disaster are over estimated

I could see clearly that I had been depressed for years

But I was slowly eliminating many of the symptoms

The Girl in the photo (aged 37)

March 28th – photo shoot… I couldn't get to sleep the night before worrying about it, despite my Quetiapine sedation. I was up at 6.30 cleaning, tidying, and airing my tiny flat. Jasmine (the make-up professional) arrived on time, and I was just about ready, although I didn't have time to do my nails. She was really friendly and we chatted as she straightened my hair and put it into curlers, then applied heavy make-up and fake eyelashes – not my taste, to wear all that makeup but she said it would open my eyes up in the photos. Tony (professional photographer for magazines and celebrities) arrived next and he seemed really nice, but I wasn't completely at ease. We took lots of photos in the flat, of me with flowers. Then we went down the seafront, and he took shots of me walking, standing, and leaning on the railings, and I just about kept up the smiles, bar a couple of shaky ones, due to nerves.

So there I was, and I was coping, I had found a level of control, even if it was with drugs – only this time prescription ones. And I was worthy of being written about.

I got the prescription for the Citalopram straight after the appointment with the psychiatrist. I'd read the information leaflet several times and had looked up various peoples' experiences of the drug on the internet. Some felt that they were a lifeline – they had more energy, felt much happier, more able to socialise and their OCD was greatly improved. Others said they nearly ruined their lives – lack of libido, feeling too carefree which led to loss of job, no energy – on and on I searched, and I found more that confused me and put me off taking them. Of course, medications that change brain chemistry like these and many others are a trial – what works for one may not for another; we are all different, individual. We are, in essence, made up of our own unique jigsaw pieces, some shaped like others and some not.

My brother Ian, Michelle and Elsa had all come back to the UK – all three brothers had now returned to live in the UK. They lived near me and I was enjoying seeing them. I didn't want to take brain changing drugs while I was visiting my eleven year old niece… So, after a lot of procrastination and worry, I began taking the Citalopram on the 8th April 2011, but I logged how I felt so that I could see if any undesirable side effects were occurring and whether they worked to make me feel better.

Day one – Had one 20mg pill in the morning, had frequent trips to the toilet with diarrhoea. It made me lethargic. My jaw kept locking.

Day two, three, four and five – Seemed better. I was freer from paranoia.

Day six and seven – Just tiredness, no other obvious problems.

Days eight and nine – I was depressed. I worked all day, pulling my hair anxiously and was restless, yet couldn't bring myself to go out. Day nine and I blew out a family get together with Ian and Peter, for fear of feeling claustrophobic on the two and a half hour journey each way. They thought I just didn't want to go which made me feel very guilty, since I hadn't seen Peter and Mel and my three nephews for nearly a year as usual.

Day ten – Felt more content today. Not excited, not depressed, just sort of normal.

Day eleven – Felt OK.

Day twelve – Woke feeling pretty good and got a lot done. Chris came round and I had a cigarette and felt shaky but it soon passed. Had a twitch near my knee all day and night.

Day thirteen to sixteen – Bad days, but I kept telling myself they were not miracle drugs.

Eventually, after four weeks and changing my dose, I adjusted, I felt better able to concentrate, had reduced anxiety, and felt less depressed, although I did have a couple of two day episodes. I was hopeful the pills were working. The Doctor told me I should have them for at least six months anyway, for them to work properly, so I would have to be patient.

27th April 2011 – *Last appointment with Dr Lamb*

I felt abandoned, upset, and angry inside about Dr Lamb leaving me to it on my own. We discussed the fact that a break needs to occur after therapies so that the things that have been learnt can be utilised and can sink in properly. She advised that after a few months, she might be able to offer me some more sessions if they would be helpful, or group therapy in the psychotherapy department or individual psychotherapy, but that I should wait. I was lost again for a few weeks. However, when I thought about what she said about time to sink in, I realised that all those past therapies, all those years of digging and delving and support that I'd had from various therapists, that wasn't all a waste of time. Time was actually key here and I finally realised that the reason I had taken so well to Dr Lamb, CBT methods, and all the changes she had helped me make, were because of all those therapies as well. One reason was that I was ready to change and understand, but the second was that I had actually learnt so many skills, techniques and understanding of my past through writing my life and all those hours with varying therapy ideals, that I was now armed and able to put it all into practise and learn new things and action them much more easily, to suit me. I guess that is why Dr Lamb had told me I was insightful throughout my therapy with her.

Last letter from Dr Lamb to Dr Singh about my end of therapy – 22nd June 2011

Dear Dr Singh,

Further to my letter dated 14th February 2011, this is a closing report regarding the outcome of therapy with Ms Green. She was offered a total of twenty one sessions and she attended nineteen of them, the last of which took place on 27th April 2011.

The focus of therapy, as you will be aware, was on helping Ms Green develop constructive skills to cope with the anxiety and anger she experiences when she finds herself in a situation that according to her perception she does not have the ability to handle and she does not receive adequate support from her environment.

During the course of therapy Ms Green had to move out of her partner's house and live on her own. She said that this transition period was quite stressful for her. In particular, she reported feeling quite anxious about safety issues. For example, she was concerned that she has not turned off safely the electric and gas devices and as a consequence, she kept checking them before leaving the house. When outdoors she kept worrying about this issue and she was only able to stop thinking about it after going back home to check them again. She also stated feeling "paranoid" about her neighbours as she believed that they do not talk to her because they do not like her. She also reported feeling depressed and explained that she stopped going out for her everyday activities or to socializing with other people. Ms Green told me that in order to cope with her anxiety and depression she started drinking alcohol again on a daily basis.

*A number of cognitive and behavioural interventions were employed in order to help Ms Green bring some structure on her daily routine so to **consequently effectively manage her anxiety and depression.** These included mood and activity monitoring, behavioural activations and guided discovery for identification, challenging and reconstruction of her negative automatic thoughts and assumptions.* **The reconstruction of her dysfunctional thoughts was attempted through the identification of cognitive errors** *she makes in challenging situations and through reality testing that enabled her to gather evidence that disconfirm her dysfunctional beliefs. Ms Green was able to engage with the therapeutic interventions and put them in practice both in the session and at home. She reported that her* **depression and anxiety gradually decreased** *and that her confidence regarding* **her ability to live independently increased.** *In particular, she managed to introduce and establish a* **number of activities** *in her daily schedule and* **to socialize more** *with the people in her environment.*

Ms Green has reported that she has difficult interpersonal relationships and this is a source of distress for her. Several sessions were devoted in helping Ms Green understand the dysfunctional beliefs and assumptions that are activated in her interactions with other people and constructively reconstruct them according to realistic evidence. In particular Ms Green has reported that she needs to have other people's approval and attention at all times and when this does not happen she then feels rejected and unworthy. Exploration of a number of incidents helped us understand that Ms Green tends to see rejection in ambiguous situations and to disregard evidence that does not confirm her dysfunctional beliefs. Ms Green was able to apply the cognitive interventions in a number of occasions and in some situations she **managed to disagree with other people's behaviour without feeling angry with them for rejecting her or criticizing herself.** *Ms Green reflected that she* **needs to further work on her interpersonal relationships as she realizes that her fear of abandonment is still an issue** *for her, although it is not as severe as it used to be and she still has difficulty to have stable relationships with other people.*

*Ms Green stated that her psychology sessions have been helpful as the cognitive and behavioural interventions have helped her to better her difficulties. In addition, the CBT conceptualization of her difficulties has helped her to be more aware about the factors that maintain her problems. She considered that **her mood swings are not as intense as they used** to be, that she **doubts less her abilities to handle everyday responsibilities** and that she **is less self-critical**. She considered that living on her own has helped her to **be less impulsive** and more proactive and that she is now in a position to understand better herself as she is able to clarify the things that she likes and does not like. She also stated that she is **now more able to cope with her depression and denied experiencing any suicidal thoughts**. At this point I would like to mention that in my first letter to you dated 16th December 2010 it was mentioned that in the beginning of therapy Ms Green denied having any suicidal thoughts. Please note that this is a mistake and that in the beginning of therapy Ms Green stated that she had suicidal thoughts, but denied having the intention or plan to act on them.*

*In our final session we considered that it would be helpful for Ms Green **to take some time off therapy to independently put in practice the skills she learnt during therapy so to further consolidate them.** We also discussed about her future therapy options should she require further therapeutic input in the future. In particular, we considered that Ms Green could be referred again to the psychology service should she wish to work again on **anxiety and depression management through a CBT perspective.** We also discussed that she could be referred to the Psychotherapy Service should she wish to work on her interpersonal* *difficulties in a group setting that will give her the opportunity to identify and challenge in practice dysfunctional interpersonal dynamics.*

In conclusion, Ms Green's case is now closed for the Psychology Service.

So, there we have it. In conclusion, CBT is a perfect therapy dynamic for depression, anxiety and OCD. Then we have to look at some symptoms of BPD – five of the nine - fear of abandonment – loss of self - paranoid/dissociation – suicidal thoughts – feeling empty inside – all helped also within the therapy and let's face it they are also interlinked with each other – depression/OCD/anxiety/BPD. So I reiterate that it is about looking at the personal symptoms you have, NOT a name, or a list of possible symptoms, its about the 'individual' and I cannot say that enough. And then, once those symptoms are helped, we look at the other four BPD symptoms – relationships/anger/mood swings/impulsive behaviours. They were still there, but much easier to deal with once many of the other suffocating symptoms were manageable. They had already softened so I was feeling very positive when I checked my checklist again – I had seventy-eight of them throughout my life and slowly, one by one, they were being ticked off.

Journal: May 2011

Don't listen or react to Chris's comments anymore

I feel free in my mind – I can feel many of my symptoms are going as I work on them. I love my flat and my freedom and I don't have to please anyone anymore.

My inner strength and desire to be something has kept me going – I do believe that doing my websites and book have kept me alive.

Without them I am not sure I would have had the strength or will to live. Not one person gave me that power (only myself) until I got CBT and realised it. My inner strength is powered by desire. I said that I would be able to die once I had written my book, but it is taking so much longer than I expected; something good absolutely HAS to come of it. Like my company, putting all my eggs in one basket, I seem to have done it again and if let down it will be harder. I cannot fail.

Although I was no longer in therapy I wrote every day; charted my progress. I continued to fill in my forms and check on my reactions to things that occurred. I began to feel better on my own. Better and better. Every day. Gradually I would make realisations that I had learnt in therapy. They hadn't perhaps fully sunk in at the time but eventually they did. What I was taught in all the therapies were firmly stuck in my mind and I was now armed to naturally deal with my issues. I could pluck a relevant and helpful skill out of my mind for each issue that arose. And I was able to forgive everyone who had wronged me in my past, release the resentment I had for them.

    Imagine that? Look at how far I'd come.

Chapter 20

Knowing myself helped me understand others

I find it very helpful to keep using my checklist as a way to see improvements of each symptom.

I was still seeing my psychiatrist even when I stopped seeing Dr Lamb.

I had been waiting weeks for an appointment to discuss my medications and issues, but the day before found myself in a dark cave. I couldn't get out. I got drunk, very drunk. I couldn't possibly drive in the morning so I had to ask Chris to take me. He did. He waited outside. But all I did during the session was cry. I took my well organised list, but said virtually nothing that was on it. I didn't want to talk. I didn't want to be there. For the tiredness the psychiatrist said I could half my dose of Quetiapine but to keep taking the Citalopram. He said it could take six months for the Citalopram to work. He told me again that I didn't have depression. My mood swings were too short lived to be Bipolar. I had a personality disorder, he reminded me.

I realised I was never going to be cured but I could keep reading my check list as a guide, to show how far I had come and how I could stop myself falling.

I could look at me from the outside, assess myself. Feeling hopeless, worrying and playing with my hair endlessly, nervousness… When I noticed these things arising, I could check on myself closely, and try to look after myself and abstain from allowing those negative thoughts to take over – not to give in to my thoughts and feelings, but to do something else more helpful instead. Keeping busy was good, wallowing was bad.

A few days later, when I had emerged from my little cave of despair, I received an email from a woman named Laura, from California who had read about me on my website and who was a fellow sufferer of BPD. I felt good that someone had taken the time to read my story and write to me. It made me realise something very important about my book. That it *could* help others; I knew it, but I needed proof. And I also found myself fascinated by her story as she too was writing about her life and had been for many years. I got excited, thinking that I might be able to make a friend who understood me; perhaps we could support one another. I even considered in a flurry of impulsiveness I wanted to go to California to meet her. But I didn't. I took control and instead I wrote back to her with a series of questions about herself, her life and her disorder. I wanted to learn how it affected her. Was she like me?

She responded with almost a book, just as I would have. Thousands of words outlining a sad but true story, much of which I could relate to and much of which was exactly how I felt or the same things had happened to both of us.

I took a long time to respond. Not that I didn't want to, but because I wanted to do it right. When I did, I found myself opening up about my life and experiences to this stranger. But how quickly strangers stop being strangers. I decided, because of something she said, I wanted to have another tattoo. She said it was like self-harming but beautiful and positive.

I have chosen four things: for when I do it.

Survivor
Courage
Inner strength
Human nature; human heart; human spirit; kindness; sympathy

And I think I will have them done on my wrists to cover the area I have thought of slashing so many times. That way I can see them and be reminded to stay strong, courageous and with kindness and that I am a survivor and will continue to be until my time is up. I will have one done first to make sure I am happy with it. I think I will be – it's only a pattern on my body and my body will die one day anyway.

Laura taught me something really important. That my book can help someone, and even if it helps one person to understand, one person who feels they're not alone, one person to realise these words, it will have been worth it.

We are all different. We are all the same.

Chapter 21

Always forwards, no matter what life brings

Peter's wife Mel was diagnosed with breast cancer.

It happened the first time when she was pregnant with Sasha, her third child, in May 2009. Sasha was born in July and she was then able to have the mastectomy to eradicate the cancer.

It worked that first time.

She was doing really well and then in 2011 she found another lump. The cancer was back. She would not have chemotherapy as advised as her dad had had chemotherapy and had died anyway. So, from April 2011, she took up an expensive and gruelling alternative therapy which involved steaming the whole body, taking supplements, eating organically and doing things to support and boost the body's natural immune system. But this time it had reached the bone.

She was losing weight, but looked very well despite her issues and she did not complain; not to us. Her family kept her going. And her faith in God. But on Friday 19th August 2011, she went into hospital for the last time.

I got a call on Saturday evening from Dad and later I spoke to Peter. He said she was holding on.

I told him that I prayed for Mel, that I prayed for her, for them. He asked me who I prayed to. I told him God and Jesus, not just the sky. We talked about Mel. I told him I don't do what Christians do and go to church but that I feel he – God - is there. Maybe the roots of those feelings, my earlier questions about religion, about faith, answered themselves when I told him that; like I'd somehow managed to work it out on my journey. For me going to church is about community I heard myself tell him; people supporting one another. It all made sense now.

We discussed the stigma surrounding religion and how people go to church so that they are with like minded people, people who wouldn't judge. I said that it was because of stigma that I hadn't told anyone of my belief in God. Perhaps, also, because I didn't believe in all of it, just that God existed, not that any one religion was right and another wrong and that rituals are nothing more than OCD. And I knew about that. .

Peter prayed for me. During that call and in spite of what was happening to Mel he prayed for me. I told him I loved him, I loved Mel. I loved them all. Despite rarely seeing them since we were worlds apart in our lives – only once or twice a year.

I ended the call at midnight.

Mel died at 2.30am.

My brother never made it to the hospital to see her when she went. But she phoned him, just after he put the phone down to me; she said she didn't feel too good. He told her about me and she felt blessed. He said, "Goodnight sweetheart, you go to sleep now."

Final words.

I have never been good with endings.

After the funeral I felt depressed; suicidal. It brought up those feelings, those questions, like it did with Aunt Agnes. I guess it reminded me how none of us are immortal.

I told Peter I was there if he needed anything.

My sympathy card to Peter:

I have very fond memories of my sister in law, Mel, since I was a child, particularly when I came to stay with you all in Australia in 1994/95 where we had quality time and I could share in six months of Jamie's early life. She was also a great cook and always put so much effort into feeding her guests a multitude of delicious, healthy foods. The last thing was the delicious chocolate cake at your 50th birthday (Dad's 80th and Jamie's 18th celebrated on that day too) just 3 weeks ago on the 30th July 2011. I so appreciated her organising that day so that we could all be together – it was perfect.

To lose a wife and mother is so very sad indeed and you will need all your strength to get though this very difficult time. Mel will be sadly missed but remembered as a true family woman, achieving a long lasting happy marriage and two very well behaved, intelligent and loving children and a gorgeous baby who always smiles.

I am so glad that we all got to be together (Mum, Dad, Ian, Michelle, Elsa and Peter, Mel my nephews) for that last time, celebrating three family birthdays. It's a shame David, Linda and Alfie didn't come, but we cannot control people, I realise that now.

Through my sadness I found memories of Mel a great comfort. As I did with Agnes.

But even in that time, that sadness, I could see how I'd changed. How it was OK to feel that way; that life was like that. And accepting that life is sad and it can be unpredictable is the biggest lesson of all. What's more I knew it would pass in time, and I was right. I didn't let the depression get the better of me. **I accepted it,** beat it and made it go away. Nor did I lash out at anyone and everyone which is something I would have done in the past; and in the not so distant past. This time, once I was out of the "I want to die and swap my life for hers" I realised that I *wanted to live. I really did.*

Mel has no choice, so I needed to live, for her, for Agnes, for my family. Mel dying in her forties with three children, made me realise again how life could be taken away – *just like that.* And it is taken away from so many people every day. Young, old, sick, healthy, accidents, disease, pain. It is happening every second of the day, so I decided that I would enjoy what life I had left – be it days, months or years. Back to my old ideals of 'live for today' just so long as I could take responsibility at the same time – balance is key.

I am enjoying my life but I still need those checklists to make sure I am really doing OK. And if I'm not, I know what to do now. I recognise myself – even the alien me. And she's not so bad. Of course I am up and down, as most people are, but I think I am more *normal* now.

I am aware of what is going on in my own mind (my own thought processes) and can evaluate them and stop unhealthy thought processes from happening. And I try to understand what is going on in other peoples' minds too so that I can understand them better – empathise and validate their emotions.

I also use mindfulness – the basics of meditation – to help me, where I stop what I am doing and use all my senses, one by one, to bring me back to the present moment, if I am drifting into a negative mood or a depressed state. And it continues to work.

Medications, perseverance and what I learned in therapy has helped me to put a stop to nearly all of my mental illness symptoms. I can now walk along or eat in restaurants without thinking that people are looking at me and judging me, I can go out on my own, leave my flat without worrying *have I shut the door, have I left the oven on, is the sun going to set light to my flat.*

And because of all these things, I no longer suffer with mild psychosis that was once brought on by high levels of stress, depression and anxiety. I am also no longer as anxious about everything and if I feel the stirrings of angst I can refocus my mind. I count to ten whenever I feel my moods or emotions changing, and I stop bad behaviours such as self-harming, drinking, or anger towards others, so I deal with my emotions more normally. I practiced this and have patience and I can now stop it happening.

I know my recovery is not all down to the medication. It has been the gradual change in thinking and behaviour, but I know the medication has augmented this; helped the other things to work, given me breathing space. I hope to one day free myself from medication, but for now I do still need it.

I saw my psychologist, Dr Lamb, and one of her colleagues in December 2011 to tell her about my book. Although the chairs were arranged like a therapy session I felt different. I felt the same as them. I no longer felt like a patient. Having wondered if I would benefit from more therapy with her, I realised she couldn't help me any further and I was doing OK on my own. I really was.

I feel, at the time of writing this, I only have two symptoms of BPD left, my mood swings and occasional impulsivity. But we all have those; however, I know I can change my thinking. I can deal with it. I still have issues; I still suffer from bouts of depression, IBS, anxiety and I still have lists of these symptoms. But this is more of a way of making sure I recognise myself. And that way I can make sure I stay in control and won't one day find another alien living my life.

I see my mum and dad regularly but I don't live in the pink bedroom, I have my own home. Mum and Dad get on better and go out together more now. Mum still tells Dad she hates him sometimes and Dad still looks after her, even though it has been many years since she had to be hospitalised. She still thinks I was never like her.

I continue to see the psychiatrist. This year the message finally hit about my drinking when he told me how alcohol was counteracting the effects of the anti-depressants and gave me the telephone number of an alcoholic's helpline. I guess even that I had to face up to in the end. I went home. I contemplated, and you know what? I gave up smoking and I cut my drinking right down.

Like everything, it's about setting the goals.

I gave myself a goal to drink a maximum of half a bottle of wine a day, but I rarely even drunk that amount. I found myself measuring my drink out and making it last. I have even gone days with just one glass of wine. I know, for sure, that I can do this. I don't need drink. I only felt I needed it because I needed to escape my illness. Of course it didn't help at the time, even though I couldn't see it, but now I can. Now I can see everything.

I feel confident, proud of myself and much less emotional. My relationships with people are improving since I have more patience, am less obsessive/compulsive, less self-aware and less depressed. I really can see that the lack of alcohol has lifted my mood, because the pills work better and because alcohol itself was acting as a depressant.

Much as I will always love Chris, once I left him for good on Valentine's Day 2011 it has not been the same. We still meet – we still have lunch and dinners and do things together. We still argue but not like we did, nothing he does affects me like it did. There's no commitment from my side now, and we have our own homes and space. It's easier this way. I guess I wasn't able to cut him out completely; there are some endings we can't quite reach.

Not like this one, this book. This obsession that has dominated my life for all these years, now put to rest. My story, you have read it all now, warts n all as promised.

So what now?

My next goal is to come off the medication, under medical guidance, and to stay *normal*. I cannot wait to see what my life brings. I realise I have achieved the biggest goal of all by finding myself again. I have got back to 'me'. And I've firmly closed the lid of my *Pandora's Box* of my past – and locked it. It's time to enjoy the present and look forward to the future. So, to signify this I bought a '*Pandora's Box*' charm – it is closed and locked with a heart on the outside in silver, and I wear it on my bracelet. So, my past is locked away and only love is left on the outside.

So whatever life brings I will seek fulfilment in helping others and seek balance and harmony; I will find the peace that was missing for so long. This is the promise I made to myself, and like writing my book, this is one I am going to keep.

Mel, my lovely sister-in-law, taught me when her precious life ended that with an ending there comes a new beginning. This is mine.

When we unlock the darkness of our own minds we can finally see

Make every moment count.

Part 3

Further Reading

An extensive list of my symptoms, useful websites and books

AND

Another book by this author...

'39 (memoirs of Amanda Green)' – the sequel to 'My Alien Self: My Journey Back to Me' which follows her ongoing journey of life and recovery...

Table of symptoms – past and present

I have only listed the main symptoms. Some, but not all, are covered in my story. You will see that quite a few overlap through disorders/illnesses which again will highlight the difficulty in diagnosis.

OCD SYMPTOM OVERCOME FROM THE PAST

1. Worry that I will do something that will end in me being put in prison or in trouble with the police – like harm Chris
2. Convinced I can't do my job on my way to work
3. Worrying about having my niece or nephew in my care
4. Worrying about driving other peoples cars
5. Constantly needing reassurance about my thoughts and decisions
6. Obsession with my weight and addiction to exercise and obsession with a flat stomach
7. Obsessed about having control – controlling myself and controlling others and not being happy when people don't do as I want or expect them to (this is why I felt let down by people, because they didn't reach my expectations. didn't want to control peoples whole lives, but certain things, like answering immediately to emails or texts I have sent, not arguing with me, not seeing certain people)
8. Making lists, living by lists, massive untidy lists, lists of things I cannot possibly achieve
9. Hoarding and keeping old lists, notes, emails, text messages, tickets of all kinds and lots of material objects
10. Sudden urges to admire and move things about and neaten towels and ornaments
11. Shaking my snow globes before leaving my bedroom for comfort and luck
12. Belief that the oven will turn on spontaneously while I am out – things could drop on the dials and turn it on and it will set fire (this is an electric hob!)
13. Getting addicted to working, forgetting to eat, failing to go out to get other things done, omitting to exercise, logging working hours and obsessing about not working enough
14. Deciding what to wear is sometimes a major problem. I try something on, then envisage myself in the restaurant or place and people looking at me and what they will think about what I am wearing – I think I look fat, things don't fit properly or I look frumpy. These thoughts bug me so much that I can enter the bedroom happily getting ready to go out and come out fifteen minutes later in a complete state having decided that it's all too much and I am now not going out at all. Chris and I both miss out and are bewildered at my rapid mood change over such a small thing even though it takes me some time to realise it.
15. Obsessive dreams; recurring ones about being chased and they are catching up, or I am paralysed but awake and hearing what's going on around me, but I can't wake up, all since I was a little girl.
16. Salute magpies and do not walk on three drains in a row, I have to do things three times for luck, like taking three lots of toilet paper, or touching things

three times
17. I am afraid of fire – I think the sun will shine through a glass and catch the conservatory on fire: that it would burn down.
18. I use a hairdryer and straighteners nearly every day going to work and have to phone my mum to check that I haven't left either of them on and the house would burn down and kill my parents
19. A perfectionist. I need everything done in a certain way and if it isn't perfect I reject it, like the garage leaking in the flat, which meant I had to sell the flat.
20. Counting everything – my steps as I walk along, and pavement squares. That started when I was little and trying to keep up with my dad's steps. He'd hold my hand walking along in town. We'd be alone, don't know why. But the counting the steps continued for years even without my dad there. Counting other things too; words in my head, words I say over and over in my head
21. I have quite a thing about 'fate'. Not for myself as much but negatively about others. If I make or cancel plans with any of my family, particularly my mum or dad, I am consumed by thoughts that something bad will happen to them as a consequence of my actions. For example, if I meet my mum for lunch and then she gets the bus home I feel very guilty that she might have an accident, the bus might crash or she might get mugged and it will be my fault for changing her day by making arrangements with her and changing her 'fate' as it were or not offering her a lift home in my car. But I also realise that my actions might do the opposite and save people from bad. This happens very often and is a big distraction
22. Obsessed with tasks and finishing things, so much so, that I cannot get on with the task in hand, for worrying about finishing it, or the next thing that I have to do
23. When flying in Chris' plane, I see death coming and panic when he turns sharply or there is the slightest bit of turbulence (this was not present when we first started flying together)

REMAINING SYMPTOMS OF OCD

1. Conversations in my head (not hearing voices, but my own made up conversations... that's different, isn't it?) – conversations that I can't stop, repeating the words and sentences over and over (this is hard because I sometimes believe a conversation has happened with someone when it hasn't) – this is now very occasional and only when I am very stressed)
2. Tidy one minute, messy the next
3. I have been obsessed with my book and my self therapy, but that's positive, apart from the fact that going through my life was very hard
4. I play with my hair, twiddle it endlessly annoying everyone I know, including myself.
5. Convinced that I cannot cope with responsibilities (only occasionally now)
6. Statistically working everything out – where I am in a novel, ie if I am on page 50 of 300 then I am now one sixth through the book and have five sixths left. But doing this every few pages, so that the statistics of what I am doing is actually taking over the enjoyment of what I am doing. This wasn't just books, it was writing my book and doing any kind of work, spreadsheets etc I love

numbers and statistics, what can I say!
7. I still salute magpies, but lots of people do this too
8. I still like things done in a certain way, but that's not bad
9. Still worry about getting future tasks done a bit, but I do at least get them done in better order now

BPD SYMPTOMS OVERCOME FROM THE PAST (I HAD ALL NINE OUT OF NINE)

1. **Messed up relationships** – fights, arguments, anger, jealousy (black and white thinking)
2. **Inability to deal with my emotions properly** – out of control at times, I can be happy one minute and fly off the handle at others, destroying things, sad, excited - Black and white thinking with no grey areas in the middle, someone is either wonderful or awful, loved or hated, good or bad
3. My **impulsive behaviours** that get me into situations that are not good for me (drink, drugs, promiscuity) and I self destruct and hurt myself, deprive myself of food and drink too much
4. Death and **suicide** are in my head so much, and take over many little happy events – feeling so low that death seems the only answer and self harming when in teens
5. **Out of control anger** set off by the smallest of events, changes or criticism
6. Having to **keep changing myself** and morphing into what I think people want me to be, changing jobs, where I live, clothes, hair, liking myself and feeling confident to hating myself and feeling insecure and unworthy
7. **Feeling really empty inside** like I have no part in the world or my own future
8. **Fear of abandonment by others and trying any attempt to avoid it,** sometimes its real and sometimes it is made up in my head
9. **Paranoia and dissociation caused by stress** where I think people are ganging up on me and don't like me, all sorts of delusions, self consciousness, feeling a bit unreal like I am watching the world through a TV not my own eyes, like its not the real world - only lasting a short time. Making things up in my head, stressing, counting, obsessing starts, vicious circle, going over and over words and conversations in my head to try to reassure myself

REMAINING SYMPTOMS OF BPD

I have pretty much overcome these symptoms in a way that they are not ruining my life anymore, but I still get some occasionally in periods of anxiety and stress from the environment and those around me, and when I do notice any I have to go with the flow and know that they will be short lived - those are symptoms number 2 and 3 but they are manageable now rather than terribly destructive. I have had one bout of symptoms 5 and 9 but I dealt with it as I recognised it was due to a major real issue in my life and it only lasted one day

DEPRESSION SYMPTOMS OVERCOME FROM THE PAST

1. Black and white thinking – everything is black or white, with no grey areas – good or bad with no in between or mix (shared symptom with BPD)
2. Generalising – when something is wrong, I think that EVERYTHING is wrong, when it is not the truth
3. Living by rules – Making unrealistic rules and expectations about my life and how I should be often leads to disappointment, guilt and a feeling of failure.
4. Catastrophising – When an event occurs, I see it as far worse than it is – how bad or how awful, no good at all
5. Depressed mood, feeling low, sad, guilty or useless and crying a lot
6. Feeling anxious and worried about things all the time
7. A low self esteem
8. Inability to enjoy things I do, like days out, or hobbies or exercise, lack of interest and feeling flat
9. Anger, irritability and inability to tolerate people's habits or ways (shared symptom with BPD)
10. Often confused and unable to make decisions, causing more anxiety
11. Feeling worthless, useless, disliked by others and I dislike myself
12. Suicidal and feeling hopeless and that I will never get better and happy again (shared symptom with BPD)
13. Not eating regularly leads to IBS
14. Not sleeping properly, wake easily and find it hard to get to sleep through worry, guilt and sadness
15. Inability to concentrate and scatty way of working, doing too many things at once
16. Staying in a lot and not seeing friends and family due to a withdrawal from society and normality, worry and lack of self esteem
17. Problems in my relationships in work
18. Not washing or getting dressed for days (although always working as that's my obsession)

REMAINING SYMPTOMS OF DEPRESSION

1. Aching back, tired and lethargy due to lack of exercise and 'get up and go'
2. Lack of sex drive
3. Anxiety and depressive moods come over me from time to time, usually due to some environmental factor or someone genuinely upsetting me, but they are short lived and I am able to deal with them within a couple of days or less
4. I do not yet have a full social life, but it is much better than it was and I can join in with those around me without panic - I still stay in quite a bit but it is more because I am working hard rather than avoiding people and I genuinely enjoy my own company again now
5. Getting so stressed and anxious that it leads to mild psychosis - feeling surreal, running on auto, loss of reality and feeling unreal, delusional thoughts and stories in my head about what is happening (shared symptoms with BPD) but this has occurred only once in months, lasting just one day, due to a major real issue in my life, as above

GENERAL ISSUES OVERCOME FROM THE PAST (some overlap with other disorders)

1. Paranoia that I am being watched in shops and that the security will think I am stealing even though I never am
2. Paranoia caused by sweating – most of my life I wore black because of sweating profusely at any one time. Chris got me to wear colours and I am just careful when I wear them
3. Paranoia when I went to an adventure park in 2010 with my niece alone in Australia. We were shown macadamia nut trees, and the guide broke some open and gave one to Elsa which she ate. I then was convinced that he had HIV and he may have a cut hand and gave my niece HIV. It bugged me for days as I panicked thinking it would be entirely my fault if she got HIV and died.
4. Heart thumping in my ears – For over a year (2010/2011) I suffered with beating in my ears at night, when trying to sleep. The more I got upset about it stopping me from Sleeping, the worse it got. I would toss and turn for hours sometimes, taking my earplugs out which I wore every night due to my sensitivity to noise (originally because It was so noisy in my bedroom at mum and dads), covering and uncovering my ears, leaning on my hand or arm. It went on and on and the lack of sleep was awful
5. Just replacing addictions such as sex and drugs with other addictions, such as self harm, working and making myself ill
6. Grandiose ideas of making a million pounds with my Spanish rentals company took my mind off the realities of what was going on with my money and company ie that I was losing it all
7. The way I self destruct and hurt myself, deprive myself of food and drink too much
8. The person that most people see on the outside is not the person that is me on the inside – the persona is quite different and I just want to be myself, without feeling vulnerable to show who I really am. I am ashamed of the BPD traits, so I just show my better 'real' personality traits.

REMAINING GENERAL ISSUES

1. I do not deal with change well - unless the change is being made by me and I am in control of that change but not if it is a surprise change that life or someone has thrown at me.
2. Time management still bad at times, but has, and continues to, improve
3. Behaving like a child and episodes of excitability and deliriously happy, but I think that keeps me young and I quite like it!

Useful information

I don't want anyone to go through what I have all because they didn't get help. Maybe you see something in my story that has happened to you. Maybe you have read my symptom list and can relate to it. Maybe not.

The key to feeling better is to:

- Recognise and accept that there is something wrong,
- Take responsibility for yourself
- Seek the right help and support from others
- And persist, as there are no miracle cures when it comes to the brain.

Just think of the life you have now and the life you could have if you felt better and realise that you don't have to suffer, you can feel better, supported and proud of yourself. For this reason, I have taken time to choose some web links that may be useful for each adversity or illness that I have gone through, to help you if any of these relate to you. Do not do what I did and remain in denial for years, do something now.

And for those of you who do not have any of the issues I have outlined in my story, these links will be of use for further reading, since you have read my book already you must have an interest.

There are also my recommended self help books and memoirs where applicable, which I have read personally and have found useful.

Of course, you will find a lot of information on my own website, including up to date links, my personal experiences with mental health issues, my self help guides, articles on the topics covered in my story and book reviews – **www.amandagreenauthor.co.uk** but I can recommend these resources as well, as they helped me to understand each topic I had to cover in understanding myself – self help books, memoirs and websites.

First of all, I mentioned in my story that I watched a programme on TV where psychiatrists had to diagnose a group of people, undergoing tests in front of them, some of which were not mentally ill and others who had various mental illnesses. You can see more about this programme from the Guardian newspaper website:

www.guardian.co.uk/society/tvandradioblog/2008/nov/05/horizon-how-mad-are-you

BOOKS I HAVE FOUND USEFUL AND INTERESTING

Borderline Personality Disorder memoirs

Girl, interrupted by Susanna Kaysen

The Buddha and the Borderline by Kiera Van Gelder published by New Harbinger Publications Inc in 2010

On a Knife's Edge by Michelle Karpus published by Chipmunka Publishing in 2010

Get me out of here, my recovery from borderline personality disorder by Rachel Reiland, published in 2004 by Hazelden

Borderline Personality Disorder self help books

The Borderline Personality Disorder Survival Guide Alexander L Chapman P.H.D and Kim L. Gratz P.H.D published by New Harbinger Publications in 2007

Borderline Personality Disorder for Dummies by Charles H. Elliott PHD and Laura L. Smith, published by Wiley Publishing Inc. in 2009

Depression memoir

The Bell Jar by Sylvia Plath, published by Faber in 2004 (first published by William Heinemann Ltd in 1963)

Schizophrenia memoirs

Henry's Demons by Patrick and Henry Cockburn published in 2011

I never promised you a rose garden by Joanne Greenberg (formally Hannah Green)

Substance abuse/addiction memoir:

A Million Little Pieces by James Frey, published by John Murray in 2004 (confusion as to what is true and not true about this story but it is a very well written account of addiction)

General memoirs dealing with adversity:

Eat, Pray, Love by Elizabeth Gilbert published by Bloomsbury Publishing PLC in 2007

Wife Interrupted by Amy Molloy, published in 2009 by Headline review

On my website at www.amandagreenauthor.co.uk/links

You will find useful websites – information, help and support for:

- General mental illness, therapies and charities
- Borderline Personality disorder
- Depression
- Obsessive compulsive disorder
- Bipolar
- Schizophrenia
- Anxiety/panic attacks
- Paranoia, dissociation and psychosis
- Eating disorders (Anorexia Nervosa and Bulimia)
- Thyroid issues
- Alcohol and drug abuse
- Anger management
- Children and young people – support and information for mental health and abuse issues
- Family support – abuse, mental illness, addictions etc
- Sexual & physical abuse/rape

- Self harm
- Suicide prevention
- Debt management
- Therapies such as Cognitive behavioural therapy, psychotherapy, DBT, Adlerian therapy, hypnotherapy
- Information on Yoga, Meditation, Mindfullness, Mentalising...
- Celebrities and famous people with mental health issues
- Quetiapine and Citalopram medications

I wish you all the best in your life, and much happiness – Amanda Green ☺

Made in the USA
Charleston, SC
01 July 2016